The Practical Gardener

Books by Roger B. Swain

EARTHLY PLEASURES
Tales from a Biologist's Garden

FIELD DAYS
Journal of an Itinerant Biologist

THE PRACTICAL GARDENER
A Guide to Breaking New Ground

T·H·E
PRACTICAL
GARDENER

A Guide to Breaking
New Ground

by

ROGER B. SWAIN

Illustrations by Frank Fretz

Little, Brown and Company

BOSTON   TORONTO   LONDON

FIRST EDITION

Many of the essays included in this book
originally appeared in *Horticulture*.

Library of Congress Cataloging-in-Publication Data

Swain, Roger B.
The practical gardener.

Includes index.
1. Gardening.   2. Gardening—New England.   I. Title.
SB455.3.S93   1989   635   88-13738

10   9   8   7   6   5   4   3   2   1

Designed by Marianne Perlak

RRD-VA

*Published simultaneously in Canada
by Little, Brown & Company (Canada) Limited*

PRINTED IN THE UNITED STATES OF AMERICA

For Asa and Gardner,
the one starting where the other left off

"Although an old man, I am but a young gardener"
THOMAS JEFFERSON

Contents

Acknowledgments

THIS BOOK WAS A NEIGHBORHOOD PROJECT. Special thanks go to all the residents of Columbus Street, to Jill and George Mercer, Nancy Mattei, Melanie and Wes Bockley, Bernice Chesler, Barbara Balasa, Marie and Hubert Jessup, Kim Streetman, Donald and Judy Manthei, Dawn Kramer, Steve Buck, and all the others who asked questions and offered advice and encouragement. And salutations to Costas Triantafilopoulos for serving me stuffed peppers every Wednesday noon whatever I was doing.

At *Horticulture* Thomas Cooper started me writing the columns, and Steven Krauss and John Barstow kept me going. Gordon DeWolf has always been willing to sit down and debate the merits of any garden practice. Elsie Cox and Gary Couch, of the Cooperative Extension Service, have never been never more than a phone call away. David Tresemer has more opinions about tools than anyone I know, and Robert Scagnetti has been inordinately generous with the tools themselves.

In New Hampshire, Peter Dekker, Dennis Kilar, and Gary Martell have all at one time or another aided and abetted me in growing far more of something than was strictly necessary, except that when you have grown a dozen kinds of onions, or a quarter of an acre of potatoes, you get to know the plants pretty well.

Although I have been writing about my garden experiences for many years, a disproportionate number of people know me by face rather than name thanks to WGBH television's nationally broadcast "Victory Garden" show. The phenomenon takes some getting used to, but I want to thank Russell Morash, John Pelrine, Kip Anderson, and the rest of the show's crew for all their behind-the-scenes assistance and support.

Fred McGourty and Frances Tenenbaum both kept after me to publish these writings as a book. Michael Congdon, my agent, and

William Phillips and Christina Ward at Little, Brown and Company get the credit for the volume you now hold.

The illustrations herein are all from the gifted pen of Frank Fretz, as patient and good-natured a collaborator as anyone ever had. Just about the only part of the book that I do not have anyone to thank for are the words themselves.

Introduction

AMONG GARDENERS, enthusiasm and experience rarely exist in equal measures. The beginner dreams of home-grown bouquets and baskets of ripe fruit, the veteran of many seasons has learned to expect slugs, mildew, and frost. Granted the experience also brings tomatoes that ripen earlier and petunias that bloom longer. But too often the raw excitement of the novice, the feeling that anything is possible, is replaced by more limited ambitions. This book is dedicated to keeping the frontier open. All of us, no matter how many spading forks we have been through, still look ahead — to persimmons or tropical waterlilies or a surfeit of strawberries. Enthusiasm is indispensable, and optimism can always be justified. What we learn during our education as gardeners goes directly toward improving the odds that our dreams will come true. And the more we can learn from other people, the shorter the path to success.

This book originated with our family's move into a new home, an 1872 brown-shingled Victorian house just west of Boston. This is a streetcar suburb, a community of older homes on quarter-acre lots. The sidewalks are shaded by maple trees and so are many of the backyards. The yews and rhododendrons planted around foundations have grown up to screen the windows. Most people mow their lawns most of the time. The last spring frost is sometime in early May; the first in the fall sometime in mid-October. Summer temperatures usually reach 95 degrees Fahrenheit, winter ones 10 below zero.

Though I have traveled widely, New England has always been my home. It is where I learned to garden as a child. It is where I have a small farm in southern New Hampshire, a piece of land that has given me ample room to experiment. It is where I work as Science Editor of *Horticulture* magazine and as a host of PBS's "The Victory Garden" television show. To deny that this land has shaped my attitudes about gardening would be as foolish as denying that glaciers have shaped this land. Readers in other parts of the country faced with different conditions may freely adapt my prescriptions to fit your needs. The nicest thing about a common sense approach to gardening is that it travels well.

Like every new house, ours brought with it a chance for a fresh start, a chance to break new ground. This time around not to be as a child planting radishes beside the sandbox, or as a graduate student growing pumpkins, but as a survivor of many of gardening's pitfalls. This time we had chosen a house with lots of sunlight, both indoors and out. The soil was good, neighbors were friendly, the office was only half an hour away. It was easy to be enthusiastic.

Some homeowners want to landscape a new yard all at once and be done with it. At best, this results in a simple dramatic display composed of a few ingredients. On the other hand, I confess that I am the sort of gardener who is forever adding plants and moving them around. My garden is destined to eventually have one of everything, though never for long in the same place.

Compensating for this splendid confusion has been a certain amount of efficiency that has come from examining the way I garden. Reviewing first principles has led to the sharpening of some of my prejudices and a cutting back on unnecessary effort. Gardening's oldest traditions date from a time when hired labor was both cheap and plentiful. Today, when gardening is largely done as a personal hobby, it must be enjoyable to both the spectator and the participant. Practical gardening is the successful culture of plants which leaves you with time, energy, and a sense of humor to spare.

The chapters that make up this book were mostly written during our first five years in this house. Readers of *Horticulture* magazine followed our progress in monthly installments under the heading of "20 Columbus St." For those who wondered, yes, this is where we live. Sometimes I was a little late with the weeding because the writing had to be done. I can happily say, though, that more often it was the other way around.

The Practical Gardener

Enough Sunlight

THE REAL-ESTATE AGENT couldn't understand why we rejected houses without good southern exposures, why we carried a pocket compass and a set of tables showing the elevation of the sun at different seasons. For her the important issues were kitchen cabinets and bathrooms. Every time we turned down an otherwise perfect house because the yard was overshadowed by neighboring trees or buildings, I had to explain again that we planned to garden. Soil, water, fertilizer — these are things that can be changed, but nobody has ever repositioned the sun.

Had we been content to grow a limited assortment of flowers and shrubs, we might have been more tolerant of shade, but we didn't want to be limited. We wanted the option of growing vegetables, and vegetables need at least six hours of full sun each day. Less light than that and you might as well forget tomatoes. The bean plants will be spindly, the leaves spaced far apart along the stem, the yield miserable. Vegetables grown for their leaves — crops like loose-leaf lettuce and Swiss chard — will do better but will still be disappointing. The simplest rule for gardening — whether you intend to grow flowers or fruit or vegetables — is full sun and lots of it.

At noon on a clear day in midsummer, full sunlight has an intensity of 10,000 foot-candles. The most that any individual leaf can utilize is about 1,200 foot-candles, so full sun would seem to be much brighter than necessary. But plants don't have their leaves arranged in a single layer. The lower leaves are usually partially shaded by those higher up the stem. Sunlight that is brighter than necessary for the leaves on top is just right for the ones underneath. Furthermore, there are many days when the sky isn't perfectly clear, when clouds or haze reduce the sunlight's intensity. The same reduction also occurs when the sun is low in the sky, which happens every morning and evening, and all winter long. Outdoors on a cloudy day in December, "full sunlight" may mean only 600 foot-candles of light. It is safe to assume that most plants will use all the sunlight a gardener can provide, responding with increased growth.

If you own acres of open land, locating a garden where it receives full sun is a trivial matter. But if your property is a modest house lot, in a neighborhood well appointed with trees and other dwellings, finding which part of the yard receives the most sunlight takes a bit of figuring.

Those who are patient can wait and see, jotting down notes from day to day and month to month, recording where the sun fell at what hour. It isn't enough, however, to collect measurements for a week or so. The path of the sun across the sky changes dramatically with the seasons — in summer crossing directly overhead, in winter slicing low above the horizon — and a location that is in full sun one month may be in shade another. The shortest days cast the longest shadows.

Those too impatient to wait from one solstice to the next (the longest to the shortest day or vice versa) can set about computing how many hours of sunlight a given patch of ground receives each day. First you need to know the sun's position during the day at different times of year. This information varies with latitude and is the sort of data sailors use to determine their position at sea. Lately the figures have become much more available because of the popularity of solar-heated structures. Nearly every book about alternative architecture or appropriate technology contains charts listing this basic information. Select the numbers that pertain to the latitude closest to the one you live in, but don't worry if the latitude isn't exact. Being exact is much more important for sailors than gardeners.

The accompanying table presents the solar-position figures for 40 degrees north latitude, which is the latitude of Philadelphia, to be precise, but close enough to Boston's for my purposes. Note that for every time, there are two figures that determine the sun's position. The first is altitude (denoted by α), which is simply the number of degrees that the sun is above the horizon. The second is azimuth angle (denoted by a_s and sometimes referred to as bearing), which refers to the number of degrees to the east or west that the sun is located. Note that the sun's azimuth angle at noon is always zero.

You can use these numbers to plot the various paths of the sun on a piece of graph paper. The horizontal axis is azimuth, the vertical axis is altitude. Linking the various points, each of which is a com-

DATE	SOLAR TIME		SOLAR POSITION	
	AM	PM	ALT	AZM
DEC 21	8	4	5.5	53.0
	9	3	14.0	41.9
	10	2	20.7	29.4
	11	1	25.0	15.2
		12	26.6	0.0
JAN 21	8	4	8.1	55.3
	9	3	16.8	44.0
	10	2	23.8	30.9
	11	1	28.4	16.0
		12	30.0	0.0
FEB 21	7	5	4.8	72.7
	8	4	15.4	62.2
	9	3	25.0	50.2
	10	2	32.8	35.9
	11	1	38.1	18.9
		12	40.0	0.0
MAR 21	7	5	11.4	80.2
	8	4	22.5	69.6
	9	3	32.8	57.3
	10	2	41.6	41.9
	11	1	47.7	22.6
		12	50.0	0.0
APR 21	6	6	7.4	98.9
	7	5	18.9	89.5
	8	4	30.3	79.3
	9	3	41.3	67.2
	10	2	51.2	51.4
	11	1	58.7	29.2
		12	61.6	0.0
MAY 21	5	7	1.9	114.7
	6	6	12.7	105.6
	7	5	24.0	96.6
	8	4	35.4	87.2
	9	3	46.8	76.0
	10	2	57.5	60.9
	11	1	66.2	37.1
		12	70.0	0.0
JUN 21	5	7	4.2	117.3
	6	6	14.8	108.4
	7	5	26.0	99.7
	8	4	37.4	90.7
	9	3	48.8	80.2
	10	2	59.8	65.8
	11	1	69.2	41.9
		12	73.5	0.0

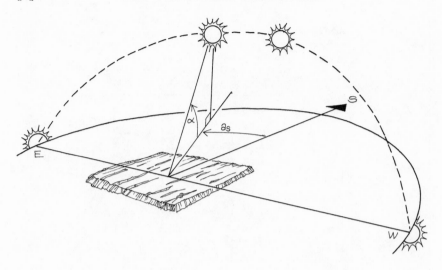

bination of altitude and azimuth, produces a series of smooth lines, such as those shown in the illustration on page 8. Note that you only have to plot seven lines: June and December are unique; the other months form five pairs.

When you complete this graph, gather together a compass that shows degrees on the dial, a protractor, and a plumb bob. The plumb bob can be simply a foot or so of thread with a small weight on one end. Go outside and sit down in your proposed garden spot. First, use the compass to measure azimuth angles for the obstructions on the horizon that seem most likely to shade your spot. There will be two azimuth angles for most obstructions — one for the left edge of the obstruction, one for the right edge. Then measure altitude angles, using the protractor and plumb bob. Turn the protractor upside down so you are sighting along the flat side. Aim it at the top of the tree or building you are measuring and suspend the plumb bob from the midpoint of the protractor. Then read off the degrees between where the thread hangs and the 90-degree mark on the protractor. This is the altitude angle. You now have all the necessary information to compute the number of hours of sunlight this plot will receive. But first you will have to correct the azimuth angles by adding or subtracting the magnetic deviation from the value shown on the compass. Magnetic deviations vary with longitude — from 21 degrees east in Seattle to 15 degrees west in Boston. If you cannot find

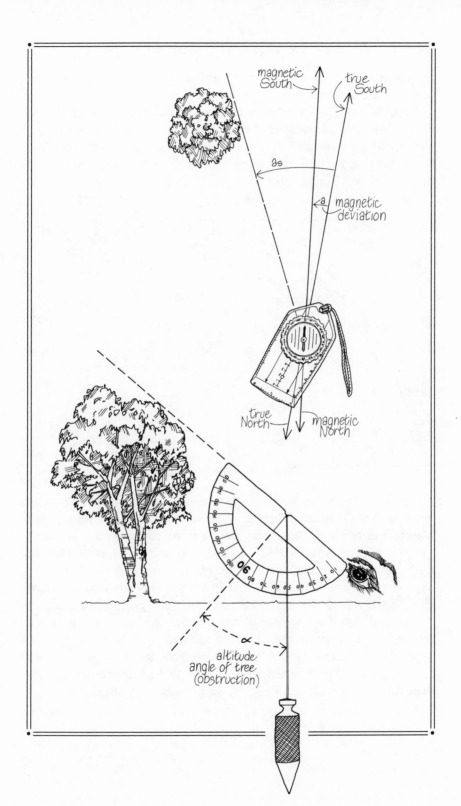

the values elsewhere, the deviations are usually shown in the margin of geological survey maps.

Back indoors, you can then use these azimuths and altitudes to draw silhouettes of trees and buildings on your graph of sun paths. The illustration shows a tree and a house that have been profiled. With this plot it is easy to determine exactly how many hours a day the ground will get full sun.

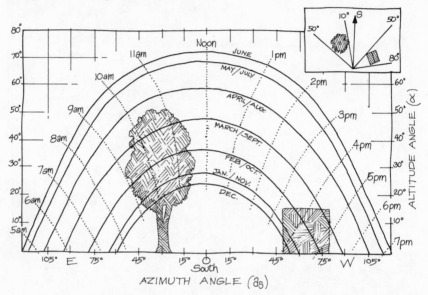

In this example the proposed garden site will get full sun all day from April to August. Starting in September and continuing until March, the tree will shade the garden from about 9:00 A.M. until 11:30 A.M. The house will also provide a couple of hours of shade in midwinter, but the shadows will fall on the garden at the end of the day, when the sun is already so low in the sky that the light is of low intensity. Overall, this would be a fine site for a garden, receiving as it does full sun during most of the growing season. Cutting down the tree would increase the supply of light in the fall.

Whatever means one uses to determine the sunniest part of one's property, the effort is worthwhile. Nothing brings greater rewards than time spent ensuring a maximum amount of sunlight.

Backyard Logging

A NEW GARDEN often begins with the destruction of an old one. Or what is left of one. Lilac, forsythia, privet, and yew are the legacies of previous owners. A few crocuses by the back porch, a grape vine, bittersweet under the kitchen window are reminders that someone gardened here. But the foundation plantings are now so overgrown that the arborvitae and yew brush against the second story. On the north side, a hemlock towers ten feet above the ridgepole. It shelters us from the north wind and is welcome. The overgrown evergreens on the south side are not. They block out all the winter sun and are, no doubt, shortening the life of our wooden shingles. Yews can be rejuvenated by heavy pruning, but for much of the existing vegetation, the only sensible cut is one made a couple of inches above the ground.

It is hard for gardeners to cut down mature trees, or even full-grown shrubs: most think of themselves as midwives, not morticians. There is, however, a time for sowing and a time for logging, and the latter, in many cases, comes first. We sharpen our resolve with the thought that the pruning provides light and space for other, more desirable plants. What's more, the soil must be reasonably fertile for the greenery to have grown so thick.

The lilac, the yew, the maple seedlings look like they could be cut down with pruning shears, but they can't. Not even with heavy-duty long-handled loppers. Advertisements claim that these tools have a cutting capacity of 2 inches, or 1¾, or 1¼. But unless you are cutting balsa wood, material this thick will spring the jaws of pruning shears so that they never again close tightly and never again cut cleanly. Save your shears, and use a saw.

Saws for cutting green wood are designed differently from those used to cut dry boards. First of all, their teeth are much coarser. Coarseness is measured in points — the number of teeth per inch.

The typical carpenter's crosscut saw has ten or twelve points. Pruning saws, even those intended for making very fine cuts, have only seven or eight points, and those intended for the roughest work have as few as four points. Not only are the teeth coarser but they usually cut a wider groove, or kerf, than saws for dry wood, the result of alternate teeth being set, or bent, far to the left or right. This wider groove reduces the chance that the saw will bind. To clear sawdust out of the cut and further reduce binding, many pruning saws have deep gullets between sets of teeth, and some have additional noncutting teeth called rakers, which help sweep sawdust out of the groove and into an adjacent gullet.

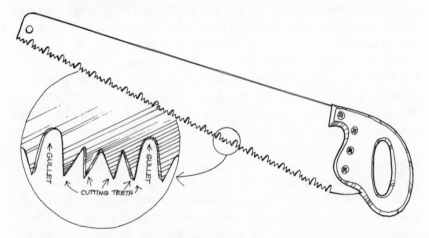

Pruning saws also differ from carpentry saws in the way they are sharpened. While most carpenters' saws cut only on the push stroke, many pruning saws cut only on the pull stroke. The reasons for this are not entirely clear to me, but may have something to do with whether the wood being cut is above or below the person holding the saw. Some pruning saws are sharpened on both the push and the pull stroke. These cut the fastest.

For cutting down shrubs and trees, many people like a bow saw. This saw stretches a thin blade between the ends of a curved piece of tubular steel. Because the blade is stretched tight it can be both thin and narrow, and is unlikely to bind. Furthermore, the blades are so inexpensive that when they dull, one simply throws them away and buys replacements. The disadvantages are that the blade, being narrow, breaks easily and also is easily deflected and thus may cut on a slight curve. And the steel bow sometimes gets in the way, either by limiting the diameter of what can be sawed or by striking other parallel trunks or limbs.

The saw I prefer for heavy cutting is a Swedish steel saw. Mine has the trade name Bushman. Shaped like a carpenter's saw, the twenty-four-inch blade is divided into twenty sets of four teeth separated by gullets. Within each set of teeth, two are sharpened to cut on the push stroke and two on the pull. Costing about twenty dollars, this type of saw is more expensive than a bow saw, but with periodic sharpenings one of them will do nearly all the cutting a gardener ever needs.

Unlike pruning shears, handsaws are not limited to moderate-size wood: it's surprising how big a tree can be felled with one. Along the south side of our yard was a row of white pines planted fifty years ago as the result of a grudge, it is said, against the neighbors. They were intended to provide a more solid screen than the existing privet. But white pine makes a poor hedge even when regularly trimmed, and these were never trimmed. By the time we arrived they were three stories high and had lost all their lower branches.

For a while, we waited for a chain saw, intending to bring one back from the country, but weeks grew into months and in the end we sawed the pines down with the Bushman. It meant climbing each tree, sawing the branches off, and cutting the trunk down in sections. A chain saw would have been faster — and a lot more dangerous. Unless you plan to cut firewood on a regular basis, there is no reason to buy a chain saw. Remarkably large trees can be cut down with a handsaw.

There are, of course, limits — trees that are so big or so positioned that felling them would invite injury or lawsuit. Our limit was a huge dead elm whose many limbs rose up through electric wires and telephone lines before arching out over the neighbor's rooftop. Cutting down such a tree is a job for a professional arborist. Not only are arborists highly skilled, they also carry insurance to cover the few instances in which their skills fail them. There is an enormous variation in the fees they charge for their services; the high and low estimates for removing this elm differed by a factor of more than five. Whatever the merits of choosing the lowest bid, one shouldn't on any account choose the highest. As anyone who has sawed down even a single tree knows, half the work is cleaning up the mess. In the case of a hired arborist, it is also half the cost. One can save 50 percent by specifying that the tree simply be cut down. Then, with a handsaw, the gardener can set about cutting it up. Even if there is no need for firewood, the tree can be useful. Sections of trunk can be used for posts, or to edge raised beds. Rounds can be sliced off to use as stepping-stones. Branches can be used for trellises or bean-poles. Even the smaller twigs can be saved for use as pea brush.

The bigger the tree or shrub you remove, the bigger the hole left in the landscape. The change looks dramatic, but only because it happened so suddenly. Landscapes are constantly changing, and when they do so gradually no one notices. Sudden changes, like those from backyard logging, may be initially shocking, yet the new view soon becomes as commonplace as the old.

Digging In

ONE OF THE MOST attractive notions for gardeners in recent years is the idea that it is possible to have a successful garden without first turning over the soil. Proponents of "no-till" gardening argue that plowing or other disturbance of the soil is not only labor-intensive but is harmful to the soil and to the beneficial organisms therein. Many farmers have embraced no-till agriculture. Relying on herbicides to keep down weeds, they simply make a single pass over the field with a tractor-drawn planter, inserting seed and fertilizer into the soil. Savings in labor and fuel, plus protection from the twin evils of soil compaction and soil erosion, continue to make converts. Among home gardeners there is no shortage of similar enthusiasts, people who plant seedlings simply by pulling back the mulch or removing a neat plug of sod from the lawn.

There are too many virtues to turning over the soil for tillage to disappear completely from the gardener's repertoire. In the North, breaking up the soil in the spring helps warm it up enough that seeds will germinate. Tilling also helps discourage weeds and is a good way to work manure, compost, and other organic matter into the soil. Finally, when admiring someone's no-till plot, it helps to remember that when the plot was new it was no doubt tilled very thoroughly. New ground must be thoroughly dug up, if only to discover what is under the surface. What might be three feet of rock-free loam could just as easily prove to be a thin skin of soil barely covering a tin-can dump. Reduced tillage is the privilege of a seasoned gardener.

The work of digging up a garden is traditionally confined to the spring, when the exuberance of being released from winter helps with the task. This is unfortunate, for breaking new ground is unquestionably the hardest part of gardening, and after a winter's sloth the lower back is ill-equipped for earth-moving. It helps to take small

bites with the spading fork, but it would help even more to do some of the work in the fall. You will save your back and get a head start on the spring planting season.

New ground is best addressed with a spading fork, a short-handled, four-tined tool. With this, one can handle soil much as one would with a spade, but the fork's sharpened tines push into the ground more readily than a spade's blade. This is particularly welcome when working heavy sod. With the fork embedded to its hilt, the handle is worked back and forth a couple of times, tearing the smaller roots and separating the forkful from the rest of the ground.

At this point the gardener has a number of choices as to what to do with the forkful of soil. The English, tireless gardeners that they are, favor putting that forkful aside and going still deeper. They loosen the soil beneath, working in additional organic matter. This approach is called double digging because it involves digging the soil to the depth of two spading forks, or nearly two feet. In this country double digging is much discussed but seldom practiced, because it requires a staggering amount of work. If the soil is heavy clay, or if there is hardpan (a hard layer of impermeable soil) a few inches below the surface, a double digging may indeed be beneficial, but for most soils in this country double digging doesn't improve the soil enough to justify the exertion. Eight to ten inches of fertile soil are all that is needed to grow most plants with complete success.

Though most of us are content with single digging, there is still the matter of how to deal with the sod. Turning it over (as a plow does) before putting it back in the hole buries the grass and weeds down where they will rot and add to the soil's fertility. Some people worry that this inverts the natural stratification of the soil. I don't know about preserving this stratification, but I do know that invert-ing the forkfuls doesn't guarantee that the grass won't turn around and grow right back up. I prefer to remove the sod completely before stirring up the soil beneath. If the sods are left lying upside down in the sun for a few hours, it is easier to shake the soil out of them. Then they are added to the compost pile or simply piled in a heap of their own. A year or so later the decayed organic matter that results gets worked back into the soil.

If the spading fork slid cleanly into the ground every time, it would be one thing, but at least in our soil, it seldom does. Either it doesn't go in at all because it has hit a rock, or the forkful can't be lifted up because the tines have hold of a root. Half the time I end up putting down the spading fork and reaching for the mattock, a hybrid between an adze and an axe. One end is designed for digging out rocks, the other for cutting roots. Spading forks are useless for roots, and trying to pry a rock out with one bends the tines into something that resembles a textbook case for orthodontics, except that once bent, the tines are harder to straighten than an adolescent's teeth.

Here in New England, where rocks can make up to half of the soil volume, there is no sense removing all of them. This only creates a hole in the ground that collects water. Big rocks, a hand or so beneath the surface, are allowed to remain and soil combed up over them. Any stone small enough to slip between the tines of the spading fork is also left in the garden.

Forking through the entire garden tells one something about the soil, but doesn't really answer the question of how good it is. The notion of "goodness" actually isn't terribly useful in the abstract, for soil that is kind to one plant may not be kind to another. The final judgment of a soil's merit will come only from trying plants and seeing how they prosper.

While goodness may not be a specific term, "badness" unfortunately is. Some soils are sufficiently contaminated with cadmium, arsenic, or lead that they are dangerous to gardeners. At some point, perhaps even before the plot is tilled for the first time, the soil in a new garden should be tested. Not all state agricultural stations test for lead, but many do, and all of them should.

We proposed to have our salad garden along the south side of our house. The house is more than a century old, and before being covered with shingles it had red clapboards. We wanted the soil tested because the lead-based paint had flaked off for a couple of generations, and vegetables, especially root and leaf crops, can pick up such lead from the soil. We would have had the soil tested even if it hadn't been alongside a house, because there might well have been a previous building on the site, or perhaps an orchard where compounds of lead and arsenic had been routinely used as pesticides.

For five dollars we received a special envelope and instructions to take twenty samples from different sections of the "field" (read "yard"), mix these together, air-dry the mix, and then place a single cup of it in the sample bag. We had to be reasonable about selecting the samples. Mixing soil from opposite sides of the yard would have created an average with no meaning. Instead, we chose samples from an area where it was reasonable to suspect that soil might get mixed together in the course of normal tilling and cultivating.

Ten days after we sent in the soil sample we knew a great deal about our soil, but the details of pH and nutrients were overridden by the confirmation of our suspicions: the soil was high in lead. Removing that soil and adding a foot of lead-free topsoil was work, but nowhere near as painful as it would have been to discover later that the soil was contaminated with lead. The reassurance that comes from going through a new garden plot once thoroughly is more than enough balm for the sore muscles.

The Basics of
Soil Acidity

I AM THE SON of two chemists. In the matter of explaining pH, I ought to be a natural. But of things ionic, I am laconic. I write now only to report that one doesn't have to understand much about soil pH to garden successfully. I have been doing it for years.

All you need to know is that the pH scale ranges from 1 to 14. Soils with values below 7 are termed acid, those above 7, alkaline (or basic). Any soil with a pH of 7 is called neutral. The pH scale is logarithmic, meaning that pH 5 is ten times as acid as pH 6, pH 4 a hundred times, pH 3 a thousand times, and so forth.

The soil in most regions of the United States is acid, because ample rainfall tends to make soils acid. Where there is scant rainfall, as in deserts, soils tend to be neutral or alkaline. The Southwest, the Great Plains, the high western plateaus, and many of the valleys in the Rocky Mountains have neutral or alkaline soils.

The most acid peat soils are pH 3 (about the same as lemon juice), the most alkaline soils no more than pH 10. For all practical purposes, no plants grow in soil with a pH below 3.5 or above 8.5. Gardeners are most likely to be dealing with soils in the range of between 4.5 and 7.5. Because this range is skewed toward the acid, the midpoint of the gardener's pH scale ought to be 6.0 rather than the chemist's 7.0.

From the point of view of most plants, 6.0 is a perfectly acceptable pH. Soils, however, needn't be precisely this value for plants to grow well. Most plants have a wide range of tolerance, and generally speaking any value between 6.0 and 7.0 is fine. It is only at the extremes of acidity and alkalinity that real problems appear, often nutrient deficiencies. In strongly acid soils calcium and molybdenum, both necessary for plant growth, are less available. Similarly, boron, copper, iron, manganese, and zinc are unavailable in strongly alkaline ones. Acid soils with a pH below 5 may, in addition, contain enough aluminum to be toxic to some plants.

The pH in a particular soil can only be determined accurately with a soil test. There are other, more important things to be learned from having soil professionally tested (such as whether or not it contains lead), but pH data is part of the package. The soil in my yard proved to be pH 5.2. Using the values in the table as a guide, I therefore added some 80 pounds of ground limestone per 1000 square feet when I was preparing the ground in the spring, working it into the top few inches of soil. I used dolomitic limestone, as it contains magnesium in addition to calcium. If my soil had been more acid, or less sandy, I would have had to add more lime than that. There are, however, risks to adding much more than this amount of ground limestone all at one time. Excessive applications of lime can cause lime-induced chlorosis in some plants, a condition marked by mottled leaves with dark green veins. If this occurs, it can be rectified by watering the plants with chelated iron: ¼ ounce dissolved in each gallon of water. It is safer, however, when adding large amounts of lime to split the total amount, adding half one year, half the next.

You can usually see the effect of fertilizer immediately. Not so with ground limestone. The response of plants to limestone is slow, of long duration, and not very conspicuous. If you begin to wonder whether the pH has changed at all, don't rush to send in another sample for soil testing. A pH test is easily done at home with a roll of pHydrion paper, which can be purchased from scientific-supply houses and comes in a wide assortment of pH ranges. The narrower the range of the particular paper, however, the more accurate it will be; so if you can, select paper that narrowly covers the pH you expect

Pounds of Ground Limestone to Add per 1000 Square Feet

	SOIL TYPE		
Soil Acidity	*Sandy Soil*	*Loam*	*Clay*
pH 4.5	100	150	200
pH 5.0	80	125	150
pH 5.5	60	100	120
pH 6.0	none	none	none

your soil to be. To use this paper you mix a soil sample with distilled water, tear off a short length of paper, and dip it in the soil solution. Depending on the pH, the paper will turn one of various colors; to determine the pH you compare the shade to a color chart that comes with the paper. Accuracy is only plus or minus one tenth of a pH point, but this is more than enough accuracy as far as plants are concerned. Beware the $20 pH meters that have come on the market lately. While there are glass-electrode pH meters that do work, all of the inexpensive metal probe ones I have seen or heard about do not.

Just as the pH of a soil can be raised by adding ground limestone, it can be lowered by adding ground sulfur or aluminum sulfate. The table on page 20 lists the amounts of each necessary to cause a range of changes in pH. The aluminum sulfate will give a faster response than the sulfur, but you must use more of it, it is more expensive, and you risk accumulating toxic levels of aluminum in the soil. Slower than sulfur, but an ideal way to lower the pH, is to add lots (up to half of soil content) of acid-producing organic matter such as acid peat, oak-leaf mold, or finely ground sphagnum moss. As this decays, it will acidify the soil in an entirely natural manner.

Gardeners are usually adding organic matter to the soil anyway, and it turns out that the higher the organic content, the more acidic a soil can be without suffering nutrient deficiencies. As it also turns out, this is a good thing, since the higher the organic content, the harder it is to render the soil more alkaline. Muck soils, with their high levels of organic matter, require even more lime than clay soils to induce an equal change in pH.

The fact that most gardeners are successful in any soil with adequate organic matter and moderate fertility has led me to conclude that the whole matter of pH tends to get much more attention than it really deserves. The numbers are nice and precise, but they don't mean a great deal. Most plants will grow well whatever the number turns out to be. No wonder then many backyard gardeners pay little attention to the pH of the soil under a particular plant. It isn't practical to be that specific in a mixed planting. It isn't practical even in large nurseries, most of which end up raising a wide variety of plants in soil of the same pH. As long as the soil isn't terribly acid or terribly alkaline, whatever you plant in it is going to prosper.

There are admittedly a few special cases where it may be worth making an intentional adjustment in the pH. Azaleas, rhododendrons, blueberries, and their kin like decidedly acid soils. Delphiniums, on the other hand, like it alkaline. The incidence of certain plant diseases depends on the pH of the soil the plants are growing

Pounds of Sulfur or Aluminum Sulfate to Add per 100 Square Feet

pH Change	Sulfur	Aluminum Sulfate
8.0–7.0	2	4.5
8.0–6.5	3	7
8.0–6.0	4	10
7.5–7.0	1.75	3.5
7.5–6.5	2	5
7.5–6.0	3.5	7.5
7.0–6.5	1.5	2.5
7.0–6.0	2	5.5
7.0–5.5	3.5	9
7.0–5.0	13	13
6.5–6.0	1.5	3
6.5–5.5	2.5	6.5
6.5–5.0	4	10.5
6.0–5.5	1.5	3.5
6.0–5.0	3	7.5
5.5–5.0	1.5	4

in. Potato scab is not a problem below pH 5.5. Neither is clubroot of cabbage above pH 7.2.

And finally, if you want to see something dramatic, try changing the flower color of big-leaf hydrangeas (*Hydrangea macrophylla* and cultivars). The flowers are either pink or blue depending on how acid the soil is. At a pH between 4.5 and 5.0, the flowers are blue as a result of aluminum in the soil; between 5.5 and 6.5, mauve; between 7.0 and 7.5, pink. Above that the plants become chlorotic. If you have a plant that is producing pink flowers you can switch it over to making blue ones by spreading a pound of dry aluminum sulfate per square yard under the bush in the spring and again in the fall. When the bush produces blue flowers, you can apply a pound of ground limestone to make it turn pink again. I have never done it; I think hydrangeas are homely in any hue. But I invite those more enthusiastic than I to experiment and let me know how it works. In the meantime, I will continue gardening in the soil I've got, which I'm certain is basically acid, more or less.

Fertilizers

I still remember a discarded combination lock I found as a boy, the kind that was used on school lockers. By carefully listening for clicks as I turned the dial, first one way and then the other, I discovered the combination and got the lock opened. Flushed with success, I imagined a bright future as a safecracker and kept the lock as proof of my prowess. It was not until much later that I discovered, by accident I suppose, that any three numbers whatsoever could be used to open the lock. All that mattered was that the dial be turned first to the left, then to the right, and then back to the left.

I remember that lock now as I think about fertilizer. By law every bag of synthetic fertilizer must carry an analysis of its ingredients. This analysis lists the percentages by weight of the nitrogen, phosphorus, and potassium contained in the fertilizer. The range of numbers is enormous: 5–10–10, 7–6–19, 23–15–18, 9–45–15, 4–12–5, and so on. If you begin by using one particular fertilizer, you could easily conclude that your zucchini depend on that particular analysis. It might take you years to discover the truth: with gardens, and certain cheap combination locks, almost any three numbers will do.

All the average flower or vegetable garden really needs is a complete and balanced fertilizer. To be considered complete, a fertilizer must contain significant amounts of nitrogen, phosphorus, and potassium. To be balanced, the amounts must be roughly equal, or, at least, one number should not be more than twice any of the others. Both a 5–10–10 and a 9–45–15 fertilizer are complete, but only the 5–10–10 is balanced.

The nitrogen, phosphorus, and potassium contained in fertilizer are only three of some sixteen chemical elements that have been shown to be essential to plant growth. The others aren't usually included in fertilizer because they aren't usually in short supply. (In a few regions of the country, zinc and boron are naturally deficient. To find out whether you need to worry, ask your Cooperative Extension Service agent.)

The three major fertilizer elements each do different things for plants when added to the soil. Nitrogen enhances the growth of leaves and stems. Phosphorus is important for the production of flowers, fruits, seeds, and roots. Potassium ensures general vigor and increases plants' resistance to disease. The three elements are often referred to by their chemical symbols, N, P, and K, as when the analysis is given in terms of total nitrogen (N), available phosphoric acid (P_2O_5), and soluble potash (K_2O). If you're like me and forget whether the "K" stands for potassium or phosphorus, remember that the ingredients in fertilizer are always listed in alphabetical order.

Unbalanced and even incomplete fertilizers have their places. The starter solutions I use at transplant time in the spring have high levels of phosphorus because the element is needed for root growth, and plants have trouble absorbing phosphorus in cool soil. If I were trying to green up the lawn or rush along a row of lettuce I might use a fertilizer high in nitrogen. In general, however, I prefer to use balanced fertilizers, believing that there is no harm in having a few extra nutrients, even if you don't need them at present.

Two general types of fertilizer are available: the so-called natural or organic fertilizers on the one hand, and inorganic or chemical fertilizers on the other. There is no law requiring nutrient analysis of natural fertilizers, and, indeed, the figures vary widely between samples. The accompanying table lists approximate analyses for a number of natural fertilizers.

Approximate Analyses of Natural Fertilizers

Bonemeal	2.5–24–0
Cow Manure (dried)	2–1.5–2
Cottonseed Meal	7–3–2
Dried Blood	12–0–0
Fish Meal	9–7–3
Horn and Hoof Meal	14–1–0
Poultry Manure (dried)	5–3–1.5
Dried Seaweed	1.5–.5–5
Sheep Manure (dried)	2–1.5–3
Wood Ashes	0–2–5

It is a waste of breath to argue the merits of natural versus chemical fertilizers. As far as the plants are concerned, the nutrients are the same. Natural fertilizers may contain trace amounts of other elements, but these aren't needed in most garden soils. Some natural fertilizers have the advantage of releasing their nutrients slowly, but there are slow-release synthetic fertilizers too. The only thing I can find that distinguishes natural fertilizers from chemical ones is the price. If you have to buy your fertilizer and you are short on cash, buy chemical fertilizer. (The tables may be turned in the future, when the petroleum required to produce chemical fertilizer becomes more expensive.)

Chemical fertilizers come in granules, powders, and liquids. The granules tend to be least expensive. Being less soluble, they release their nutrients over a longer period of time but may injure roots or leaves if they come into direct contact. Soluble powders and liquids, when diluted with water, aren't likely to injure plants, but their effects are short-lived since they are often rapidly leached from the soil.

I always purchase fertilizer in as large a quantity as I can conveniently use. The price per pound of active ingredient decreases dramatically as the size of the package increases. Faced with different analyses, I buy whichever fertilizer gives me the most actual nutrient for my dollar. The calculations would be easy if you could buy fertilizer in 100-pound quantities (percents would equal pounds), but the largest bag of fertilizer sold is 80 pounds. I wish I believed that that size was intended to make it easier to carry your purchases rather than to make it harder to comparison-shop.

Whenever I am comparing two balanced fertilizers, I concentrate on the first number in the analysis, which represents nitrogen. Because its manufacture consumes a lot of natural gas, nitrogen is nearly twice as expensive as potassium or phosphorus. It is also the element that is lost most quickly from soil. The farmer's supply store near me sells the following three fertilizers in 80-pound bags: 5–10–10 — $9; 10–10–10 — $10; and 15–15–15 — $11. Which is the best bargain? The bags contain 4, 8, and 12 pounds of nitrogen respectively, so I am faced with paying either $2.25, $1.25, or $0.92 per pound. I choose the 15–15–15 every time. The only thing I have to remember is that a more concentrated fertilizer should not be put on quite so heavily.

When I had my soil tested for lead content, the report that came back suggested I add 5 pounds of 5–10–10 per 100 square feet if I wanted to grow vegetables and 2 pounds per 100 square feet if I wanted flowers. I took the advice, more or less, broadcasting roughly half that amount of my 15–15–15 and digging it into the soil before planting. I like to spread fertilizer by hand, going back and forth over the ground several times to get an even distribution. Fertilizer is a salt that will dry out your skin and irritate open cuts, but other than that it doesn't harm bare hands.

In general, one application of fertilizer is all my plants get. But if I find a plant that looks a little peaked, or I want to get the most out of a row of leeks, I top-dress the plants with a second, lighter scattering of granular fertilizer when they are half grown, being careful not to get it directly on the foliage. This I don't dig in.

Some people like to feed their plants with liquid fertilizer during the summer. In the days when manure was common, a bag of it was soaked in a bucket of water and the resulting manure tea was ladled onto plants. Today dilute mixtures of soluble fertilizers can be sprayed directly on the foliage, where the nutrients are taken in through the leaves.

The effects of adding fertilizer may be dramatic, but they are not instantaneous. Wait two to four weeks before concluding that you haven't added enough. Too much fertilizer can do more harm than good. Excess nitrogen causes carrots to fork and keeps eggplants from flowering. In the meantime you can do a little experiment to see what all the talk about fertilizer burn is about. Select a young plant you don't mind sacrificing (the effect on an older one is less dramatic) and dump half a cup of granular fertilizer on it. When you see the leaves shrivel and dry up, you'll understand the hazards of fertilizer application. An overabundance of fertilizer salts draws water out of plant roots, injuring them and ultimately the leaves they supply.

Devout organic gardeners will claim that the use of chemical fertilizers leads relentlessly to the destruction of soil, plants, and ultimately us. By this point it should be clear that I disagree. Chemical fertilizers can be abused, but so can cow manure. Anyone who uses both chemical and natural fertilizers risks being impaled on the fence by one faction or the other. Under pressure from either camp, I will seek refuge in the observation that it doesn't really matter whether you are hauling bags of synthetic urea or bushel baskets of manure. It's the time spent hauling that we all ought to be focusing on.

Although I think chemical fertilizers are still the most inexpensive way to supplement soil nutrients, the proponents of natural fertilizer are correct in pointing out that you can't count on chemical fertilizers to maintain soil fertility. The soil must be deep enough and of a texture that allows free movement of air and water. Its pH must be within an acceptable range, and it must contain adequate moisture. An exclusive reliance on chemical fertilizers dooms the gardener to using ever-increasing quantities, since the organic matter in soil is constantly declining, most rapidly in soils aerated through regular cultivation. The lower the organic content of soil, the more quickly added nutrients are washed away and lost.

Whenever I fertilize my garden, I add organic matter as well. Compost, peat moss, old horse manure, and rotted sawdust — they are all the same. Half an inch or an inch spread over the surface makes a big difference. After all, a soil with 5 percent organic matter is considered rich. Adding these organic materials to my garden doesn't add nutrients directly, but it might as well because all of them reduce the amount of fertilizer I must use. Already I am using much less than originally recommended. Someday maybe I'll find that I can get away with o–o–o.

Water Works

RAINBOWS are all the more marvelous because they signal an abundance of both sunshine and water. Under the arching spectrum the lawns are luxuriant, the cucumbers fat and sweet, the lobelia blossoms a cool cobalt blue. The long days of summer come with enough light. Water is another matter. Average rainfall most often consists of too much followed by too little. This spring the rains were so frequent and the soil so sodden that pea seed rotted. With the help of trenches and raised beds, we drained the vegetable garden just in time for the drought. Weeks of uninterrupted sun soon turned the muck to dust. As the lawns dried up and even the lilac leaves began to wilt, the weatherman, as always, continued to refer to the rain that never fell as "a threat of showers."

Weatherman aside, none of the rest of us care to stand by idly and watch emeralds turn to straw. If the sky doesn't provide, we must. But this is easier said than done. A plant uses somewhere between 50 and 3,000 pounds of water for every pound of dry matter it produces, depending on its species. Five hundred pounds is about average. Some of this water is used to transport nutrients within the plant, some to maintain turgor pressure in the cells, and some for photosynthesis. The soil a plant is growing in must contain even more water than this, however, because a certain percentage will be lost to evaporation and some will remain permanently bound to the particles of soil.

Clay soils contain a higher percentage of this so-called unavailable water than do sandy ones. But they also have a higher field capacity — the maximum amount of water a soil will hold after gravity has drained away the excess. Available water, or capillary water, as it is also called, is the difference between a soil's field capacity and the unavailable water that remains when the plants begin to wilt.

Approximate Soil-Water Characteristics for Typical Soil Classes

	Sandy Soil	Loamy Soil	Clayey Soil
Dry weight 1 cu. ft.	90 lb.	80 lb.	75 lb.
Field capacity — % of dry weight	10%	20%	35%
Unavailable water	5%	10%	19%
Percent available water	5%	10%	16%
Water available to plants — lb./cu. ft.	4 lb.	8 lb.	12 lb.
Approximate depth of soil that will be wetted by each 1 in. of water applied if half the available water has been used	24 in.	16 in.	11 in.

Department of Irrigation, University of California, Davis.

As a rule of thumb, lawns and gardens need about an inch of water a week (two inches in arid regions). A tin can makes a simple rain gauge, which will show the gardener how much he must provide to make up for shortfalls. This is not as simple as it may sound. The week's ration for a 10-foot-by-10-foot plot amounts to 525 pounds. And since the water should be applied in one watering so that it has a chance to soak in and encourage deep roots rather than shallow ones, the gardener who has only a watering can wears out the grass and himself traveling to and from the faucet.

Moving the water is much easier with a hose. These long, thin "buckets" are constructed of vinyl or rubber or a combination of the two, and are best reinforced with nylon or other synthetic fiber. Rubber hoses have a higher burst strength, stay flexible at lower temperatures, and withstand more heat than vinyl hoses. They last longer, and they cost more. I think they are worth every penny. When I'm not using it in the garden I coil mine away where it will be out of full sun, trying not to drag the coupling across the asphalt driveway. In the fall, I drain it and store it in a dry place. I expect it to last as long as I do.

The diameter of a hose determines the rate at which it delivers water. A ¾-inch hose may be only 50 percent greater in diameter than a ½-inch one, but it delivers water more than twice as fast. The advantages to using a larger-diameter hose diminish, however, once

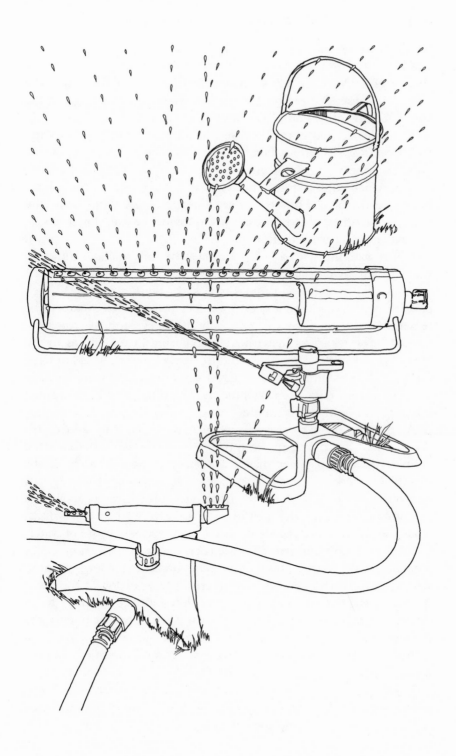

the diameter of the hose exceeds the diameter of the plumbing it is attached to. For most household use, a ⅝-inch-diameter hose is about right. Don't use a hose longer than necessary either, since the longer the hose, the greater the drop in water pressure between the faucet and the other end of the hose.

A nozzle screwed onto the hose end further reduces the pressure and hence slows the flow, but it does spread the water out so that it does not simply run off downhill in a narrow stream. A solid-brass nozzle, which adjusts from a fine mist to a narrow blast, should last as long as the hose. For seeds or seedlings, a nozzle with many tiny holes, sometimes called a rose, will provide gentle, low-pressure water that won't wash them out.

When watering with a hose, you must be sure to allow sufficient water to fall. A rain gauge is the surest way to measure how much water has fallen, but you can also check this with a trowel; an inch of water will wet soil to a depth of a foot or more. It is hard to be patient when hand-watering, especially in the evening. At this time of day the water soaks in without evaporating as quickly as in the heat of the day, but this is also the time when mosquitoes are most active. When blood is draining out of you only slightly more slowly than the water drains from the hose, it is hard not simply to dampen the dust and head for the house.

A sprinkler doesn't demand such attention. Set it up and go indoors. Here the problem becomes one of placement: the area the sprinkler waters may not match the shape of one's garden. If the sprinkler waters too much, one ends up soaking the driveway, the patio, the street. If it covers too little, you must move it about and risk double-watering the area of overlap. Overwetting isn't disastrous, nor is watering the street. Each, however, is a waste of water.

Here on Columbus Street we are charged about a tenth of a cent a gallon for city water, plus a 75 percent surcharge for sewage unless we can prove with a second water meter that a portion of the water we used went outdoors where it didn't flow into the sewer. A tenth of a cent a gallon is a great bargain when you compare it to even the cheapest bottled water, enough of a bargain that people don't seem to mind wasting water. But waste the water, and the price can only go up.

Oscillating sprinklers have a perforated bar that swings back and forth, watering a rectangle the size of which can be regulated by adjusting the faucet. Impulse sprinklers shoot a jet of water, which is broken into small droplets, and cover circles or portions thereof. Whirling sprinklers have two or more arms that spin around. Most wet a circle, but some wet a square. (The design of the latter is the sort of problem assigned to engineering students at MIT.) The best sprinkler is simply one that uniformly waters the area one wants watered. Nothing more.

All sprinklers have the disadvantage of throwing the water through the air, giving it a chance to evaporate before it hits the ground. As much as 10 percent of the water from a sprinkler may be lost this way. The only device I know that provides slow, well-defined water without much risk of premature evaporation is a soaker hose. A flat plastic hose with many perforations becomes a soaker hose when turned hole-side down. I like an old-fashioned canvas soaker, a simple tube of canvas that looks like a smaller version of the fireman's hose. I use one to water a very narrow border of petunias and zinnias at the edge of a stone retaining wall. By weaving the hose among the plants and leaving it on for hours at a time I can completely soak the soil without getting any water on the sidewalk or the zinnia leaves. If I wish to shorten the hose, I simply tie a knot in it. The only disadvantage of the canvas compared with some of the newer water-permeable synthetics that are now available is that I must gather the hose up after each use, hang it over the clothesline to dry, and store it inside. Otherwise, it rots.

Sprinklers and soakers both allow the gardener to go away and forget that the water is still running. To prevent this, a timer attached to the faucet will shut off the water when a certain time has elapsed. The best regulators, however, are not timers at all but meters. Since water pressure varies from moment to moment as toilets are flushed and dishwashers are turned on, time itself is a poor measure of how much water has flowed from a faucet. The meter records exactly how many gallons have passed. I calculate how many gallons I want to apply (remembering that there are roughly eight gallons to a cubic foot of water), dial the setting, and forget everything.

Indoors, there is always a drought. Perhaps the best argument for moving houseplants outdoors for the summer is that their owner gets a brief vacation from watering. Otherwise it is a weekly chore, month in and month out. Elisabeth won't let me use a hose indoors, fearing I will leave it coiled on the living-room rug, the nozzle dripping down behind the sofa cushions. And so the water gets carried by the watering-canful, the potful, the glassful. I wear out the carpet and myself shuttling back and forth to the sink. Outdoors, the soil has a great buffering capacity, so a bit of over- or underwatering doesn't hurt. Indoors, plants are either drying up and dying or succumbing to root rot and dying. Overwatering is the more likely possibility, especially in plastic pots sitting in watertight saucers.

In an effort not to leave the plants drowning in a pool of water, many gardeners tend to underwater. Hanging plants are especially easy to underwater, since their saucers don't just fill up but overflow, cascading down onto the stereo and the bookshelf. Some people recommend ice cubes for hanging plants, explaining that they melt slowly and the water can soak in; but I can't justify the price of this slow-release water. I end up simply clearing the spillway of anything valuable.

As in all arid-zone gardening, the buildup of salt left by evaporating water can become a problem. The only solution is to carry the houseplants to the sink every six months and flush the soil thoroughly with lots of water to dissolve and rinse out the salt. In fact, carrying the pots to the water is probably the right way to water them every time, but I can't face it. Too much work.

What's in a Name?

MORE THAN 20,000 species of plants are currently being nurtured by gardeners in the United States. Add to that countless cultivated varieties and you have a staggering number of names. The more experienced a gardener, the more names in her repertoire. But even the most prodigious mind is eventually overloaded. The botany professor was clearly at this point when upon being introduced to a new student he said, "Don't expect me to remember your name, young man; it will mean forgetting the name of a plant."

Plant names are important. They are the grips by which we handle plants. Names enable us to order a second specimen of something, permit us to describe the plant's properties to someone long-distance, assure us that the advice we are reading applies to what we are growing. Nonetheless, errors creep in, especially in the use of common names. Lady's slipper, for example, can refer to any of three different genera of orchids: *Cypripedium, Paphiopedilum,* or *Phragmipedium.*

Such confusion is dramatically lessened by the use of the Latin names of plants. In the system of naming made famous by the Swedish botanist Carolus Linnaeus, every known plant is assigned a two-word name. The first word is the genus name, the second is the specific epithet, a Latin adjective that modifies the genus. Thus within the genus *Acer,* the maples, there are several species: *Acer saccharum,* the sugar maple; *Acer rubrum,* the swamp maple; and so on. Because the names are a foreign language, they are usually printed in italics. The genus is capitalized, the specific epithet ordinarily not.

Every plant has a unique Latin name, but this doesn't eliminate the confusion. Botanists, in their efforts to improve taxonomy, keep changing plant names. The little wild flower called Quaker-ladies isn't in the genus *Houstonia* anymore; it has been moved to the genus *Hedyotis.* Not only do plants move from genus to genus, but whole species disappear, consumed in a burst of botanical simplification. When one species is declared synonymous with another, the older name takes precedence. When a particular species is found to be invalid, the plant itself doesn't disappear, of course. Only the name is jettisoned.

There is also the matter of cultivar (cultivated variety) names. Although each new cultivar now gets an official name when it is registered, there was in the past a proliferation of names for some plants, and different nurseries still sometimes use different names for the same plant, further confusing beleaguered nurserymen. *Hortus Third* (Macmillan, 1976), a dictionary of the plants cultivated in the United States and Canada, is the most comprehensive, up-to-date account of what a particular plant should be called.

Botanical debates over which name is correct look like academic niceties when a gardener is confronted with the problem of identifying a plant that is either totally misidentified or has somehow lost its name altogether. Last spring I bought a flat of young Italian parsley seedlings clearly labeled as such. I put them in the garden, mixing them up with blue ageratum as an experiment in edible landscaping. After being away in England for three weeks I returned to find that the plants were flourishing. But the leafstalks were standing upright instead of sticking out in all directions as parsley should. It took only a moment to reach over and break a leaf and taste it. Celery. This was no great loss; I simply pulled out the ageratum and raised celery instead. However, I can't help but wonder if mine was a unique case, or was the scenario repeated in gardens all over the city?

A more serious error showed up later the same summer in a grapevine I had planted three years earlier. The vine was supposed to be 'Ontario', whose medium-size, yellowish-white fruit ripens three weeks before 'Concord'. It ripened at the right time, but the grapes were large, not medium, and, more damning still, they were purple-black, not yellow. What am I to do with this plant? I have invested three years' work in it. It is growing magnificently, and the fruit is delicious. I have decided to call it 'Isn't Ontario' grape.

Gardeners can't do much about controlling what happens to name tags at nurseries, but they can do something about keeping track of the names once the plants arrive. First and foremost, keep track of the order form — it contains a list of what you ordered. When you

put the plants into the ground you can put a tag alongside them, but these tags are notoriously impermanent. Weather obliterates them, frost and children toss them around. Before long they have as little value as the small wooden label I found on the sidewalk in front of a house down the street, a house with an old and burgeoning garden. The penciled markings said, "Crocus [illegible] one foot North."

Better than labels are garden plans, kept in some sort of garden journal. Lecturing people about the importance of garden journals is like lecturing people about flossing their teeth. Some people are better record keepers than others, and most people are slow to change. But if you can sketch a map and put it in a drawer along with your order form, you will have some clue to what is planted when you can no longer remember.

Sometimes, of course, you have no choice. Suppose you have moved into a home where someone else planted the rosebushes and never knew the names, or at least left no records. What are you to do? In some cases you can assign a name with reasonable accuracy. In the case of a flowering shrub, this can often be done with the aid of a good book. In the case of a particular cultivar of iris, it would require the efforts of an expert.

My own anonymous inheritance is a cluster of five apple trees. They were planted forty years ago by a retired economist. That I know. He took enough care to wrap their trunks with hardware cloth. But by the time I came along the man had been dead many years, and the collars were girdling a number of the trunks. With pruning and fertilizing and spraying, I have gotten all the trees to bear regularly. They are all different — some are dessert apples, some are storage apples. Some of the fruit is soft and yellow, others hard and red. The first kind ripens by the first of August, the last not until the middle of October. Experience has taught me a great deal about these trees. I know them intimately — everything, that is, except their names. I have carried fruit around to commercial orchardists, who have been able to tell me only that the fruit isn't any of the common apples. I will keep searching.

But in the meantime I have been thinking about this issue of names. It is possible to get too caught up in them. Referring to everything by its Latin name is at best an affectation, at worst silly. Who wants *Fragaria* × *ananassa* with cream? Use names to make yourself clear; use the right names to eliminate confusion. But using a name correctly does not make you a gardener. You have to get to know the plant, and that takes years of acquaintance. When you get to the point where you are raising something well, it doesn't really matter what it is called. Does a mother who calls her children by the wrong names love them any less?

Seed Catalogs

"SCENES OF UTOPIA" would be a more precise term for seed catalogs. On their shiny pages, all the flowers blossom at once, the pansies with the petunias, the columbines with the sunflowers. No wind or rain has battered these blooms, nor has any errant dog or rabbit left its mark. Most of the pictures are closeups, but when we get a glimpse of a plant's surroundings, we see ground that is weed-free, lawns that are neatly edged and freshly mown.

The vegetables in these catalogs are marvelous. Here, too, we are offered all the delights of spring, summer, and fall in a single serving. Ripe tomatoes jostle one another for space, crowded by Swiss chard on one side of the alphabet and turnips on the other. A few pages away a dozen kinds of lettuce are laid out head to head. Not only do the vegetables rival the flowers in opulence, but many of them seem to have prepared themselves for the table. The watermelons and muskmelons are sliced open; the butternut squash is peeled and baked. The broccoli is boiled, the cabbage is shredded, the onion sliced and atop a hamburger. The vegetable garden in the seed cata-log resembles some modern-day Cockaigne, that fanciful land where food was so abundantly available that it came running to be eaten.

All gardeners are optimistic, and none more so than the beginner at the start of a new year. What these catalogs are offering might as well be magic beans. Even the veteran gardener, hardened by the wisdom that comes from having dreams fail to germinate, opens each new catalog and imagines planting some of everything. Even if one discounts the superlatives in the text, there is no denying that some-one raised these flowers. Why not me?

Trying to grow everything is like approaching a huge buffet table carrying a small plate. The portions of each dish we sample become too small even to taste, let alone enjoy, and many of them end up cascading off the plate and are lost altogether. Each of us has a finite garden, which in proportion to the offerings of a seed catalog becomes a small plate indeed.

Deciding what to grow is ultimately a personal decision, but the final choice is easier if you begin by deciding what not to grow. First, there are all those plants that can be raised from seed but rarely are. And usually with good reason. Before you order African violet seed, ask yourself how many people you know have grown their African violets from seed (as opposed to starting with a severed leaf, a division, or a purchased plant) and whether you want to be one of them. Seed is lightweight and easy to package, making it attractive to mail-order concerns, but it is often a lot easier for the gardener to buy at least his perennial flowers from a nursery that has raised the plants through infancy.

In general, one should be wary of trying to grow plants that no one else seems to know about. The absence of gazania in the neighborhood may not be due simply to ignorance. Gazania does much better in the heat of the Southwest than in the cool of the Northeast. If you are thinking of growing something that seems exotic, ask an experienced gardener living nearby. Seed companies are doing a nationwide business and aren't entirely at fault for regional limitations.

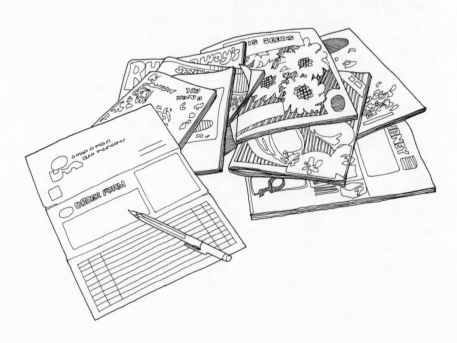

That said, however, I wish the seedsmen would give us some advance warning in their catalogs about how long it takes for a particular flower to bloom from the time we sow the seed. Flowers vary enormously in this. In northern areas most flowers must be sown indoors and seedlings transplanted outdoors, but the period they must spend indoors varies from weeks to months. As it is now, we must wait until the seed packets arrive to discover how many weeks before the last frost to sow the seeds indoors. And even then you don't know how long it will be until the plants flower. Experienced gardeners try to keep records, a sort of sowing timetable with notations about when the seeds were sown, when they were first transplanted, when they were planted outdoors, and when they bloomed. Commercial growers raising flowering plants for sale keep similar records, and they are every bit as valuable to the home gardener. Beginners shouldn't avoid flowers simply because of these uncertainties; but proceed cautiously until you have worked out your own timetable and discovered which flowers you have the time and energy to grow from seed.

Choosing among vegetables is made easier by knowing the precise number of days to maturity — a figure that is given in the seed catalogs and usually appears right after the vegetable's name. Obviously, one does not want to try to grow 'Blue Hubbard' squash with its requirement of 120 days from seed to maturity in an area with only 90 frost-free days, or if you can't get it sown until fewer than 120 days of the season remain. Because the number of days to maturity is influenced by temperature, fertilizer, and water, I always figure on the conservative side and add 7 to 10 days to my calculations of when to start the seeds.

Bush beans that take 50 days to mature will still be yielding beans a week later, though they won't bear all summer long, as pole beans will. Therefore it doesn't make sense to sow at once one kind of bush bean that ripens in 50 days and another in 56 unless you want to be picking both at once. To spread out the harvest, plan on repeated sowings or choose cultivars whose numbers of days to maturity are generously spaced.

The exception to the general accuracy with which seed catalogs report the growing period for vegetables concerns celery, peppers, eggplants, and tomatoes. The number of days to maturity listed after these plants refers to the time after transplants are set in the garden.

For celery this means 10 to 12 weeks should be added to the stated number of days, 8 to 10 weeks for peppers and eggplants, and 6 to 8 for tomatoes. In the rush to demonstrate how early their vegetables mature, the catalogs have done a disservice in suggesting that 'Early Girl' hybrid tomatoes, for example, can be grown in 54 days, when the actual figure is at least 96.

In deciding how to simplify our choices still further, we are confronted with the question of whether to buy hybrid seed or seed from so-called open-pollinated cultivars. Seeds from the latter have been produced without human intervention. Hybrid seed, on the other hand, comes from crossing two different parent lines. It combines the genetic traits of both parents and often exhibits something termed "hybrid vigor," a healthy exuberance that seems to result from the good qualities of one parent canceling out the bad of the other and vice versa. Hybrid offspring are often more robust and productive than either parent, but because they are of mixed ancestry their own offspring will be quite varied, making it impossible for gardeners to save their own seed. The production of the hybrid seed also requires maintaining both parent lines and often performing laborious hand-pollinations. As a result, hybrid seed is more expensive than non-hybrid seed. Hybrid tomato seeds now cost three to four cents apiece; seeds of nonhybrid tomatoes, which will breed true provided they are grown in isolation, cost less than a penny.

One of the major concerns of plant breeders is disease, and gardeners are wise to choose cultivars reported to exhibit disease tolerance or resistance. It will be easier for the gardener if the plants themselves control the various mildews, anthracnose, mosaic, and wilts to which they will no doubt be exposed.

The seed companies have their own favorites, and often identify the cultivars they recommend. In addition, industry-based selection was standardized back in 1932, when producers of vegetable and flower seeds organized the All-America Selections (AAS), a national network of trial gardens that tests new cultivars of flowers and vegetables. The seeds are submitted by the producer, a committee selects a comparison cultivar, and the two are grown side by side in trial gardens. An elaborate scoring system is used to measure performance: less than 5 percent of the entries are judged sufficiently different from existing cultivars to merit a prize. Prior to 1983, there were three categories of medals given: bronze, silver, and gold. Of the opinion that bronze was beginning to sound like "third place," the executive board decided as of January 1983 to lump silver and bronze into a single category called AAS Winner. I agree with the AAS committee that even a bronze medal makes a flower or a vegetable worthy of a gardener's attention, but I am sorry to see the silver medalists disappear.

How many different flowers and vegetables you end up ordering will depend on your circumstances. I usually end up growing a couple of cultivars of each: two peas, two broccoli, two carrots. This

---

All-America Award Gold Medal Winners Still in General Commerce

FLOWERS

Coreopsis 'Early Sunrise' 1989
Cosmos 'Sunset' 1966
Linaria 'Fairy Bouquet' 1934
Lobelia 'Rosemund' 1934
Morning Glory 'Scarlett O'Hara' 1939
Nasturtium 'Golden Gleam' 1935
Nasturtium 'Scarlet Gleam' 1935
Petunia 'Firechief' 1950
Zinnia 'Peter Pan Pink' Hybrid 1971
Zinnia 'Peter Pan Plum' Hybrid 1971
Zinnia 'Scarlet Ruffles' Hybrid 1974
Zinnia 'Thumbelina' 1963

VEGETABLES

Bean 'Topcrop' 1950
Broccoli 'Green Comet' Hybrid 1969
Cabbage 'Ruby Ball' Hybrid 1972
Cabbage 'Savoy Ace' Hybrid 1977
Cantaloupe 'Honey Rock' 1933
Corn 'Iochief' Hybrid 1951
Lettuce 'Salad Bowl' 1952
Pea Edible Podded 'Sugar Snap' 1979
Squash 'Caserta' 1949
Watermelon 'New Hampshire Midget' 1951

practice gives me a chance to compare them, like the AAS commit-tee. By growing the best cultivar in each pair next year alongside something new, I am assured that at least half of what I grow will do well; any failures with the unfamiliar cultivars I chalk up to ed-ucation.

One final caveat: Don't order more seed than you need. Catalogs are fairly good at specifying how many seeds you get or how long a row a packet will sow. And though there seem to be fewer seeds in a packet every year, in most cases there are still plenty. Despite one's best intentions, leftover seed packets are unlikely to be reopened.

Making out one's seed order isn't half as complicated as all this may sound. Whatever effort goes into making intelligent choices will be more than repaid by the results. Gardens are never perfect, but seed catalogs are a step in the right direction.

The Seed You Need

NOWHERE is the gardener's tendency toward excess more apparent than in the case of ordering seed. Year after year even the most experienced gardeners end up buying more seed than they can use. From a plant's point of view extra seed is just insurance that some will germinate, but to a gardener the sight of two- or three-year-old packets still partially filled with now-defunct seed is depressing. Dreams that died on the shelf.

It doesn't seem to matter whether you are buying from one catalog or ten, whether you have put off ordering until the last minute or have been poring over the pages for weeks. The descriptions are all so attractive that you end up ordering some of everything, and an excess of most things.

Even if the sight of wasted seed does not bother you, the steadily rising price of seed should catch your attention. Despite reductions in the number of seeds contained, the price of most seed packets is now over a dollar. If all you want is a half-dozen petunia plants, it is more economical to buy a flat of six seedlings raised by someone else than to buy 150 seeds for roughly the same price and spend three months rearing the plants yourself.

Years ago, when I began growing vegetables, my seed order was subsidized by an aunt who included the stipulation that some of the money had to be used to buy flower seed. Now, hundreds of dozens of home-grown annual flowers later, I confess that I am buying fewer and fewer flower seeds. Partly this is because the bedding-plant industry, which now produces some three billion flowering annuals each year, offers a diversity of choice that I cannot easily match. Partly it is because a great many of the flowers I grow are perennials, which don't have to be started again every year.

But I continue to buy vegetable seed. Except for asparagus, horseradish, Jerusalem artichoke, and rhubarb, there aren't any perennial vegetables. And the vegetable seedlings sold commercially don't match the flowers in number or variety. Only one vegetable seedling, usually of some widely grown cultivar, is grown for every three flowers.

Deciding not to grow one's own flowers from seed doesn't greatly ease the task of deciding what seed to order. Every year there are new catalogs with yet more possibilities. The most recent invitation to excess comes in the form of a catalog of catalogs. *The Garden Seed Inventory: 2nd Edition,* edited by Kent Whealy of the Seed Savers' Exchange (Rural Route 3, Box 239, Decorah, Iowa 52101), is a compilation of more than five thousand nonhybrid vegetables and the 215 companies that currently offer the seed. From cover to cover are companies and cultivars I have never heard of. But so far I am resisting the temptation.

At the heart of the matter is the fact that my garden, like everyone else's, is a finite size. Over the winter it may swell in my imagination, but if I took a tape measure to its snowy expanse I would find that it has the same old dimensions. We all know the sizes of our respective gardens, and sooner or later we will have to come to terms with their capacities. Experience teaches us that trying to grow too many kinds of vegetables in limited space invariably means wasting seed. If you only have room for a couple dozen tomato plants and want to try growing six kinds, you would use four or five seeds out of each packet and end up with six packets all still 90 percent full.

In England gardeners with very small plots regularly devote all of their space to achieving the perfect culture of a single vegetable — a particular cultivar of leek, or parsnip, or Brussels sprout. What at first seems to be a peculiar preoccupation with a single crop comes to seem quite sensible when you have experienced the chaos and waste resulting from trying to do everything at once in too little space. There is more than pleasure in growing a few things extremely well.

We Americans are unlikely to abandon our taste for variety and passion for self-sufficiency. So the problem is to estimate how many different kinds of vegetables can be grown in a garden of a given size. The technique that I have worked out begins by considering how much garden space the progeny of a given packet will occupy.

Because seeds of different vegetables vary considerably in cost, seed companies put differing numbers of them into packets so that these sell for roughly the same price. To guide the consumer, most com-

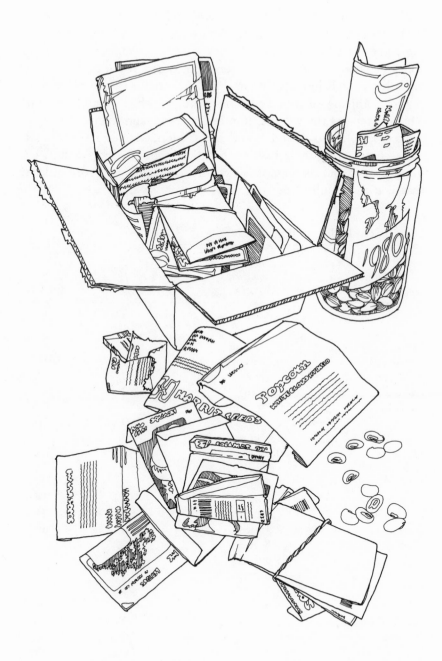

panies tell you somewhere in their catalogs how many feet of row one of their seed packets will plant. More recently they have started telling you exactly how many seeds they are selling you as well — probably in response to the complaints of customers horrified to discover only thirty seeds in a packet that used to contain two hundred.

One company deserving commendation for the thoroughness with which it reports the weight, number of seeds, and sowing rate of its packets is Johnny's Selected Seeds, of Albion, Maine. The figures in the accompanying table have been culled from a recent catalog. Using numbers such as these it is possible to prepare your seed order so that you make fullest use not only of your garden space but of the

What a Seed Packet Will Sow

Vegetable	Size of Smallest Packet	No. of Seeds It Contains	Approx. Feet It Will Sow
Beans	2 ounces	175	20–25
Beets	5 grams	385	30
Broccoli	1.5 grams	300	30
Brussels sprouts	0.5 grams	80	15
Cabbage	1 gram	240	25
Carrots	2 grams	1200	40
Cauliflower	0.75 gram	200	20
Corn	2 ounces	300	75
Cucumbers	2.5 grams	90	15
Eggplant	0.25 gram	50	n/a
Kale	1.5 grams	360	24
Leeks	1.5 grams	525	21
Lettuce	1 gram	830	34
Muskmelon	1.5 grams	60	15
Okra	2 grams	30	n/a
Onions	1.5 grams	345	17
Peas	3 ounces	375	15
Peppers	0.5 gram	70	n/a
Radishes	4.5 grams	395	15
Spinach	5 grams	440	35
Summer squash	4 grams	30	10
Tomatoes	0.5 gram	50	n/a
Watermelon	2.5 grams	60	15
Winter squash	variable	30	10–15

seeds you order. If you are going to plant beets, plan on a row that is 30 feet long. If you want to plant two kinds of beets, plan either to double the space or to share half of each packet with another gardener. It quickly becomes clear that your garden must be very large indeed if you are to use up a significant portion of all the seed packets of all the cultivars you might like to order. The only way to do justice to seed packets of ten different tomatoes is to plant a couple of hundred tomato plants. Which I have done, but it meant dealing with about a ton of ripe fruit.

The stated number of feet of row that a packet will sow is only approximate. If you intend to sow your carrots in a wide row — say, a band 8 to 12 inches wide — then a packet of seed won't go as far as listed. On the other hand, estimates of how many plants you will get from a packet assume average in-garden germination rates. In cold soil with an uneven water supply, a great deal of seed will not germinate. The estimates take that into account. But if you sow your seeds indoors under optimum conditions, the percentage of germination can be much higher, as high in fact as the laboratory-tested percentage listed on the back of the seed packet. Indoors, germinating every tomato seed you sow is entirely possible.

Even if you do your sowing directly outdoors there are ways to get the most out of a packet of seed. First, wait for conditions to be right. In the case of corn, wait until the soil temperature has reached 75 degrees. (If you must plant earlier, be sure that the seed is treated with thiram fungicide to prevent it from rotting before it germinates.) Then space the seed so that you don't do as much thinning of excess seedlings. Instead of sowing corn seed every four inches, as is usually recommended, and later thinning to stand a foot apart, I sow two seeds every 16 inches, spacing the two seeds a couple of inches apart, and then do no thinning. In most places both seeds will germinate; in some places one. I usually end up with approximately one plant per foot of row, and I use only half as much seed.

All of this is to say that it really takes very little seed to plant a vegetable garden. If we want to grow some of everything, we will have seed left over. So what does one do with the extra seed? If you store it cool and dry it will remain viable for a couple of years. Put the packets of unused seed with a tissue-packet of powdered milk inside a screw-top jar and store the jar in the refrigerator. The dried milk will serve as a desiccant, soaking up moisture from the air inside the jar that would otherwise get into the seeds.

Next year you can inventory the contents of the jar and make allowances when you order seeds. But you know what is going to happen, don't you? You aren't going to trust what you have. Perhaps it was already old seed; perhaps there isn't as much seed in the packet as you thought there was; perhaps something will happen to it and it won't come up. You aren't going to take the time to test the viability of the seed by seeing how many germinate when wrapped in a damp paper towel. It would be best to buy some more seed, wouldn't it? Well, no, it wouldn't. It would be best to buy less in the first place. If you have trouble remembering that, just repeat over and over as you go through the seed catalogs: "I have only one garden. I am only buying for one year. I have only one bank account." It helps.

Sowing Seeds Indoors

SEEDLINGS ON A WINDOWSILL are as sure a sign of impending spring as snowdrops and crocuses. Even where the growing season is long enough for outdoor-sown plants to reach maturity, most gardeners start some of their flowers and vegetables indoors. We may think that we want marigolds to bloom earlier or tomatoes to bear longer, but our efforts are as much a measure of our impatience with winter.

As much as we might like it to be spring, we must be careful not to sow seeds prematurely. Seeds planted too soon will produce over-sized transplants — large but so stunted by their small pots that they will fail to make good growth when planted in the garden. Calculating when to sow seeds indoors is a matter of noting on the seed packet the number of weeks needed to produce a transplant of suitable size. Then count backwards from the average date of the last frost in your locality (or whatever other date the packet says is safe to let one's progeny outdoors). If these calculations reveal that it is still too early, eager gardeners will have to content themselves with setting up.

The first step is to select a container that will serve as a seed flat. You can sow seeds directly in individual pots and allow them to grow undisturbed until they are transplanted outdoors. This is the preferred method for melon, cucumber, squash, and other seedlings that resent having their roots handled. For most plants, however, it is more efficient to sow a number of seeds in a single container. This way you don't have to worry if germination proves to be less than 100 percent, or if some of the seedlings emerge less robust than others. When the seedlings in the flat are big enough to handle, you can select the best and transplant these into individual pots.

Seedlings suffer from wet feet, so whatever you use as a seed flat should have ample drainage holes in the bottom. The flats I use are plastic and measure 4½ inches by 6 inches. They are 2½ inches deep and have six generous drain holes. I prefer to use small flats like these, sowing only one kind of seed in a given flat. If I used larger flats, I could plant the seeds of several cultivars in each flat. But then I would risk mixing up cultivars. It is easier to sex newly hatched chicks than to tell two petunia seedlings apart.

What the seed flat is made of — wood, plastic, or aluminum — is unimportant, provided it is a material that can be cleaned. Cleanliness is crucial to ensure that your seedlings don't contract some lethal disease. Before I use my flats, I run them through the dishwasher. If the plastic isn't dishwasher-safe, it can be sterilized with a 1:10 solution of bleach and water. Follow with a thorough rinse of plain water.

The soil used in seed flats need not be fancy. Again, it should be clean, it should hold moisture, and it should allow sufficient air to reach the seedlings' roots. Traditionally, gardeners have satisfied these requirements with a mix of one part fine peat and one part coarse sand. These materials are relatively free of harmful organisms, and they hold moisture and provide aeration, respectively. If the seedlings are going to be transplanted immediately, it doesn't matter that such a mix contains virtually no nutrients. The seed provides all the nourishment needed for germination.

Seedlings usually aren't transplanted immediately, however; they are allowed to grow a second set of leaves. The traditional means of providing a bit of nourishment has been to add one part of soil to the mix. But soil is not clean. Adding soil to the sand and peat also adds bacteria, fungi, and nematodes. To control these you must treat the soil, usually with heat. A temperature of 140 degrees Fahrenheit for 40 minutes won't sterilize a mix, but it will pasteurize it, making it safe for seedlings. Heaped in shallow pans, the mix can be heated in an ordinary oven, or even a microwave oven. Avoid heat above 185 degrees, because it can break down some of the complex chemical compounds in the soil, releasing toxic byproducts such as ammonia.

It is a nuisance to pasteurize the mix, and the loam and sand add considerable weight. These objections have prompted the invention of a number of soilless mixes, which are principally mixtures of peat and vermiculite. The latter is a material that consists of gray sponge-like kernels, each made up of many accordion layers. Vermiculite originates as a micaceous mineral mined in Montana and North Carolina. The crude ore has microscopic amounts of water trapped in its layers. Heated in a furnace at 2000 degrees Fahrenheit, the water turns to steam and pops the layers of ore apart, creating the kernels. These are highly porous, but, unlike sand, weigh no more than 10 pounds per cubic foot.

To this mix of peat and vermiculite, synthetic fertilizer and ground limestone are added. The formula for one such mix, Cornell Peat-Lite, intended for germinating seeds, is as follows:

1 bushel shredded sphagnum peat moss
1 bushel horticultural (not construction) vermiculite (No. 4–fine)
4 level tbsp. ammonium nitrate
2 level tbsp. powdered superphosphate (20 percent)
10 level tbsp. finely ground dolomitic limestone

Such a mix, which usually needs no pasteurization, is a delight to use. And what's more, it doesn't have to be homemade. Premixed commercial versions are widely available and make a great deal of sense for the home gardener who, after all, doesn't need very much each year.

When the date on which you have determined to sow a particular seed arrives, wash your hands and fill a clean flat with mix. Press it down with the backs of your fingers so that the mix is level and about half an inch below the rim of the flat. I find that the unmoist-ened soilless mix flows rather freely through the drain holes in my seed flats, so I set them on shallow plastic-foam trays saved from the packages of meat one buys at the supermarket. Later, when the flats have been moistened, the trays keep excess water from dripping on the floor.

Before you do anything else, make out a label with the name of the cultivar being sown and the date and stick it in the seed flat. Then cut the corner off the seed packet. If you are sowing large seeds (like tomato or zinnia) you can place them one at a time on the surface of the mix. If they are lettuce or nicotiana, you will have to tap the open packet with your fingers as you move it back and forth over the flat. With luck, the seeds will roll out a few at a time. Whether the seeds are sown one at a time or broadcast, they should be about half an inch apart. Resist the temptation to sow a few extra, for if they all germinated those seedlings would be so crowded they'd be hard to separate.

Seeds must be kept moist, and one way to assure this is to cover them. The smallest seeds won't need any covering at all, but larger ones will. A rule of thumb is to cover them to a depth twice the diameter of the seed. This means never more than half an inch. I have trouble judging how deep the seed has been covered, so I use a layer of pure vermiculite to cover my seeds. Not only is it easy to see the gray vermiculite against the brown soilless mix, but the vermiculite is rough enough not to erode if I choose to water the seed flats from above. It is safer to water the sown flat from below, however. Set the flat in a pan containing an inch of water. The water will move to the surface by capillary action, and when the surface is damp the flat can be lifted up and drained of excess water. Some people like to set a sheet of glass over the flat to hold in moisture; plastic wrap would do as well. I find a rectangle of newspaper cut to fit neatly on top of the vermiculite works, too. Keep the paper damp by sprinkling it lightly every few days until the seeds germinate, but be careful not to overwater. Seeds should be kept moist, not wet. When seedlings begin to push up the paper, discard it.

Although light is important for seedlings, many seeds will germinate in the dark. Exceptions among vegetables are celery, dandelion, garden cress, lettuce, mustard, and witloof chicory, all of which need light to sprout. Most seeds, however, will germinate in the dark provided they are kept moist. And warm. Germination is essentially a series of chemical reactions that proceed more rapidly the higher the temperature (see the table on page 54). Up to a point, the warmer the soil the faster the germination. If there is no recommendation on the seed packet, try to find a location where the temperature is between 75 and 80 degrees Fahrenheit. Since this is above the normal winter temperature in most homes, it will take some hunting with a thermometer to discover where in the house these conditions exist. Try on top of the refrigerator, above a radiator, or in a gas oven with the pilot on. Given warm enough conditions, seeds will be up in a surprisingly short time, and this year's garden will be on its way.

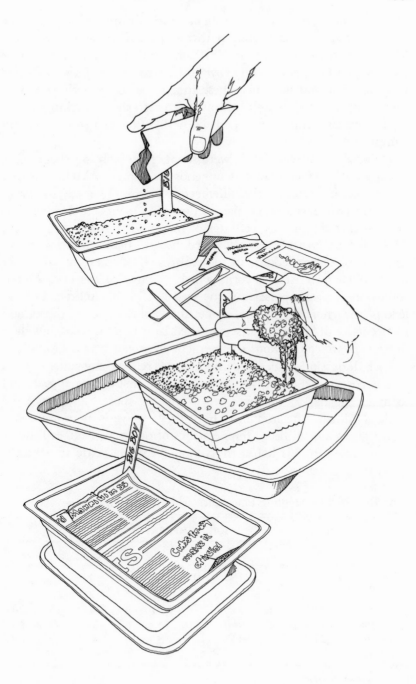

If you have ever sprouted alfalfa seeds or mung beans in the kitchen, you may have noticed that roots emerge and grow quite long before the shoots appear. This is how all seeds germinate. Since roots respond to gravity and grow downward, if the seeds are buried in a seed flat you will miss these first stages of growth. The first visible signs that all is well are tiny pale green shoots sticking up out of the planting mix, a few perhaps with split-open seed coats still clinging to them.

Depending on what seeds were sown, the emerging shoots have either a hook, which gradually unbends, or a spike. Although it isn't of practical importance, the difference is a convenient way to distinguish the two classes into which all flowering plants are divided. The hook is characteristic of seedlings of marigold, tomato, and zinnia, which belong to the class Dicotyledonae — plants possessing two seed leaves, or cotyledons, in the embryo. The spike, on the other hand, is characteristic of corn, which belongs to the class Monocotyledonae, plants possessing one seed leaf in the embryo. Dicotyledons and monocotyledons, sometimes abbreviated as dicots and monocots, will be further distinguished later in their lives, but their differences are conspicuous the moment the shoot breaks ground.

Such digressions aside, it is important to remove any paper or glass that is covering the seed flat as soon as the first shoots appear, and to move the flat to wherever it will get the most light. Once the seeds germinate, the amount of light they receive is more important than the amount of heat. Temperatures of 60 to 70 degrees Fahrenheit are fine. In this house the young seedlings settle in a south-

Days Required for Seedling Emergence at Various Temperatures

Vegetable	SOIL TEMPERATURE (°F)								
	32°	41°	50°	59°	68°	77°	86°	95°	104°
Cabbage			15	9	6	5	4		
Eggplant					13	8	5		
Onion	136	31	13	7	5	4	4	13	NG
Pepper	NG	NG	NG	25	13	8	8	9	NG
Tomato	NG	NG	43	14	8	6	6	9	NG
Watermelon					12	5	4	3	

NG — No Germination

facing bay window on the second floor, where, even though the sun is still low in the sky, the house next door doesn't shade them, and they benefit from the heat that rises inexorably up the front stairs.

It is impossible to give seedlings too much light, but it is all too easy to give them too much water. This will likely result in a dreaded disease called damping-off, the symptoms of which are seedlings that suddenly topple over and die. This is the result of fungi attacking the stem at soil level. Overwatering, lack of drainage, poor ventilation, and crowding of seedlings all promote the growth of several species of fungi that are responsible for damping-off. Like most plant diseases, damping-off is much easier to prevent than it is to cure. I have had some success with dusting powdered sulfur over the surfaces of infected flats. The sulfur probably just dries out the surface, and it is easier to keep the surface dry in the first place. Don't water the seed flats any more than necessary. Also, don't rush to fertilize unless the seedlings begin to look pale, and then use only a water-soluble fertilizer diluted to half the recommended strength. The mix the seedlings are growing in usually has enough nutrients to sustain them until they are ready to be transplanted.

The first leaves of seedlings are seldom what one expects. They usually don't look anything like the leaves of an adult plant. In some cases, beans for example, the first leaves are actually the two cotyledons of the seed, which have turned green and are photosynthesizing. But even in peas, where the two cotyledons remain underground, the first leaves are atypical. (One of the advantages of sowing seeds indoors in a pasteurized mix is that you don't have to worry about which infant seedlings are flowers and vegetables, and which are weeds.)

The second set of leaves produced by seedlings may not look entirely normal either, but they are a step in the right direction, and their appearance signals that it is time to move the seedlings out of the seed flat and into individual pots. Before this the seedlings are so delicate they are easily crushed: after this, injury is likely to occur from pulling apart the intergrown roots.

Whatever type one chooses, individual pots must be large enough to accommodate the seedling's growth until it is eventually transplanted into the garden outdoors. Certain seedlings, onions and lettuce for example, can be grown in pots as small as one inch square.

Tomatoes, on the other hand, should get pots at least two inches square (four times as large). In general the larger the container, the stronger and stockier the seedling will ultimately be. Smaller pots, on the other hand, save space. There never seems to be enough room on windowsills, and this is incentive enough to use the smallest containers possible.

Many home gardeners use small pots made of pressed peat. These are widely sold and have the virtue that they can be planted straight in the ground, seedling and all, the roots of the plant eventually growing through the sides of the pot. I have quit using these as often as I once did, partly because of their cost and partly because I found that unless I was careful to break away the rim of the pot down to soil level before I planted the seedling, the pot stayed so dry that the seedling's roots had difficulty penetrating the peat walls.

Commercial growers use multicelled plastic containers that resemble ice-cube trays. These are sold in garden centers and the like, and if handled carefully will last for several seasons. Do not emulate the few nurseries that still grow seedlings all in one box, allowing the roots of the plants to commingle. Tearing these plants apart invariably results in severe transplant shock when the seedlings are set out in the garden.

Egg cartons, sawed-off milk cartons, and cardboard orange juice cans have all been used successfully to raise seedlings. The containers I have used for many years and continue to recommend are plastic-foam drinking cups. Whether you buy them in the store or salvage them from the wastebasket after church on Sunday, these cups need only three small holes punched in the bottoms with a sharp pencil to become ideal seedling pots. They are large enough to support even big tomato seedlings, yet small enough for a dozen to be parked on a windowsill. Their tapered sides make it easy to knock out the seedling's root ball without disturbance, and they can be washed out and reused.

You can fill the containers with whatever you used to germinate the seedlings, but I prefer to stretch the soilless mix I use for germination with perlite. Perlite, like vermiculite, is a naturally occurring material. The crude gray-white siliceous ore is mined from lava flows, crushed, and heated to 1400 degrees Fahrenheit, at which point small amounts of water in the particles turn to steam, expanding the particles to light spongy kernels. Perlite is less likely than vermiculite to disintegrate with handling. If it has any fault it is that it lasts too long; the whitish granules are visible in garden soil for years. But I find that one part perlite mixed with two parts soilless mix provides excellent drainage and aeration for the roots of the developing seedlings.

Some people like to fill their containers and then poke holes in the mix into which they stick the roots of the seedling. The British expression for transplanting seedlings out of a seed flat is "pricking out," in reference to making these holes with a pointed tool. I find that I tend to kink the roots trying to get them into a hole like this, so I prefer to suspend the seedling over a partially filled pot with my left hand as I fill it with soilless mix from my right.

But first one must disengage the seedlings from the seed flat. For this I prefer a kitchen fork (or rather, a kitchen-type fork, since there is some ill feeling about my expropriating the daily cutlery). Provided that the seedlings have not been sown too close together, it is easy to dig out a seedling, roots and all. If the flat has been sprinkled beforehand, ample mix should adhere to the roots. Once the seedling has been uprooted with the fork it can be grasped with your fingers, but be careful never to squeeze the stem. Rather, hold the seedling by its leaves. The stem is far too tender to risk bruising, and any bruising will be fatal. However, the seedling can quickly compensate for injury to the leaves by growing new ones. I usually grasp the seedling just under its first leaves, cradling it between the first two fingers and the thumb of one hand.

Then, holding it over a partially filled foam cup, I add potting mix with my other hand until the seedling is positioned slightly lower in the mix than it was in the seed flat. Do not plant the seedling so deep that the first leaves are buried. There should also be at least half an inch of freeboard between the mix and the rim to allow for watering. Finally, press the mix down gently with your fingers to ensure it is snug against the roots, and water the pot until water runs out the drainage holes.

Handling tiny seedlings can make your neck stiff as you strain not to injure them. It helps to remember that, like human babies, they are remarkably tolerant of accidental mishandling. This isn't an invitation to abuse, just a reminder not to worry overly much about their survival.

I like to keep my seedlings out of full sun for half a day or so just after transplanting. This allows them a chance to recover. But then they need full sunlight again. The most obvious sign of insufficient

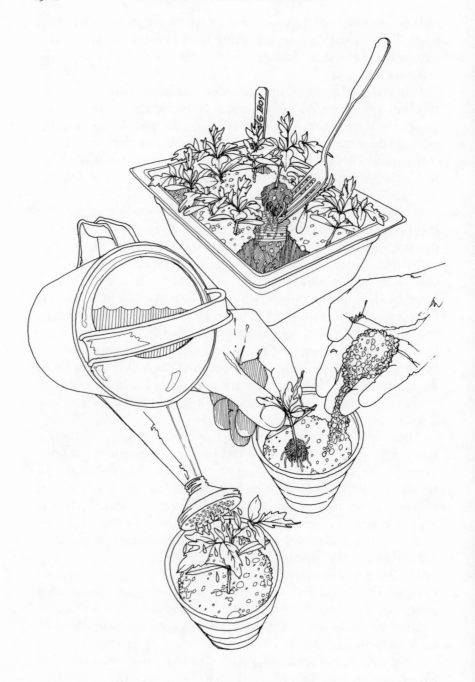

light is an excessively large gap between leaves or sets of leaves. This
legginess, and the accompanying paleness of stems and leaves, can
be corrected only by more light.

Even if the seedlings are receiving enough light, they will tend to
grow toward it. Plants on a windowsill bend toward the outdoors.
To compensate for this, turn the pots every few days, or erect a re-
flective barrier on the room side of the seedlings to bounce some
sunlight against them from the opposite direction.

The older the seedling the less likely it is to succumb to damping-
off, but it is still important not to overwater. Don't be alarmed if
your seedlings occasionally dry out so much they wilt. Provided the
leaves aren't crisp, they will recover from even severe prostration once
they are watered. Every two or three weeks, water with a half-
strength soluble fertilizer.

The less-than-ideal light conditions found indoors are a major reason for not starting seeds too soon, and a reason to move the seedlings
outdoors as soon as possible. It is disastrous, however, to move seedlings suddenly outdoors for good. All indoor seedlings must be gradually acclimated to life outdoors, a process termed "hardening off."
It isn't just the colder temperatures that the seedlings need to adjust
to but also the bright light, particularly the ultraviolet light. Indoor
seedlings have been exposed to very little UV, since ordinary window
glass filters out much of it. I once made the mistake of leaving two
dozen pepper plants in full sun for a full day their first time outdoors.
By dusk they had all but perished from sunburn, their dark green
leaves bleached to a translucent whiteness.

Plan to start hardening off seedlings at least two weeks before you
intend to plant them. I find the best way to harden off seedlings is
to put them in a cold frame. Keep them quite warm for the first few
days and then gradually open the cover of the cold frame more and
more on successive days until it can be removed altogether. Remember, however, that although the seedlings may have become acclimated to cooler temperatures and increased sunlight, the frost-sensitive ones will still be frost-sensitive. If the thermometer threatens
to dip below 32 degrees Fahrenheit, close up the frame.

If you don't have a cold frame, you will have to move the seedlings
in and out of the house for the first week. Put them outside in the
shade at first, and only for a couple of hours, then on succeeding days
lengthen their time outdoors and increase their exposure to sunlight.

Seedlings under Lights

WINDOWSILLS ARE FINE PLACES to raise a few seedlings, provided that the space isn't already taken up by houseplants. But even the most spacious windowsill is too small for a couple dozen seedlings each of peppers, eggplants, tomatoes, and melons, not to mention an accompanying assortment of flowers.

When I was in college, I started my annuals in the spare space of someone else's greenhouse, and if I had a greenhouse of my own today I would certainly use it, because I still believe that a beginning under glass is the best a plant can have. As it is, however, with a limited bank account and limited windowsills, I have found that I can successfully start most of my annuals down in the cellar, under the light of fluorescent lamps.

Artificial illumination has its advantages. Seedlings can be raised in a well-insulated room where heat loss is insignificant compared with that of a greenhouse. Indeed, heat generated by the lamps can be used to warm the space. And when the young plants are moved outdoors for the summer, the fluorescent lights can be put away or used for something else altogether.

To raise seedlings, you don't need to use the special wide-spectrum bulbs with their characteristically purplish light. These bulbs have been designed not only to provide the right wavelengths of light for photosynthesis but also to give off enough light in the red end of the spectrum to trigger flowering. Annual seedlings, however, are not supposed to flower indoors; it would stunt them. Unless you need to worry about flowering, there is no reason to purchase the more expensive wide-spectrum bulbs; standard cool-white or warm-white fluorescent lamps serve just as well.

Although the kind of light that seedlings get is not particularly important, it is important that they get enough. To assure adequate intensity, I space my fluorescent bulbs no more than six inches apart and hang them no more than six inches above the plants. To make it possible to water, I have attached the lights to a panel, which, with the help of two pulleys, I can move up out of the way. This also allows me to move the lights as the plants grow, keeping the bulbs a fixed distance from the top of the foliage.

A 24-by-48-inch sheet of ½-inch plywood serves as the mount for my three fluorescent fixtures, each of which holds two four-foot, 40-watt bulbs. (Department stores frequently sell such fixtures, described as shop lights, at discount prices.) I bolt the fixtures to the underside of the panel, spacing them so that the bulbs in adjacent fixtures are no more than six inches apart on center. If the fixtures

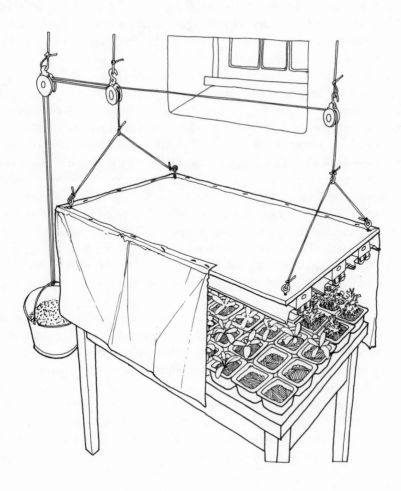

don't come with attached reflectors, you can paint the underside of the panel white to bounce errant light back toward the seedlings.

By attaching eyebolts to each of the four corners and running rope from these through pulleys hanging from the joists in the cellar ceiling, I can raise and lower the lights at will. The eyebolts, the rope, and the pulleys must be good and strong because the fluorescent fixtures with their ballasts are surprisingly heavy. It would be disastrous to have the whole arrangement come crashing down on top of the seedlings. A counterweight on the other end of the ropes makes it easier to raise and lower the lights. The illustration shows the arrangement of lights, eyebolts, ropes, and pulleys.

The temperature in our cellar hovers in the mid-50s all winter, which is a bit chilly for tender seedlings. But by tacking a strip of old sheet around the edge of the light panel so that it hangs down like a skirt, I can hold in heat given off by the lamps and keep the air around the seedlings in the 80s.

Constant illumination is bad for seedlings. They need at least 6 hours of dark in every 24-hour period. This period of dark can occur at any time — it can even be broken into several shorter periods — but turning the lamps off and on shortens their life. With the help of an electric timer, I start seedlings with a 16-hour period of illumination each day; this keeps them stocky. Once true leaves appear it is safe to cut back to 12 hours of light a day, to slow their growth a bit and toughen them up in preparation for the move outdoors. If you wish, you can continue to use 16 hours of light a day, but it means spending more money on electricity. (The costs are not trivial. Six 40-watt bulbs running 16 hours a day consume roughly 4 kilowatt-hours a day. Multiply this times the number of cents a kilowatt-hour your public utility charges to compute the cost of raising your seedlings.)

There are always ways to justify raising your own, if only that it allows you to grow certain flowers and vegetables that aren't commonly sold as plants. Nevertheless, it is wise to use space under the lights efficiently. I pot up my transplants in square pots so that no space is wasted, and I move the hardier seedlings out into the cold frame as soon as possible to make room for others. When schedules are properly synchronized, an impressive production line can be set in motion, spitting out flat after flat of perfect seedlings like trays of cookies emerging from the oven.

Garden Geometry

THE SPACING OF PLANTS is something we all deal with sooner or later. Foresighted gardeners handle it all in advance, carefully laying out their plots on sheets of paper. The rest of us put off the matter until the last minute, until we are kneeling in freshly dug earth, a trowel in one hand, a tray of transplants in the other. Only then do we discover that (1) the area is not as large as we thought it was, and (2) we were overgenerous in our estimates of how many plants we needed to fill it. Unable to enlarge the garden, and unwilling to discard perfectly good plants, we end up crowding them all in. Our rationalization is that some of the plants will probably die, and besides, young plants are so small that the garden looks better with a few extra.

All too soon we discover that everything has survived. "Too soon" may be a few weeks for annuals, a few years for trees and shrubs. Either way, there is no bare ground to be seen. Individual plants are shouldering one another, and the stronger will soon overwhelm the weaker. From a distance, the garden looks like a solid hedge. Though pleased by the verdancy of it all, we cannot help but wonder how many more flowers or fruits the plants might bear if we had spaced them differently. If we had set them farther apart originally we could at least be enjoying their individual shapes.

For any plant to achieve its full size and natural form, it must have room to grow. "Room" means a competition-free zone where the plant's roots do not have to struggle with other roots for water and nutrients, where its leaves are not shaded by the leaves of other plants. As a guide to spacing, it helps to think of each plant as requiring a circular domain, which might be illustrated thus:

The center of the circle represents the plant's stem, the periphery the farthest reach of roots and branches. The diameter of the circle will depend on the plant; apple trees require more room than zinnias. Giving an individual plant more room than it needs will not affect its growth; giving it less will. Whenever two plants are close enough that their domains overlap, they will conflict with one another, and one or both will suffer as a result. Picture the conflict like this:

OVERLAPPING
DOMAINS

The two plants need not be the same kind. A weed will likely emerge the victor in competition with a cultivated plant because weeds are much more adept at getting theirs than most cultivated plants are. Two plants of the same kind will tend to impair each other equally because both have roughly the same requirements. Only when two plants have widely differing needs or means of satisfying them — say, an impatiens and a Japanese maple — can they thrive in close proximity. Even though one may seem to be growing in the shadow of the other, their domains do not overlap as much as geography suggests.

Asked to position three or more plants in a garden, most of us will instinctively line them up in a row, whether we are planting tulips or tomatoes. Few of us realize that in doing so we pay homage to the English agriculturist and inventor Jethro Tull (1674–1741). The traditional spacing of crop plants in Tull's time was obtained by broadcasting seed. This flinging of seed by hand across prepared ground resulted in plants that were more or less randomly spaced.

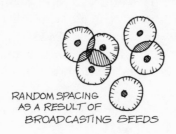

RANDOM SPACING
AS A RESULT OF
BROADCASTING SEEDS

When seeds are sown in this manner, some of the resulting plants end up competing with one another. Many end up competing with weeds since the irregular spacing of the plants makes it impossible to enter the field to remove the weeds without damaging the crop. Jethro Tull invented both a seed drill, a machine with which he sowed seed in neat rows, and a horse-drawn hoe that could be used to cultivate the ground between the rows once the seed had germinated. The great virtue of Tull's method of cultivation was that it essentially eliminated competition from weeds. It also produced much greater yields, hardly a surprise to modern gardeners but a revelation in Tull's time. In the centuries since Tull's discovery, neatly weeded rows have become indelibly printed in our perception of how to grow plants.

Even in a row, there are various patterns in which plants can be spaced. Three of these are:

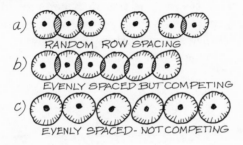

Pattern A is a more or less random spacing of plants in the row, such as one might achieve from sowing carrots by hand and not thinning the seedlings that result. The plants that are unrestricted will grow to maximum size; the ones that are competing with one another will not. Among carrots, this produces an undesirably wide variation, but in a shrub border it gives a natural look.

Patterns B and C contain evenly spaced plants. In C there is no competition between plants, and each can reach full size. In B all plants hinder each other slightly but almost equally. Curiously, experiments have shown that in terms of pounds per square foot yielded, the best results come from growing plants close enough together that they are competing somewhat. For specimen plants of maximum size, whether a focal point in the landscape or a prize-winner in a vegetable contest, plants should have all the space they can use. But the overall yield of the garden will not be as great as when plants are slightly crowded. In this case, individual specimens will not be as big, but the increase in numbers will more than offset the drop, resulting in a greater yield per row. Increasing the density of the planting still further beyond the optimum point will result in smaller and smaller plants. With some crops, such as carrots, the total production in pounds remains at the maximum as numbers increase; the carrots simply get smaller and smaller. With other crops, such as beets, beyond a certain density there is a rapid decline in total yield.

The great advantage of rows is that they make it easy to eliminate weeds. The disadvantage is that they waste space. So much of the advice about spacing assumes that you will be running a cultivator between the rows: if not a horse- or tractor-drawn tool, then a gasoline-powered tiller, or at least a wheeled hoe.

Much of so-called intensive gardening is based on finding ways to minimize the space between rows that does not support the growth of plants. One way to do this is simply to move the rows close enough together that the domains of the plants in one row just touch those in the next. The simplest such spacing is a square grid that looks like this:

SQUARE SPACING

Square grids save space, but some is still wasted in the gaps between the circles. Some of this wasted space can be eliminated by shifting the positions of the plants in every other row one half-space. This produces a staggered pattern resembling a honeycomb. Called hexagonal close-packing, this arrangement is the most space-efficient way to place your plants.

HEXAGONAL CLOSE-PACKING

There are a number of elaborate methods for positioning seeds or plants in a hexagonal pattern. I find it easiest to break a stick to the length of the spacing I want and then use it to keep each plant or seed equidistant from its nearest neighbors; I position the seeds in a series of interlocking triangles that add up to hexagonal spacing. The additional advantage of using a stick is that it makes 12 inches an invariable distance. Otherwise, when I try to squeeze in just a few more plants, the 12 shrinks to 10 and then 8, and so on until the pattern is ruined.

Spacing between Centers of Mature Plants*

VEGETABLES

Beans, bush 6–8″	Chard 8″	Peppers 12″
Beans, pole	Corn 12–18″	Potatoes 12″
poles 18″ apart	Cucumbers 12″	Pumpkins 30″
(4–6 beans per	Eggplant 16″	Radishes 1″
pole)	Kale 12″	Rutabagas 6″
Beets 4–6″	Kohlrabi 6″	Salsify 3″
Broccoli 15″	Leeks 4″	Spinach, New
Brussels sprouts 18″	Lettuce, head 12″	Zealand 12″
Cabbage,	Lettuce, leaf 8″	Spinach, regular 4″
Chinese 10″	Melon 16″	Squash, summer
Cabbage,	Mustard greens 6″	16″
regular 15″	Okra 12″	Squash, winter 30″
Carrots 2–3″	Onions 4″	Tomatoes 18–24″
Cauliflower 18″	Parsley 4″	Turnips 3″
Celery 8″	Parsnips 4″	Watermelon 24″
	Peas 3″	

FLOWERS

Ageratum 8″	Marigolds, African	Salvia 12″
Asters 10–12″	18″	Scabiosa 16″
Bachelor's buttons	Marigolds, French	Snapdragons 12″
12″	8–12″	Stocks 12″
California poppies	Nasturtium 8″	Strawflowers 16″
12″	Nicotiana 18″	Sweet peas 12″
Calendula 12″	Petunias 12″	Zinnia 12–16″
Cosmos 18″	Phlox (annual) 9″	
Hollyhocks 12″	Portulaca 6″	

*Spacings are for standard-sized cultivars.
Dwarf cultivars should be spaced proportionately closer.

While intent on using all the available space in a garden, one must still be careful to leave some room to get in to weed the plants. If the plants are spaced far enough apart that one can walk between them, there is no need for aisles. But with closely spaced plants I try not to plant any bed so wide that I can't reach into the middle of it. As plants arranged in hexagons begin to mature, less and less weeding is required because the foliage of adjacent plants just touches, shading the ground underneath and preventing weed growth.

As with so much advice on gardening, specific instructions for spacing plants depend on what it is that you are growing and where exactly you are growing it. The table on page 67 contains suggested spacing for common vegetables and flowers. Note that the distances between plants correspond roughly to what the seed packets recommend for spacing within the row. One simply ignores the much larger between-row spacings that the packets advise; they are echoes of Jethro Tull.

Switching from straight lines to polygons is not easy. Our vision of a well-kept garden is expressed in orderly rows. But hexagonal grids can be every bit as orderly. They can also be informal, much more informal than any plot laid out row by row. The only thing hexagonal spacing assures is that as many plants as possible have room to grow.

The Regular Season

PLANT A GARDEN TOO EARLY, and you will probably end up planting it again. Much of the seed sown outdoors in cold wet soil rots before it has time to germinate. Some gardeners turn to treated seed, seed that has been coated with fungicide; others presprout their seed before they sow it. It is easiest simply to wait until the soil warms and is no longer sodden. I like to think of the garden plot as a bed, and I try not to plant seed in soil that I wouldn't be comfortable lying down in.

Raised beds, created by heaping up soil with or without enclosures to keep it that way, drain quickly and warm up earlier in the spring. Shallow ditches, provided they drain somewhere, have the same effects on the soil. A layer of thin plastic, either the clear or the black polyethylene that is sold as garden mulch, hastens the sun's warming of the soil beneath it, although plastic will hold in moisture. Any cultivating that breaks up the ground will also warm the soil since it increases the surface area exposed to warm air. Whenever you are spading up wet ground you are in danger of packing it down with your feet, however. If you must venture onto wet ground, lay down an old piece of lumber to stand on. It will spread out your weight and compact the soil less. Be especially careful not to use a power tiller on wet soil. The soil's granular structure will be destroyed, or puddled, by the fast-spinning tines. Once puddled, soil takes months or years to recover its natural consistency.

The date when flowers and vegetables are planted out — what I consider the start of the regular season as opposed to the preseason plantings — depends on the weather. Soil is dry enough for sowing when a ball formed by hand breaks apart readily upon poking with a finger. The proper temperature depends on what you are planting. Plants like lettuce, cabbage, and radish tolerate cold soil. Peas, for instance, can be sown as soon as the soil is dry enough to dig. At a soil temperature of 50 degrees Fahrenheit, peas take 14 days to come up. At 40 degrees they take 36 days, but at least they do germinate. Other plants, like cucumber, okra, peppers, and beans, need warm soil to germinate at all. There is no sense in sowing beans, for instance, until the soil is above 60 degrees, unless you want to practice sowing beans.

Plants produced by seeds sown outdoors are usually left to grow where they came up. Because no transplanting will be involved, only thinning (by which unwanted plants are destroyed), it is best to sow thinly. Sow only enough extra seed to compensate for poor germination. Rather than scatter seeds in rows, and thin the resulting seedlings to desired positions, I have taken to sowing several seeds in the proper position in the first place — several cabbage seeds every 15 inches, two corn seeds every 18 inches, and so on. By thinning out any extra seedlings that appear in each location, I find I can achieve a more precise spacing of plants than I can when I sow seeds every 4 inches or so.

The smaller the seed, the more finely prepared the soil should be to ensure that each seed closely contacts moist earth. Lettuce, with 25,000 seeds to the ounce, requires that you rake out even the pebbles from the seed bed. Corn, with only 150 seeds to the ounce, will come up even in soil with rocks as big as your fist. Whether you make holes one by one and drop in seed, sow it in a furrow, or scatter it lightly in a broad band, you should then cover the seed with soil to a depth roughly four times the seed's diameter. Then press the soil down firmly to increase seed-to-soil contact. I use my hands or the back of a garden rake. Some people use their feet, but I am too afraid of compacting the soil excessively to imitate their example.

Under ideal conditions the soil will stay warm and moist, and nearly all the seed will germinate quickly. But all too often it rains heavily and the seed rots, or no rain falls and the ground dries so much that the seed fails to sprout. The latter problem can be corrected by watering the seeds after they have been sown. The trouble with this is that when the soil dries out after being watered it often develops a hard crust, which young seedlings have difficulty penetrating. Once you begin watering you almost have to continue it, keeping the surface soft until the seedlings are up. Alternatively, you can cover the seeds with something that doesn't form a crust when it dries, finely sifted compost for instance. Whatever your solution, nature has a way of confounding it. The fact is, sowing seeds outdoors is a calculated risk, in which you are betting against a great many things over which you have no control.

Transplants — seedlings that have been raised indoors — are a form of insurance. Even if certain plants didn't have to be sown indoors to give them a long enough growing season, I think most gardeners would still raise a few peppers and tomatoes indoors just to guarantee themselves something in the garden should all the outdoor-sown seeds fail to germinate.

Before you plant transplants out, the soil should be well dug and fertilized; give it essentially as much preparation as you would for sowing seeds. There is even less reason to rush the start of the season with transplants, since they are growing comfortably in the containers they are in. Unless, of course, they were started too soon and are in danger of becoming stunted. For eggplant and melons, I wait a full week or two after the last frost to put the plants in the garden. By that time the soil is warm enough that the plants aren't checked in their growth.

Choose a day that is cloudy or wait until late afternoon to do your transplanting. This will give plants several hours to recover from the shock of being transplanted (during which time plants stop growing and often wilt) before being subjected to full sun. If you have to transplant in the heat of the day, you can put a half-bushel basket or even a sheet of newspaper over the plants to shade them until they recover. If a newly transplanted plant is wilting it is unlikely to need water. What it needs is shade.

Use a trowel to dig the hole for each transplant. If the transplants are growing in peat pots, break off the edge of the pot down to the soil line. This will help the plant's roots penetrate the pot wall by preventing the rim from acting as a wick and drying the peat even when the pot is buried in the ground. If the transplants are in a nonbiodegradable container, turn the plant upside-down and hold it in the palm of your hand so that the stem of the transplant is against the web of your middle two fingers. Gently tap the bottom of the container with your hand or the back of the trowel until the root ball slides into your hand. Grasping the root ball (not the stem of the plant), set it right-side-up in its hole and fill in around it with soil. The transplant should end up no deeper in the garden soil than it

was in the pot. Finally, press down firmly on the root ball and surrounding soil. It is important that no air spaces remain either under
or beside the root ball. One way to help ensure this is to water each
transplant well after setting it. This helps wash soil into close contact
with the root ball.

I use a transplant solution to water my transplants. Transplant
solutions are soluble fertilizers dissolved in water. They greatly reduce
the incidence of transplant shock, and their use also results in higher
yields. Almost any soluble houseplant fertilizer will serve as a transplant solution, and you can water transplants before or after setting
them in the garden. For vegetables, the most beneficial starter fertilizers are ones that contain at least two or three times as much
phosphorus as nitrogen or potassium. Typical formulas of such starter
fertilizers are 9–45–15, 10–55–10, and 15–30–15. Regardless of the
formula, the mixing ratio is two tablespoons per gallon, and the
application rate is a cup per plant.

Starter solutions can also be used when sowing seeds. These solutions are too expensive to be broadcast, but spot application near
cucumber seeds, for example, has resulted in greatly improved yields
in test plantings.

The extra phosphorus in these starter solutions is beneficial because
phosphorus, essential for root growth, is not readily available to
plants when soil temperatures are below 60 degrees Fahrenheit. The
additional phosphorus compensates for low soil temperatures, mini-
mizing transplant shock and getting seedlings off to a fast start. You
can't do much more to improve your chances on opening day.

Cloches

IT IS ALL BUT IMPOSSIBLE for the backyard vegetable gardener
to justify building a greenhouse for the sake of early tomatoes or
cucumbers. And while cold frames are an economical alternative,
their limited space makes them best suited to raising young plants
for transplanting. What most of us vegetable gardeners really need
in the weeks before and after the last spring frost is a way to improve
the climate right in the garden, where a large number of plants are
spaced at considerable distances from one another. In short, we could
all use some sort of cloche.

The word comes from the French for bell, referring to heavy, glass
bell jars that were used in French vegetable gardens at least as far
back as 1623. These bells were set over individual plants or over
small groups of seedlings. Sunlight warmed the air and the soil beneath the glass, and the plants inside were protected from wind, rain,
light frosts, and pests. As the demand for winter- and spring-grown
vegetables increased, so did the use of these bell jars. By the start of
the twentieth century some two million were being set out in Paris
alone.

Today these original cloches are no longer in use, which is just as
well, for they had their disadvantages. They were fragile, and they
were heavy. The 17-inch-high and 15-inch-diameter bells weighed
5½ pounds apiece. What is more, on warm sunny days each of them
had to be propped up slightly on a wooden "tilt" to prevent the plants
inside from overheating.

The glass bell jars may be gone, but not the practice of improving
the environment in the vicinity of individual plants. Low temperature is the main factor limiting the growth of vegetables in the open.
Increase the air temperature around a plant only 10 degrees and you
roughly double its relative growth rate (expressed as increase of
weight per unit weight per day). To do this, a host of devices have

been invented, some to cover individual plants, some to cover whole rows. All are temporary structures consisting of some sort of transparent or translucent material that lets in light and holds in heat. All work on the so-called greenhouse principle: they admit radiant energy from the sun but restrict the loss of longer-wavelength thermal radiation and cut down on convection.

Americans have been slower to use cloches than Europeans. But in the last twenty years, their use has become more common as vegetable gardeners, amateurs and professionals alike, have discovered how much can be grown on a given piece of land.

The simplest cloche is nothing more than a plastic gallon milk jug with its bottom cut out. Milk-jug cloches don't have the wind resistance of glass bell jars, but if you push them into the soil they won't be blown over. Or bend the bottom to one side and put a brick on it. They have one advantage over the old bells: remove the cap and they won't overheat. In the home garden these milk-jug cloches have all but replaced the paper hot tent, or hot cap, that used to be set out over pumpkin and tomato seedlings.

The problem with the milk-jug cloche is that the plant inside soon outgrows the space, which is only six inches across. A cone-shaped cloche a foot and a half in diameter or larger can be fashioned from fiberglass-reinforced plastic. But even if you do the work yourself, the materials end up costing you several dollars per cloche. If you have the money to spend, I recommend trying a water-filled conical cloche. Sold under the trade name Wall-O-Water, this is a double cylinder of flexible plastic that becomes a semirigid cone when filled with three gallons of water, heavy enough to stay put in a breeze, and the water stores up heat during the day, then radiates it into the interior at night.

The newest cloche design, in the semitraditional category, is also the largest. It is called the umbrella cloche, and it is made by whacking the handle off one of those high-crowned, transparent-plastic umbrellas. Like all umbrellas, this cloche should only be used where the wind is not a problem.

The trend in cloches lately, however, has been away from round shapes that cover individual plants. For years English gardeners have constructed cloches from sheets of glass, connecting them in barnlike configurations with clever clips. Several of these sheet-glass cloches lined up one after the other can cover an entire row. But sheets of glass have the disadvantages of being fragile and, unless the edges have been smoothed over, dangerously sharp. Not surprisingly, there has not been wholesale adoption of the technique in this country.

I have used sheets of glass set in wooden frames — to wit, discarded storm windows — to cover rows of tomato plants. A couple of nails driven into the top edge of each enables pairs to be wired together. The difficulty with storm-window cloches is that they are heavier to move about than bell jars (which is why the windows were discarded in the first place) and prone to injury from flying baseballs and the like.

The lightest, cheapest, safest cloches available are plastic row covers. The most durable of these tunnellike cloches are constructed of corrugated fiberglass. A 26-inch by 4-foot panel bent into a semicircle and secured with heavy wire becomes a sort of Quonset hut that can be set out over a row of plants. Alternatively, row covers can be constructed from clear polyethylene film held above the plants by stiff wire hoops. A wire of #8 or #9 gauge is usually sufficiently strong. The lighter the plastic, the more important it is that the cloche be secured against wind, usually by burying the edges of the plastic in soil. A number of companies sell plastic tunnel cloches as kits, with hoops and plastic provided, but it is easy enough to make your own.

The most recent form of the cloche is the most amorphous of all. It is simply a layer of fabric draped loosely over a row of plants and held down along the edges. As the plants grow, their foliage lifts up the fabric. The fabric being used for this is either spunbonded (nonwoven) polypropylene or polyester. The latter is currently sold under the trade name Reemay. Whether these floating row covers deserve to be called cloches is certainly debatable, but their ability to enhance the growth of vegetables is not.

It is important to remember that whatever cloche you choose, you will be using it only temporarily. Depending on the vegetable, and where you garden, the cloche season can be as short as two weeks or as long as eight. It is not simply that the plants will outgrow the cloches. As the season advances the temperature inside a cloche gets too high for the plants' own good. For example, temperatures above 85 degrees Fahrenheit damage the blossoms of peppers and tomatoes. Not all plants are equally affected, however. Muskmelons and water-

melons can tolerate temperatures well above this and thus are well adapted to an extended cloche season.

If you are growing things like lettuce or spinach and don't want them to go to seed, it is important that the temperatures don't get too high under the cloches. Opening or removing the cloches every time the mercury rises is too time-consuming for most gardeners. Consequently the trend is toward cloches with built-in ventilation. Leaving the tops off the milk jugs allows hot air to rise by convection. Likewise, most conical cloches have holes a couple of inches in diameter at their tops that serve the same function, as do the gaps in the English glassbarn cloches. Plastic row covers are now being made with two rows of closely spaced five-inch-long slits running their lengths. The slits open just enough to keep the temperature inside from getting out of hand. In the case of the fabric covers, ventilation is not an issue because the fabrics are sufficiently porous that a certain amount of air gets through them. Whatever cloche design you use, once the weather has warmed up the cloches should be taken up and put away. Most can be reused for a number of years.

Although the air temperature inside cloches rises dramatically during the day, at night most offer much less frost protection than you might expect. Polyethylene is 70 percent transparent to thermal radiation, so heat stored during the day is readily lost at night. Under a polyethylene row cover, for example, or a sheet of spunbonded polyester, the nighttime temperature is only 2 degrees Fahrenheit above ambient at most. What frost protection polyethylene tunnels do provide comes not from the plastic but from the thin layer of condensation that forms on the underside of the plastic as falling nighttime temperatures reach the dew point. The water is opaque to thermal radiation and serves as a heat barrier.

The foregoing is part of the reason that water-filled cloches are better than other cloches on below-freezing nights. Reportedly they provide up to 16 degrees of frost protection. Not only does the water serve as a thermal barrier, but a great deal of heat is released if the water freezes.

There are also a number of minor benefits gained by using cloches. Cucumber beetles, for example, have difficulty finding young melon vines under a layer of fabric. Cabbage maggots are less likely to attack broccoli. Of course, the protection from airborne-insect attack lasts only as long as the cloches are in place, and where insect pollination is required cloches can be a hindrance.

Principally, however, cloches are of value because they raise the daytime temperature and, consequently, the relative growth rate of vegetables. Like money earning interest in a bank, the increased growth of a vegetable under a cloche is constantly compounded. The end result is a dramatically earlier and heavier harvest. In one experiment at the University of New Hampshire, the yield of muskmelons planted in black-plastic mulch and covered with row covers was twice that of melons planted in the mulch alone. Evidence like this has been responsible for altering the appearance of spring market gardens across the country. The home vegetable gardener, with more time to experiment, and less at risk, is free to devise even more successful ways of applying spot warmth to newly planted vegetables.

War of the Weeds

THERE ARE no pacifist gardeners. To decide to grow anything — be it strawberries or snapdragons — is to join in a never-ending war with weeds. Even those with the greatest reverence for wild flowers will soon find themselves armed with hoes or down on their knees in hand-to-hand combat.

The contested ground, the site of the struggle between weeds and the gardener, is bare soil, especially bare soil that has been freshly dug and fertilized in preparation for sowing beans and corn, for setting out tomato and pepper plants, for planting a rosebush or a cherry tree. The gardener scarcely turns her back when the first weeds appear — tens, hundreds, thousands of them. The tiny seedlings are so numerous they turn the soil green. Any hope that they come from the seeds the gardener sowed is dashed by their sheer abundance.

The seeds that those weeds come from have been lying dormant, part of the seed bank in the soil. Soil in which weeds have grown in the past may contain as many as 5000 weed seeds per square foot, and when the ground is disturbed some of them germinate. Most of them, however, do not. In fact, less than one-twentieth of the seeds in the soil germinate at any one time, yet this is enough to fill the garden with unwanted plants.

Though the young weed seedlings belong to different species, all have some things in common: They will grow rapidly, flower quickly, and produce large numbers of seeds. A single large specimen of *Chenopodium album,* variously called lamb's-quarters, pigweed, white goosefoot, or fat hen, may produce 70,000 seeds. Such fecundity requires ample amounts of food and drink, and weeds are adept at snatching up the water and nutrients they need. In a garden they do so at the expense of cultivated plants. Cultivated plants tend to lose out in competition with weeds because all the breeding that went into them concentrated on attributes like color, size, taste, earliness, and disease resistance rather than competitive ability. Breeders expect cultivated plants to be grown comfortably far apart from one another in weed-free soil.

While both weed seedlings and crop plants are small, the weeds do not interfere, but the grace period is short-lived. As a rule of thumb, gardeners have about three weeks to get rid of weeds. After that the presence of the weeds will begin to affect the cultivated plants. Onions are especially susceptible. Experiments have shown that once competition sets in, weeds reduce the ultimate yield of onion bulbs by 4 percent a day. That adds up to more than a 50-percent reduction in a fortnight. Not all plants are as affected by weeds as onions are. Beans, for example, by virtue of their large seedlings, seem able to coexist with weeds. But wise gardeners set about removing weeds whenever they appear in the garden.

The younger the weed the easier it is to remove. In close quarters, a gardener may have to weed by hand, but hoeing is a quicker and easier way to dispatch large numbers of weeds. Keep the blade of the

hoe sharp and your strokes shallow. Hoeing too deeply can disturb the roots of cultivated plants, hasten the loss of soil moisture, and worst of all can bring more weed seeds to the surface.

Even if one hoes shallowly, however, some of the ungerminated weed seeds near the surface will sprout. Certain kinds of weeds are more likely to germinate at one time of year or another, but there is no time when weeds aren't coming up. The good news is that not all the seeds present in the soil will germinate in any one year. As the cultivated plants grow, their leaves shade the ground, and this seems to inhibit the germination of weed seed, perhaps by depriving seeds of the light they need to sprout. Some weed seeds will germinate, but so deep in the soil that they exhaust their food reserves and starve before the seedlings reach light. Other seeds simply die. The supply of viable weed seed in soil is depleted roughly by half for each year that the soil is kept cultivated.

Most of the seeds that germinate are from short-lived weeds. Some are annuals, others are winter annuals, still others are biennials. Annuals germinate in the spring, flower, set seed, and die the same year. Winter annuals germinate in the fall, overwinter as seedlings, then flower, and set seed the next spring. Biennials germinate in spring, overwinter, flower during the second year, and then die.

If these were the only weeds that the novice gardener had to contend with, keeping a garden weed-free might not be such a battle. But new gardens usually contain perennial weeds as well. Perennial weeds live for many years, and rather than investing their energy in rapid growth and large numbers of seeds, perennials invest in permanence.

The first sign of trouble in a new garden may be a few green shoots of grass. Pulling on them, one finds they come from a fat white rootstock. This is *Agropyron repens,* variously known as quack grass, couch grass, or witchgrass. Ridding soil of this weed is a long and arduous process, because even a small section of root left in the garden can become a new plant. The use of a high-speed tiller that chops the roots into small bits only aggravates the problem. Perennial weeds can be eradicated, but often only by diligently starving the plant until it has no reserves with which to make new foliage. The presence of perennial weeds in a garden is a strong argument for growing nothing but annual crop plants until the pest is controlled (annual plants offer more opportunity to work the soil than perennials do). In among perennials, whether asparagus or raspberries or iris, perennial weeds run amok.

The broadest definition of a weed is a plant that is out of place, a definition that allows for the weediness of a number of cultivated plants. All garden mints are terribly weedy, spreading rapidly unless enclosed in tight containers. Many bamboos are similarly invasive. No gardener who once plants horseradish is ever without it. So too with Jerusalem artichokes. The weediness of these plants is not a reason to avoid growing them, but gardeners should be careful.

Any weed can be put to some use. Lamb's-quarters, for example, is an effortless alternative to spinach. Weeds can be used to prevent soil erosion, and might be encouraged if the only alternative is bare ground. Weeds contribute to the organic matter of the soil, and they may hang on to nutrients in their tissues that would otherwise leach out of the soil.

This is not to say gardeners should give weeds a break. Under no circumstances should perennial weeds be allowed to spread, or annual weeds allowed to produce seeds. "One year's seeding equals seven years' weeding" is an old aphorism. Given that the seed bank in cultivated soil is depleted by half every year, it takes roughly seven years to reach one percent, or 50 weed seeds per square foot, which is as weed-free as garden soil ever gets. Once gardeners get their soil to that point, it would be tragic to let up. The war against weeds is never over, but after seven years of struggle any lull in the action seems like an armistice.

Mulch, Mulch, Mulch

MUCH has been said about mulch. Too much in many instances. Not that I disagree with the claims made for its efficacy. Mulch is marvelous. A good thick blanket of it tucked in around one's plants dramatically reduces the need for watering and weeding. If it did nothing more, I would mulch, but mulch also reduces soil erosion, and the biodegradable ones like straw and leaves slowly enrich the soil as they decay. For many crops, mulching increases total yield and hastens maturity. This is especially true for heat-loving plants like tomatoes, peppers, eggplants, and watermelons when they are grown in the chilly North. Four inches below a layer of clear polyethylene mulch, the soil during the day is 20 degrees warmer than unmulched soil at the same depth. At night, some of this trapped heat radiates upward through the plastic and warms the foliage.

I don't object to the promotion of mulching in general. What bothers me is the parochial nature of people's enthusiasms. To wit, gardeners who advocate mulching usually advocate a particular material. Members of the peat party tout peat moss as the universal mulch. Equally determined are gardeners in the sawdust set, the corncob caucus, the grass-clippings guild, and the bark brigade. Each of them proclaims that their mulch is the true key to successful gardening. And while this is going on, every now and then someone comes up and whispers "plastic." It isn't just confusing; it's dangerous. Such conspicuous enthusiasm tends to create spot shortages of particular mulches.

There is no universal mulch, of course, nothing that will result in low maintenance and improved growth for all plants. A good mulch will be one that is light and easy to apply but does not blow away readily or break down too quickly. The material should hold moisture in the soil beneath, yet allow rainfall to pass through. In general, it should be something that can be applied thickly enough to inhibit

weeds without depriving the soil of oxygen. Although mulches can be applied at any time, they are usually applied during transplanting or when seedlings are high enough not to be buried.

Two of the essential requirements for a good mulch are that the material be readily available and also inexpensive. If you are going to cover your garden with several inches of a mulch, you will need a lot of whatever material you decide to use. Unfortunately, when gardeners begin lobbying in favor of a specific mulch, the material suddenly becomes hard to find, as both demand and price skyrocket. It wasn't long after Ruth Stout started talking about the glories of a garden covered in decaying hay that the once-abundant resource virtually disappeared (unless you were willing to look long and hard for a few bales and pay an outrageous price when you found them). I would sooner publicize the location of a mountain bog filled with pitcher plants and orchids than I would announce my favorite mulch.

The particular mulch gardeners use will depend on what part of the country they live in (and hence what is readily and inexpensively available). Experiments are in order until one discovers which mulches work best for which plants. In general, however, the only incorrect choice one can make about mulching is not to do it.

The following is a list of commonly used mulches. If my comments seem even-handed, it's because I am trying to prevent a run on my favorites.

Bark   Bark mulch is readily available now that sawmills are grinding the bark off logs before they are sawn. This not only yields another source of cash for the mill but it reduces the need to resharpen the saw, because much of the dirt and stones embedded in the log surface are removed with the bark. Bark mulch decays slowly and remains an attractive deep brown, making it especially good for mulching permanent plantings.

Leaves   Dead leaves are an inexpensive mulch. Shredding them with a shredder, or wheeling a rotary mower back and forth over them, reduces the likelihood that they will be scattered by the wind. Raking leaves into a shrub border or simply letting the wind take care of this is also an excellent way to mulch, provided the leaves are not so deep that they smother the roots. I am amazed every spring to see people patiently raking leaves out of shrubbery instead of leaving them to feed their lilacs and forsythia.

Peat Moss   I think peat moss is too expensive to use as a mulch, though many gardeners still feel otherwise. When peat moss is wet it holds a huge amount of water. Once it dries out, however, it becomes exceedingly hard to rewet. Thus a serious drought may result in peat-moss mulch forming a dry crust that sheds water, preventing rain from reaching the underlying soil.

Pine Needles   Like leaves, these are available for the gathering and make a very attractive mulch. If additional needles are added annually this mulch will, in time, form the same rich mat of humus that nourishes trees in the forest. The acid in pine-needle mulch can be moderated, if desired, by a light broadcasting of ground limestone every few years.

Grass Clippings   I believe that grass clippings should be left on the lawn, where they will dramatically reduce the need for fertilizer. If you use them as mulch, don't put them on so thick and so fresh that they make an impermeable layer. Also, never mulch with clippings that have come from a lawn treated with herbicide.

Hay/Straw/Salt-Marsh Hay   Spoiled hay is scarcely cheaper than good hay now that everyone wants it for mulch. Spoiled or not, hay contains too many seeds to make a good mulch. I prefer straw, as it is the residue from grain harvesting and hence has had the seeds removed. Salt-marsh hay contains seeds but these are of plants that grow in salt marshes, not gardens. All straw and hay mulches have a tendency to harbor rodents. In theory, one can grow potatoes by laying pieces of potato on top of prepared soil and simply covering them with hay. In practice, I have never harvested any potatoes grown this way that had not been partially eaten already.

Sawdust/Wood Chips   Like bark, both of these are long-lasting mulches. Wood chips tend to bleach to a pale whiteness and sawdust can form an impermeable cake on top if it is applied more than a couple of inches deep. As they decay both sawdust and wood chips will temporarily take up nitrogen from the underlying soil. This may cause plants mulched with these materials to turn yellow. The problem can be averted by a heavy application of complete fertilizer before the mulch is put down.

Plastic Polyethylene film (clear or black) is a comparatively recent gardening innovation, but one whose worth has been so solidly demonstrated that it can no longer be considered a novelty. Critics of polyethylene note that it is a petroleum product and hence more valuable than its price suggests. To them I reply that it should be used wisely and taken up at the end of each season. Even a film only 1½ mils thick can be used several years. Although biodegradable forms of plastic mulch are becoming available, most plastic mulches are photodegradable, not biodegradable. This means that after several years outdoors the plastic disintegrates into small pieces that never actually disappear. Better to dispose of old plastic before it falls apart completely.

Two additional problems with plastic are that it must be weighed down with rocks or soil to prevent its blowing away and that it can cause the soil to dry out unless there are holes for water to get through.

Despite all these flaws plastic can be a godsend to Northern gardeners who want to lengthen their season. Clear plastic is superior to black plastic in this respect because it lets the sunlight pass through and warms the soil more. But it also allows weeds to flourish. Commercial growers treat the soil with an herbicide before they lay clear plastic. I find weeds can be inhibited by simply stretching the plastic tight over smooth soil. To gardeners whose short growing season makes it difficult to raise eggplants, or peppers, or watermelons, I recommend plastic.

You can acquire small lots of plastic every fall by carrying off the plastic bags filled with leaves on your neighbors' curbs. Add the leaves to your compost pile or use them as mulch, and save the bags for the plastic. The dual waste of putting leaves *and* plastic in the rubbish is one of the horrors of modern times.

Exotica The list of possible mulches goes on and on: buckwheat hulls, peanut shells, bagasse, spent hops, and ground tobacco stems.

When I was a child, Baker Chocolate Company was located in Boston, and they gave the cocoa-bean shells to the Arnold Arboretum to use as mulch. My earliest memories are of plants surrounded by this aromatic mulch. The factory is gone, and the odor of chocolate has gone with it. But somewhere cocoa-bean shells must still lie in heaps, and were I gardening nearby I would be there filling the trunk of my car.

Nonbinding Ties

TAKE A MASON JAR, stuff it full of flowers and foliage, and you have a tangle, a wildly extravagant bouquet closely resembling the way plants arrange themselves if left to their own devices. Most gardeners, however, like most flower arrangers, prefer a higher degree of order. We want to control the positions of blossoms and branches. In a vase, cut flowers and foliage can be impaled, wired, or wrapped. But outdoors the restraints we use must be gentle ones, supporting and shaping the plant without injury.

Fortunately, a great many garden plants keep their shape well. This is no accident. Most vegetables are bred for commercial production, for farmers who don't have the time to stake individual corn plants or restrain errant bean runners. Plant breeders have found that one of the simplest ways to restrain a plant's growth is to dwarf it. This produces a compact, wind-resistant specimen that is not likely to grow out of bounds, flop over where it shouldn't, or break off altogether. Dwarf marigolds seldom suffer the injuries to which the tall African ones are prone. Dwarf snapdragons are similarly superior to their tall counterparts. But most gardeners quickly tire of displays in which none of the plants grow more than 14 inches tall.

Sooner or later you decide to grow hollyhocks, baby's breath, or lilies. Or perhaps pole beans, grapes, clematis, and climbing roses. With the first season comes the lesson that what grows up will grow out as well and, unless supported, is in danger of falling down at the least opportune moment. Anything that grows more than knee-high is a candidate for attention. The support will have to be strong, durable, and if not good-looking at least inconspicuous. What you use to attach the plant to the support — whether twine, wire, or cloth — will have to be just as tough. But it will have to be gentle, too, lest it injure the stem it is supposed to protect. Never wrap anything tightly around a stem, because you risk girdling that stem, in effect cutting off the plant's circulation as it grows.

In the vegetable garden, most of the plants don't need support, but pole beans and tomatoes trained as a single stem do. Also, if you are short on space you may decide to train cucumbers and melons to a fence. Looks are less important than strength and durability in the vegetable garden. A tomato vine carrying a full complement of fruit weighs roughly 25 pounds, even more when wet, and a stake that supports such a load must be strong enough to withstand the wind of an August storm. I use wooden poles at least 1½ inches in diameter that are roughly 5 feet tall after being set a foot and a half or so into the ground.

Trying to hammer such a tall and slender stake into the ground is incredibly awkward, and dangerous. Try swinging a sledgehammer atop a stepladder set on soft ground. No, don't. Use a crowbar instead. Jab it into the ground where you want the stake to be and wiggle it around until you have created a conical hole of the right depth. Then jam your stake into the hole and backfill around the stake with your feet. If you set the stake at the same time you plant the tomato plant, you avoid damaging its roots later on.

As the tomato plant grows it will have to be tied to the stake every foot or so. I use inch-wide strips of old sheet, wrapped halfway around the tomato stem and once around the stake before knotting with a square knot. Be careful not to pin a flower cluster between the stem and the stake: the developing tomatoes will go right ahead and enlarge, but like bound feet they will be horribly misshapen.

I prefer a slightly more slender pole for beans, because bean shoots have some difficulty spiraling around fat stakes. This, however, means that the stake must be especially strong for its size. I use newly cut poles if I can because thin ones are less likely to snap when green than after they have dried. Beans grip their support themselves but benefit from a little guidance early in life. Once the stems begin to run and are waving about in the air looking for something to climb up, I bend them to the pole and hold them there with a single circle of soft twine. Otherwise, the bean plants are apt to discover each other and soon become a hopelessly unsupported tangle. Cucumbers and melons grown on a trellis or fence need similar attention, even though they both possess tendrils that secure them amply once the vines are headed in the right direction. Cucumber fruit will hang unsupported from aerial vines, but full-sized melons will have to be provided with individual hammocks in which to lie. Cloth slings tied to the fence will do nicely.

The durability of any wooden stake or pole can be enhanced by applying wood preservative to the end that will be in the soil. The wood preservative you use must be one that is not harmful to the growth of plants. The only one I recommend is copper naphthenate, a green-colored liquid available under the brand name Cuprinol. Paint it onto the ends of new posts, or better yet, let the posts stand in a bucket of the solution for several days.

In the flower garden stakes can be smaller than those used for tomatoes and beans, especially if you are willing to use several of them per plant. Order without rigidity is the intent here. The supports should be as inconspicuous as possible; invisible is best. The proper time to stake is long before the need arises; otherwise the results can be far from satisfactory. As soon as a rain-soaked snapdragon falls over on its side, the tip of the spire reorients to point straight up. The gardener who isn't outside fixing things immediately soon discovers that when the fallen plant is set on its feet again the spire reorients once more, producing a pair of right-angle bends, a nasty detour in what was intended to be a straightaway.

By staking early, not only do you head off disaster but you give the plant's foliage a chance to obscure the source of its support. Double metal hoops with attached metal stakes do a rather good job of holding up peonies and are inconspicuous if installed early. The fact is, they cannot possibly be installed once the peony is in full flush. Smaller versions of this form of support can be made from heavy-gauge woven-wire fencing, the kind that is used for sheep or pigs. Cut it so that you end up with a cylinder a foot in diameter and a foot high, with prongs that can be pushed down into the ground. Jam one of these in around an emerging columbine or lupine, and it will provide all the support the plant needs later in the year.

Lilies and hollyhocks, plants with strong single stalks, require individual stakes. Prepackaged bamboo canes of various lengths and diameters will do this job. Beware of the green dye they have been treated with; some will come off immediately on your hands, the rest with weather. You can also buy metal stakes with an open loop at the top that you simply twist around the stem.

Some stems can be supported with a single stake, but many, especially the bigger and showier ones like delphinium, will do better with two or three stakes that have been tied together at several levels to create a loose cylinder. This allows the stem to move around a bit and reduces the chance that it will snap off just above a single point of attachment.

With flowers, as with tomatoes, the ties should be as gentle as possible, neither cutting into the stem nor constricting it. Green twine is more aesthetic than white sheets in the flower garden. I like the wire-reinforced paper ties called Twist-Ems. Plastic ones are also available, but I hate to use anything that isn't biodegradable in the garden if I don't have to. Again and again I come across the undisintegrated remains of last year's garden. Whatever you do, tie loosely. If you are worried about the tie's falling, knot it around the stake, not the stem.

If you want, you can erect elaborate networks of stakes and twine, through which a developing perennial can grow. This is probably the only way to keep a baby's breath in full bloom from collapsing during a rainstorm. If you insist on having everything in its place, you may want all your plants firmly corseted. At the same time, however, it is possible to overdo staking. It would be unfortunate if there were no chance for serendipity in the garden, no chance for the lucky juxtaposition of two colors brought on by a bit of heavy dew or a breeze. Surprise is an essential part of gardening. Our task is to provide just enough support so the surprises are pleasant ones.

Warding Off Wildlife

I AM NO HUNTER. It doesn't really matter how many legs are involved — two, four, six, eight. I don't even like to kill slugs, and they have no legs at all. A friend fills a pint container with slugs every morning, adds a little water, and brings them to a boil on the stove. I would as soon strangle bunnies. Not that I am unbloodied. I have done my share of squashing, drowning, poisoning, clubbing, and shooting. It was all, however, in self-defense. My garden was being attacked. Even pacifist vegetarians will reach for a rock when their own beans are at stake.

Because I don't have the temperament of a hunter, and because even if I did I doubt whether I could kill all the animals that have a taste for my fruits and vegetables, I put my effort into excluding the larger animals rather than exterminating them. This means finding ways to keep animals at a safe distance from my young lettuce and ripening grapes.

Woodchucks, rabbits, raccoons, porcupines, and assorted birds have all troubled my gardens at one time or another. These can all do a devastating amount of damage in a short time. For completeness I ought to add deer, but, though deer wreak havoc in some people's gardens, so far they haven't in any of mine.

I have learned, as have generations of gardeners before me, that as long as I am actually working in the garden, animals stay away. But if I am gone even a few minutes, let alone a whole night, they move in to feed. Stand-ins for myself, old-fashioned straw men, are notoriously ineffective. Scarcely better are the more modern scarecrows, those vinyl snakes or inflatable owls. All too quickly the enemy becomes habituated to their presence and recognizes these dummies for what they are.

The only practical way to ward off wildlife, I am now convinced, is to erect barriers: fences against the ones that walk, nets against

those that fly. These barriers are put up each year before the animals begin to feed in the garden. A naïve woodchuck will be turned back by a wire fence; not so one that has tasted peas.

Over the years I have used different materials for fencing my main vegetable garden, but the one that I have settled on is 48-inch-high chicken wire with a 1-inch mesh. Historically, chicken wire was indestructible stuff. I have been trying to tear up some that has been outdoors for at least half a century, and it is hardly tarnished. But the current lot lasts scarcely five years before it disintegrates into rusty fragments. The falling quality has not, however, prevented a rise in price. Chicken wire now sells for roughly $25 per 50-foot length, or 50¢ a foot. My vegetables are valuable, but my garden is not Fort Knox. To keep the costs of fencing within bounds, I now dismantle the fence every fall, rolling the wire up and storing it under cover until spring. I am hoping that by exposing the wire to weather for only six months of every year it will last at least twice as long.

For fence posts I use 6-foot wooden stakes that are no thicker than a bean pole. Indeed, some of them are ex–bean poles that rotted off at ground level. Instead of trying to drive these slender posts into the ground with a mallet, I ram them into conical holes made by jamming a crowbar 18 inches into the soil and rotating it. I space these posts 8 feet apart, a generous distance that saves on the number of posts needed and guarantees a floppy fence. Animals, I have found, are more reluctant to climb a floppy fence than a taut one.

Once the posts are in, I unroll the fence, leaning it up against the posts. Originally I then bent the bottom foot of the wire at a 90-degree angle because this made a barrier much more difficult for animals to burrow under (because when they began tunneling at the edge of the fence they were stymied by the wire beneath them). This left me with a three-foot-high fence that required no gate, since it was low enough to step over. The accompanying diagram illustrates how to fold the wire at the corners of the garden so that you do not have to cut it when you turn the corner. Lately, however, instead of bending the wire out at the bottom I have simply run my rototiller around the periphery of the garden each spring, churning the soil to a fine froth. I find that I can then work the bottom 4 to 6 inches of the fence down into the soft soil, which as it settles grips the lower edge firmly enough to discourage animals from pushing under. This leaves a fence that is too high to step over, and requires a gate. I hang mine between two heavier posts and use a board on edge at the bottom to make a tight sill.

The chicken wire is attached to the posts with twine, which is easy enough to cut in the fall. Each post gets two ties, one at the very bottom, another a foot or so from the top. Should an animal start climbing the fence, it will fold back on him as he nears the summit.

My fence does a good job of keeping woodchucks and rabbits and porcupines at bay. It does not, however, keep out raccoons. Raccoons are ordinarily not a problem in the vegetable garden — unless you

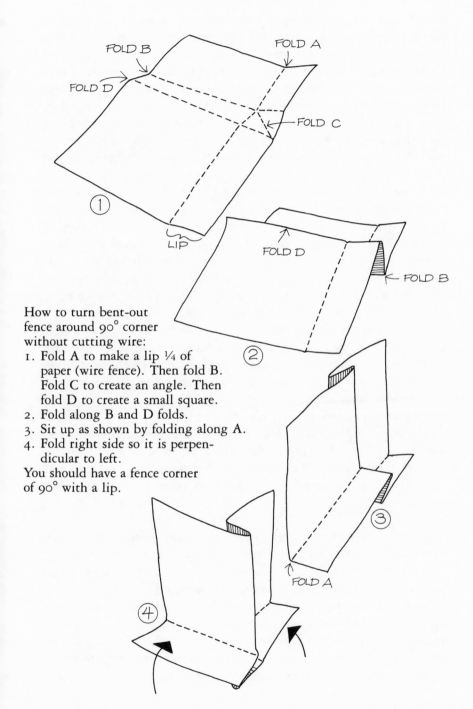

How to turn bent-out
fence around 90° corner
without cutting wire:
1. Fold A to make a lip ¼ of
   paper (wire fence). Then fold B.
   Fold C to create an angle. Then
   fold D to create a small square.
2. Fold along B and D folds.
3. Sit up as shown by folding along A.
4. Fold right side so it is perpen-
   dicular to left.
You should have a fence corner
of 90° with a lip.

are growing corn, whereupon they are guaranteed to show up the first night the corn is ripe and begin breaking down even the most robust stalks in pursuit of the sweet kernels.

Innumerable ploys for keeping raccoons away from corn have been tried. The only one that has worked for me is an electric fence, which I use in conjunction with the chicken wire. It need not be put up until the corn is nearing maturity, but installing it earlier helps keep out other animals. I purchased a standard electric fence charger intended for livestock, one that runs off a house current, though battery-powered models exist. I then made a large number of 16-inch-long stakes, each topped with a porcelain or plastic insulator. These I drive in a row around the garden about a foot outside the chicken-wire fence. Their height and distance from one another are such that when I string electric-fence wire from insulator to insulator it is always 6 to 8 inches above the ground. The only difficulty with a wire this low is that the grass and weeds grow up and short-circuit the fence. But by using a string trimmer I keep the vegetation down with only a few minutes of attention a week.

The shock that the animal, or for that matter human, gets from an electric fence of this sort is painful but not dangerous. I find it works better to leave mine on all the time, and risk an occasional zap, than to turn it off when I am working in the garden and risk forgetting to turn it on.

It looks like electricity may also be the best way to keep deer away from gardens and orchards. The setup is different, requiring multiple strands of a special kind of wire and a different charger, but the principle is the same. The Cooperative Extension Service agents will gladly provide the specifics to anyone in need of an electric deer barrier.

My two-ply fence — one woven, the other electrified — stops only those animals that walk. For those that fly, I turn to netting. My introduction to the virtues of netting came when in desperation I covered a bed of strawberries with some salvaged fish netting picked up at a nearby seaport. Draped across the bed on low-lying poles, it cut my avian losses enormously. Since then I have purchased netting intended for the purpose, some of which is made of black polypropylene, some from white nylon. I now consider it indispensable in assuring a harvest of grapes, cherries, or blueberries.

Again, netting should be installed before the crop is ripe and birds have acquired a taste for the fruits. And there must be no gaps through which birds can pass. The larger the piece of netting, the less splicing and tying will be needed. Netting that is 14 feet wide is sufficient to drape over a 6-foot-high grape trellis. A medium-size cherry tree can use a piece that is 20 feet or more square. I've found that a long pole with a forked tip serves best to put such a big piece on and take it off a tree.

Netting is even more susceptible to the elements than chicken wire. Plastic, especially polypropylene, breaks down eventually from exposure to sunlight. So I am careful to roll up and store the netting indoors as soon as the crop of fruit has been picked.

All this may sound like a huge endeavor. In season my garden — the fruit trees wrapped in netting, the vegetables encircled by chicken wire and an electric fence — is reminiscent of a Christo project. But now that I know what I am doing the fences and nets go up and down in only a few hours. And the beauty of it is knowing that I am going to be the one who gets to enjoy what I am growing. Some days I can even relax enough to admire a woodchuck eating clover outside the fence.

A Prescription
for Pests

SOMEWHERE in every garden, inscribed on the pedestal of the sundial for instance, should be the reminder to "know your foes." The print need not be large. If it takes a magnifying glass to make out the message, that's all right; a magnifying glass may be needed to make out the subjects. These are not the four-legged or two-legged pests of gardens — the yew-clipping deer, bean-consuming woodchucks, corn-pulling blackbirds, or strawberry-pinching children — but rather the much larger legion of smaller garden pests, the ones with six legs or eight legs or no legs at all. Insects, mites, slugs, snails — these invertebrates, or animals without backbones, are infamous pests of gardens. Add in a host of disease-causing fungi, bacteria, and viruses and you know what you are up against. You cannot garden and fail to meet up with these organisms sooner or later. Most are small and many are microscopic, and we might be able to ignore their presence were it not for the missing flower buds, severed stems, or moldy fruit.

What we see first is the damage. And we panic. We rush down to the garden center and tell the clerk that we need to spray our tomatoes quick because something is eating all the leaves. Unfortunately, neither the gardener nor the clerk knows what is eating the leaves. When you don't know the target, pinpoint eradication is out of the question. Of necessity the pesticide of choice is a broadspectrum one, the one with the longest list of potential victims on its label. When you should be killing caterpillars you end up using a weapon that also poisons such beneficial garden occupants as the honeybees that pollinate flowers and the ladybird beetles that feed on aphids. You don't have to be a placard-carrying environmentalist to figure out that this can be a prescription for disaster.

When people who were raised on Rachel Carson's *Silent Spring* or its sequels start gardening, many decide simply to skip trying to control pests and instead to try harmonious coexistence. The problem is that harmony isn't as contagious as gray mold. Japanese beetles have their own notions of manifest destiny. Even the most experienced and right-thinking organic gardeners have problems with pests.

In recent years the great philosophic gap separating organic gardeners and synthetic-chemical gardeners (for want of a better phrase) has dramatically narrowed. Slogans like "purveyors of death" and "hopeless optimists" are no longer hurled back and forth between the two groups. Among commercial growers, those who relied most heavily on chemical sprays have discovered that indiscriminate spraying is financially disastrous, not to mention that it promotes resistant strains, and can turn benign species into pests. As a result these growers are using fewer and fewer poisons. Meanwhile, organic gardeners are increasingly ready to concede that some spraying can be necessary. In the end, the common wisdom will be that there is a time and place for everything, even pesticide.

Deciding when to spray, and knowing what to spray, however, is only possible when you know what it is that you are spraying for. Before you do anything, you always need to discover what is bothering your plants. It may take some down-on-your-hands-and-knees close inspection. Look for the slimy trails of slugs, the round droppings of caterpillars, the sticky secretion of aphids. The culprit may be hidden — cabbage maggots feeding on the roots underground and causing the leaves to wilt — or it may be in plain view but beautifully camouflaged — a tomato hornworm stretched out along the stem of a tomato vine. Not all pests keep the same schedule as we do. It helps to go out at night and check the garden by flashlight.

When you have spotted what you think is the culprit, you are already well on your way to having a name for it. *The Gardener's Bug Book* by Cynthia Westcott (Doubleday and Company, 1973) lists garden pests by the plants they attack, and provides generous descriptions of each. The Peterson Series' *Field Guide to the Insects* by Donald Borror and Richard White (Houghton Mifflin, 1970) will teach you to recognize the key features of insect groups, the critical differences between squash bugs and cucumber beetles. Descriptive keys are useful, but I find that you can never have too many pictures of a pest when you are trying to identify it. If you get stuck, and you will sometimes, remember that you can always carry a specimen (in a jar is fine) to your nearest Cooperative Extension Service agent of the USDA. Some offices have a gardener's hotline, staffed by people who are experts at identifying things over the phone, but there is nothing like having the organism in hand to be absolutely certain.

Having trained as an entomologist, I am afraid that I have little empathy for entomophobia — a paranoid fear of insects — but I have met many people who can not bring themselves to catch a caterpillar, who shudder at the sight of aphids, who would sooner walk through broken glass than hold a June bug in their hand. Whenever I meet someone like this I try to explain that given the long and intimate association between plants and insects, a connection that goes back some 300 million years, it is unreasonable to expect to have the former in your backyard and not the latter. I tell them that there is no better reason to get to know insects and other creepie crawlies than wanting to garden.

Once you know the name of what is troubling your garden you can look up its life cycle, and you can ask other people how you should control it. But the first thing you should always try to ascertain is whether you can get away with doing nothing. I tried repeatedly to rid my globe thistles of the black aphids that cluster on their top growth and finally gave up, only to watch the aphids disappear on their own. Ladybugs arrive and decimate the aphids and the globe thistles go on to bloom just as though they were accustomed to insect attacks. Which, of course, they are.

Not all pests can be safely ignored. Full-grown tomato hornworm caterpillars, great green beasts as big as your thumb, can strip all the leaves off a tomato plant in a few days. Cutworms can go down a row of newly transplanted seedlings at night destroying every one. Striped cucumber beetles feeding on cucumber vines can infect them with fatal bacterial-wilt disease.

Where you must intervene to protect your plants, always start with a small stick and move up to a big one only when the first proves inadequate. Sometimes a simple barrier between pest and plant suffices. Setting out transplants with lightweight-cardboard collars that extend an inch below the soil line and a couple of inches above will keep cutworms at bay. Sheets of spunbonded polyester fabric, first used as floating row covers to raise daytime temperatures, are even more useful as insect screens. Spread out over plants and sealed tightly at the edges with soil or rocks, this fabric will keep away everything from flea beetles to root maggots.

Some plants are naturally unattractive to pests. Certain new cucumbers like 'Marketmore 80' have been bred to lack the bitter compounds that cucumber beetles home in on when searching for food. Less successful have been efforts to use naturally repellent plants to protect adjacent susceptible ones. There is a vast folklore on this so-called companion planting, and a number of popular books circulate

widely, but when the relationships are subjected to scientific scrutiny the benefits tend to vanish.

The best fertilizer is the gardener's shadow; the best pesticide is the gardener's footstep. Hand-picking is the euphemistic term for squashing, crushing, smearing, or otherwise killing pests directly. The smaller the insect, the easier this is both physically and emotionally. If you look for the bright orange clusters of eggs of the Colorado potato beetle on the undersides of the leaves, you can dispatch a whole population between your fingers before they even get started. With the biggest caterpillars, on the other hand, all but the least squeamish are grateful for heavy boots.

Where the pest is too fast to catch, or the row too long, or the labor force too small, sprays extend the gardener's reach but at the expense of precision. Again it is wise to start with the least powerful. Diatomaceous earth contains the remains of marine organisms, whose skeletons yield sharp fragments of silica. Dusted on plants, these fragments pierce the bodies of insects both externally and internally and cause them to die of dehydration. Sprays of *Bacillus thuringiensis,* or Bt, a naturally occurring disease-causing bacteria, kill a wide range of caterpillars from cabbage worms to corn borers when the bacterium is eaten. Rotenone, pyrethrum, and ryania are all plant-derived insecticides that break down into harmless substances soon after application. This means they have little residual effect. It is important to remember, however, that pesticides from natural sources are not necessarily safe. Rotenone is lethal to fish and it is widely used to clear ponds of trash fish before restocking. Nicotine sulfate, which is an extract of tobacco and used to control sucking insects, is a dangerous nerve poison for mammals.

In many instances, a single application of pesticide when you first spot the problem solves it. In others, however, you may have to resort to stronger, more lethal sprays that break down more slowly and thus have a longer-lasting effect. As an amateur gardener who is not trying to make a living from what you grow, you may decide that the light is not worth the candle. You may conclude that it isn't worth trying to raise that particular plant, or you may find a way to escape the problem by growing the plant differently. Late plantings of cabbage, for example, are less likely to be attacked by root maggots than early ones. Every plant pest has its own peculiar life cycle, its distinct behaviors, its own natural controls. The more that you can learn about these, the greater your chance of dealing with them safely and surely.

All of this extends to plant diseases as well, with an extra emphasis on prevention. Once a plant exhibits a full-blown case of disease there is often little that you can do. Yes, you can uproot the infected plant and discard it far enough away that it doesn't spread the disease. But your emphasis should be on preventing the disease from getting started in the first place. For starters, healthy plants resist disease the same way healthy people do. Keep your plants well watered and fertilized, give them room to grow and adequate air flow around their leaves, and they will defend themselves.

Try to rotate your annual crops from year to year so that you are not always planting the same things in the same place. It is important to remember that many related plants share the same diseases. Thus clubroot of cabbage will affect broccoli, Brussels sprouts, cauliflower, Chinese cabbage, kohlrabi, rutabagas, and turnips. Try to move members of the tomato family, the squash family, or the carrot family to different parts of the garden each year.

Although diseases like mildew of summer phlox or smut on corn are easy to recognize, most people are not plant pathologists. I confess that I am discouraged by the color atlases of sick and dying vegetation. Fortunately, many of the diseases pictured are ones I have never seen and probably never will. Credit for this goes to plant breeders who have built in genetic resistance. Many of the genes involved have come from distant and unprepossessing wild species, one of the reasons to be concerned about the declining diversity of plants in the world.

Read catalogs carefully, and you will find mention of disease resistance. Pay attention. I have given up growing *Phlox paniculata* in favor of *Phlox carolina* 'Miss Lingard', an excellent white flower that is all the more splendid because it never loses its lower leaves to mildew. I grow fireblight-resistant pears, and yellows-resistant cabbage, and verticillium wilt–resistant tomatoes. Nowhere are the words of the entomologist Neely Turner more pertinent. "Probably more pests can be controlled in an armchair in front of a February fire with a garden notebook and a seed catalog than can ever be knocked out in hand-to-hand combat in the garden."

Pesticide Safety

THE ORGANIC GARDENER with a few potato plants sees no reason not to remove potato bugs by hand. The farmer growing many acres has trouble imagining it. Though there will never be universal accord on what pesticides to use and when, the one thing that everyone has come to agree on is that whenever pesticides are used, they must be used with care. Misusing them is a threat to the user, to other animals and plants, and ultimately a threat to our being able to use these tools.

The guidelines that follow may seem conservative. They reflect my own upbringing. When I was a child, my father issued a lot of what seemed to me silly cautions — about the dangers of lead paint and the risks of too much sun. I will be pleased, but not surprised, if my own precautions turn out to be as well founded.

Every pesticide container has an extensive label giving all the necessary instructions for use and safety precautions. But this label is of absolutely no value unless it is read. The print is small. The labels are often large and sometimes folded over on themselves before being attached. But all the information is there, somewhere. Before you use any pesticide, make sure that it is intended to control the pest you propose to apply it to.

Sprays adhere to plant surfaces better than dusts do and for this reason are more common. Pesticides to be sprayed, however, must usually be diluted with water beforehand. I wear disposable plastic gloves when mixing spray. The gloves are inexpensive insurance against accidentally touching any of the concentrated pesticide; if you are mixing a tablespoon per gallon, what you start with is 250 times more toxic than the final product. For measuring out the concentrate and the water, I have a separate set of measuring spoons and containers. I never even consider borrowing ones from the kitchen. I also do my mixing outside, away from where people might come into contact with any spillage. If I pretend that what I am mixing is more dangerous than it is, then I find that I am more likely to mix the spray with the necessary care and precision.

Never mix up more spray than you intend to use. It seldom can be stored once diluted, and there is no easy way to dispose of leftovers. I try to calculate in advance how much spray I need, and I prefer to err on the short side, mixing up a little more if I run out.

When you apply the spray, wear a long-sleeved shirt and pants and, if you are spraying over your head, a hat. Better to accidentally spray your clothes than your bare skin. Plan on putting the clothes in the laundry as a separate load when you are done, and washing any exposed skin with soap and hot water. I also wear a respirator whenever I am spraying. Respirators aren't technically required for chemicals sold over the counter, but I like the margin of safety they provide. A respirator must be NIOSH-approved and equipped with filters specifically intended for pesticides. One of the great benefits of wearing a respirator is that it makes you look like a member of a hazardous-waste cleanup team, and causes anyone seeing you to keep their distance.

Every care should be taken to kill only the intended pests. You can time your spray to minimize drift. In the early morning and evening there is usually less of a breeze than at midday, and if you are applying dusts, they will better adhere to the dew-moist foliage. Honeybees, frequent unintentional victims of pesticides, are less likely to be killed by dawn and dusk spraying because they will then be safely in their hives.

When the sprayer is completely empty, wash it out, using plenty of water. Don't dump this rinse water down the drain; dump it outdoors. Then put the sprayer away where it is out of reach of children. Put the remaining pesticide away as well, being even more careful. Ideally, it should be stored in a locked cupboard or box. No matter how often you use a pesticide, it should never be stored under the kitchen sink.

Most pesticides are formulated to expire in two and a half years, so purchase only the amount you think you can use up in a couple of years, date the container when you bring it home, and go through your pesticides to discard any that are out of date. Disposing of extra pesticide properly, however, is a problem. You certainly don't want to dump it down the drain, because this is a sure way to poison water supplies. EPA policy allows homeowners to dispose of up to 1 gallon of liquid pesticide and 10 pounds of dry formulation — both hefty amounts — by wrapping the containers up securely and placing them in the trash. But this form of disposal is only slightly better, since no one knows where the chemicals will wind up. The best alternative is to turn old pesticides in to a local hazardous-waste collection station, which some towns have set up. If yours doesn't have one, consider requesting that it be established. In the meantime, the simplest way to get rid of pesticides is to use them up as they were intended and dispose of the empty container in the trash.

Pesticides can be useful tools. But they should never be thought of as household products. They are too dangerous ever to be completely domesticated. I was horrified to discover this spring that a major pesticide manufacturer was giving away samples of its products packed in a picnic hamper, alongside plates, cups, a tablecloth, and an apron. It requires a distorted sense of logic to believe that any poison, however important to food production, could possibly belong next to eating utensils.

As useful as pesticides are when applied correctly, they are never as convenient or quick a solution to pest problems as the manufacturers' advertisements would have us believe. If we are to be allowed to continue to use pesticides in our gardens, it will only be because we demonstrate that we are willing to take the trouble to use them safely. To paraphrase an old maxim, pesticides are a privilege, not a right.

Insect Traps

No one around here puts up scarecrows anymore. The birds in this neighborhood have become so accustomed to humans that they scarcely shy in the presence of real people, let alone fake ones. The effort not spent on repelling birds is going instead to trapping Japanese beetles. These voracious pests make their appearance in July and feed until Labor Day, earning more enmity than birds ever provoked. My neighbors, who are tired of drowning the beetles one by one in a container of soapy water, yet are still reluctant to resort to broad-spectrum insecticides, have hung up dozens of the familiar yellow-and-green Japanese-beetle traps in the hope that they will be a solution. Dangling from tree branches or hung on poles, the traps decorate their gardens like wind socks at a miniature airport.

The Japanese-beetle trap is almost as old as the mousetrap, and the design is nearly as unchanged. The newest models still have four bright-yellow vanes and a funnel that causes the beetles crashing into the vanes to fall into a green container underneath. Although most of the traps are made of plastic now, with easy-to-dispose-of green plastic bags, you can still buy the old-fashioned metal models. Eugenol, a flowery-smelling chemical derived from clove oil, is still the standard bait. The only substantive improvement to the traps in recent years has been the addition of a small amount of synthetic sex pheromone, the chemical that Japanese beetles naturally use to attract mates. Traps baited with both sex pheromone and eugenol capture more beetles than traps baited with only one or the other.

The traps catch Japanese beetles. That I can guarantee. In one week a few summers ago I caught 3825 Japanese beetles in a single trap. (I didn't count every last one, not after I found that there are 425 frozen Japanese beetles in a level half-cup kitchen measure.) But there is a flaw in assuming that because you are capturing a lot of insects in a trap, the trap is working. For unlike the fur trapper, who is making a living from what is in the trap, the gardener is more interested in what is in the garden. Unless an insect trap is reducing the number of insects attacking the plants, it isn't working no matter how quickly it fills up. Did the Japanese-beetle traps reduce the number of Japanese beetles in my garden? Not that I could see. The grapes, the roses, the sweet potatoes, and everything else Japanese beetles like to eat continued to be defoliated. I gave up trapping them after a couple of seasons, having decided that the only reward was a modicum of revenge.

Perhaps I gave up too soon. Maybe if I had used huge numbers of the traps I might have gotten better results. But I don't think so. In an experiment in eastern Tennessee in which 2000 traps were set out on 88 acres, the traps caught only 39 percent of the Japanese beetles; 740 traps set out on 55 acres the next year caught only 30 percent. Since a trap can attract Japanese beetles from as far away as 1500 feet, using only one Japanese beetle trap may be worse than having none at all.

Another example of an insect trap that catches insects without reducing the activity of the pest is the so-called bug-zapper, those blacklight traps surrounded by an electrified grid that are said to rid your yard and garden of mosquitoes and biting flies. Again, these traps kill a great many insects. You can hear the snap, crackle, and pop. But there is no evidence that they reduce the number of mosquitoes biting exposed skin. Quite the contrary, in fact. Two Ontario entomologists, in a controlled experiment, found that there was no significant difference between the number of mosquitoes biting people in yards equipped with bug-zappers and the number in those without.

This is not to say that traps are useless in controlling garden pests. It depends on the specific pest, its numbers respective to the number of traps, and the ease with which other individuals of the pest species can move in from other areas. Pieces of plywood a foot square that have been painted with Rust-Oleum 659 Yellow, made sticky with a coating of SAE 90 motor oil and hung between tomato plants in a greenhouse, *do* control whiteflies, because there are as many traps as plants, and because whiteflies cannot freely pour into the territory vacated by their late kin.

If a trap is inexpensive and easy to use, it is always worthwhile testing it out in your own garden, remembering that the proof lies not in the trap but in the garden. Shallow containers of beer sunk to their rims in the soil will trap and kill slugs (which are mollusks but can be considered honorary insects as far as their eating habits are concerned). One woman I know, a teetotaler who lives alongside a busy road, gets her beer supply from the cans that are flung from passing cars into her garden.

An even simpler trap is a small board or shingle laid on the soil surface in the garden. A great many night-active garden inhabitants will seek shelter here during the day, and the gardener who turns the board over will have the opportunity to exercise selective annihilation of undesirables.

The future promises an assortment of specialized insect traps for the home gardener. The incentive for their development comes from the needs of commercial growers, who use the traps to monitor for the presence or absence of a pest species so that they can spray when spraying does the most good. Many of them will prove to be useful only for monitoring (as is the Japanese-beetle trap), but some may turn out to provide direct control when used in sufficient abundance. What makes me hopeful is that I already know of one such trap.

The trap is a sticky red croquet ball, and it catches apple-maggot flies. In this part of the country, the big three insect pests of apples are plum curculios, coddling moths, and apple maggots. The first marks infant apples with crescent scars just after the petals fall and causes most of the fruit to fall off the tree a few weeks later. Codling-moth larvae burrow up into the core and leave a black mess, but one that can be at least partially removed with a paring knife at harvest time. The damage caused by apple maggots, however, cannot be pared away. These larvae of a true fruit fly (as opposed to those so-called fruit flies that like bananas) burrow throughout the flesh of an apple and leave a maze of brown tunnels.

The use of sticky-ball traps for apple maggots resulted from theoretical studies by Ron Prokopy at the University of Massachusetts at Amherst. Prokopy was investigating what sort of object attracted the adult flies. He discovered that both males and females are attracted to apple-sized spheres — the female because she is looking for a place to lay her eggs, the male because he is looking for females with which to mate. Since these flies are mating and laying eggs in

early summer, a time when most apples are green, one would expect the flies to be attracted to green spheres. Not so. The flies are maximally attracted to red spheres, specifically croquet balls painted with Sherwin-Williams Tartar Red Dark Enamel. If these red croquet balls are covered with Tangle-Trap or Bird Tanglefoot (not Tree Tanglefoot, which is smellier and less effective), any flies that land will be stuck as to flypaper.

Commercial orchardists use apple-maggot traps to determine when to spray, one sticky ball for every couple of acres. I, on the other hand, have been putting six sticky balls on each of my apple trees. This leaves them looking like out-of-season Christmas trees, but the result is that I haven't had any apple-maggot damage in my apples in four years. I know of no other trap that provides such startling, and consistent, results.

Several companies sell the traps ready-made from croquet-ball seconds. Gardeners with old croquet sets might consider repainting the balls for the purpose. Each ball should have a small screw eye screwed into it and a foot of wire attached. With a popsicle stick or a tongue depressor, coat each ball with a *thin* layer of Tangle-Trap, leaving it a little thicker at the top of the ball than at the bottom since during the summer it will slowly creep downward. Be careful — the stuff is one of the world's stickiest substances and a nuisance to remove from hair and clothing.

How many balls you should hang in each apple tree will depend on the size of the tree and the number of apples. Generally, plan on one ball for every one hundred apples. These should be precisely placed, at head height, a half to one yard inside the outermost foliage of the tree. All fruit or foliage within one foot of the balls should be removed. But beyond that radius there should be as much fruit and foliage as possible to attract flies to the general area.

I set my traps out in mid-June, before the first apple-maggot flies have emerged (check with your extension agent for the date in your locality), and leave them up all summer. I take them down in the fall, scrape off the Tangle-Trap and dead insects with a curved piece of plastic cut out of a milk jug, and wipe them clean with a kerosene-soaked rag.

These sticky balls trap all sorts of insects, and feathers on some of them indicate that an occasional bird runs afoul of them. But it is easy to spot the apple-maggot flies. They are slightly smaller than

houseflies and have distinctive black-and-white-striped wings. By the
end of the season each ball has a score of these flies on it. As with
the Japanese-beetle traps there is a small measure of satisfaction from
seeing the pests fatally mired in the goo. But the real pleasure is in
the harvest, when you slice open apple after apple and find the flesh
clean and white to the core. To my mind, red sticky balls are the
standard against which to judge the effectiveness of any trap.

Grass of Ages

For TWO MILLION YEARS our ancestors lived on the African savannas. In this grassland dotted with trees, an upright walk and free-swinging arms were well suited to daily life. Recently, a number of scientists have speculated that the human mind as well as the body may be predisposed to life on a savanna. All through recorded history, gardeners all over the world have created strikingly similar landscapes of grasses and other low-lying plants interspersed with trees. The scientists suggest that in enjoying these creations, in seeing them as beautiful, we may be responding to a deep genetic urge that drives us to seek out such a natural habitat.

In this line of argument, some will find justification for having lawns. I, however, see no reason to go that far, though I am prepared to accept a genetic basis for my taste in landscapes. Why should I spend enormous amounts of time, money, and labor to create a putting green when I can achieve equal harmony with a stand of tall grass?

All of this is a preface to the observation that many of my neighbors spend more time watering, mowing, and fertilizing their lawns than I, and yet seem no happier for it. I watch them making their rounds a couple of times each week, mowing, carefully raking up the clippings, setting up the sprinkler, spreading fertilizer and weed killer. I should be more charitable, for a lawn enthusiast is really no different from a gardener who spends all his time on roses or dahlias, but I just can't understand all that effort.

In nature, savannas take care of themselves. They are the product of reduced rainfall, fire, and grazing by large animals. Here in the eastern United States there are very few natural grasslands. The rainfall is sufficient to promote lush forests, fire is strictly regulated, and in most towns the residents no longer pasture cows or sheep in the front yard. The only way that grassland is maintained is by mowing. Regular cutting interrupts the inevitable takeover of the forest.

Mowing once or twice a year is all that is necessary to keep woody plants from springing up. Such infrequent mowing yields a rough meadow containing an assortment of coarse grasses and broad-leaved wild flowers. Daisies, asters, goldenrod, clover, orange milkweed, purple vetch — what appears will depend on what seeds are present. A meadow of this sort with its coarse-stemmed plants should never be mowed as close as a lawn made up of bent grasses, which can be cut as low as ¼ to ½ inch. Six inches is a perfectly satisfactory height for meadow mowing. Unfortunately most lawnmowers are not designed to cut that high. In the past I have occasionally exchanged the wheels of a conventional rotary mower for a set 10 inches in diameter to raise the blade's cutting height. The risk in doing this is that it becomes far easier to slip a foot under the machine. But when you are only mowing the grass once or twice a summer, there is time to be especially careful.

I have not converted this lawn into meadow just yet. I don't think the neighbors are ready for it. It is bad enough that I let my lawn get shaggy; if I let it go to hay someone might go to court. Not really, but some towns have ordinances requiring that lawns be kept mowed, and there have been several widely publicized cases in which property owners have defended their right to grow wild flowers instead of grass.

Recently I attended a wild-flower conference at which a compromise was suggested, a way to maintain meadows in densely populated areas and still please the neighbors. The suggested solution was to surround the meadow with a clearly defined section of closely mowed lawn. This border supposedly demonstrates to others that the long grass is not simply the result of slovenly habits, of the owner's having given up yard work altogether.

I like this idea. Perhaps I could let the grass grow in back and keep it cut short up front — the way I once kept my hair. I envisage a small patch of perfect lawn, just enough grass so I could cut it with a hand mower, one of those reel mowers that represent a triumph of nineteenth-century mechanical engineering.

I am not the best person to ask about how to maintain a perfect lawn of any size, since as you already know I don't have the best lawn on the block. The man across the street does. All the same, I have opinions about how it should be done, a number of which I have provided free of charge from the sidewalk, and so I offer them here again.

Small lawns are easier to perfect than large ones. Most of us ought to leave the task of maintaining vast greenswards to those with estates and endowments to match.

The closer you choose to mow grass, the more often you will have to mow. Otherwise a newly mowed lawn resembles a freshly harvested hay field. This looks bad and is not good for the lawn. As a general rule, plan on removing no more than a third of the grass's height at any one time. The higher the setting of the blade, the longer you can wait to mow again. Longer grass is also more resistant to drought, and less likely to become infested with crabgrass. Unfortunately, shaggy lawns aren't most people's idea of perfection.

If you are mowing as frequently as you should, there is no reason to remove the clippings. Doing so removes nutrients that would otherwise be returned to the living grass when the clippings rot. Reportedly this can add 50 percent to your fertilizer bill. However, if the lawn gets out of hand, say, after three weeks of steady rainy weather when you can't mow, you will have to remove the clippings or they will mat and kill the grass beneath. Add these nitrogen-rich clippings to your compost pile.

Most gardeners use far too much lawn fertilizer. Some lawns may need fertilizer some of the time; many lawns never need it. The more fertilizer you apply, the faster the grass grows and the more often you have to cut it. Fertilizer is often misapplied, creating at best zebralike patterns of green exuberance, at worst sickly yellow patches of dead turf. If you are convinced that your lawn needs fertilizer, a spring application of a ureaform fertilizer, which is a slow-release type, is probably the best choice. There is no danger of burning, and the nitrogen needs of the grass for an entire season can be supplied with one application.

Buy fertilizers that do not contain herbicides. This is a personal prejudice, I admit, but I have heard too many stories of trees killed by herbicides that had been applied to adjoining lawns, of contaminated compost piles, of people being poisoned. If you don't worry about such things, use herbicides, but follow the directions to the letter. More than the health of the grass is at stake.

There are other equally effective methods of weed control. As a child, I earned a penny per ten dandelions and prided myself on my ability to remove the entire taproot. Crabgrass requires full sun to grow; it is shaded out by dense turf that is more than 1½ inches high. Clover should be reclassified as an honorary grass. It fixes its own nitrogen, feeds the bees, and recovers from drought better than grass, which is one way that it gets established in the first place.

Unless you are in a terrible hurry to have an instant lawn, sow your own. Fall is the best time to sow seed — from late August to mid-September in the North, through October farther south. Seed should germinate in seven to ten days, provided the soil is kept moist, and will be well established by the time freezing temperatures arrive.

Lawns consisting of a single kind of grass require precisely the right conditions for that particular grass if they are to flourish. It is far safer to plant a mixture of seed from different grasses so that whatever grass matches your conditions will get a chance to take over.

Any freshly sown lawn becomes a feeding station for birds. The English recommend tightly stretching fine string six inches or so above the ground between small stakes. In theory this deters the birds because it fouls their wings the way that the wires dangling from barrage balloons fended off German bombers over London during World War II. My own solution is to spread a layer of coarse cheesecloth over the newly seeded soil. The material I use is recycled shade cloth from tobacco farms. The birds can't find the seed under the cloth, the newly germinated shoots easily penetrate the fabric, and it eventually rots in place.

New grass should not be mowed until it is a couple of inches tall, and then only a little bit should be taken off the top with a sharp mower blade. The next year, when the grass is better established, is soon enough to cut it lower.

Grass is the only groundcover that can withstand foot traffic. But ground that is regularly trodden is unlikely to support a good grass cover because the soil becomes so compacted that the grass roots do not get sufficient air. In most cases it is best to recognize that a path is a path, and stop trying to grow grass there. But if the condition is temporary — say, the swing has been moved — then aeration can provide a cure. This involves making small holes four inches or so deep every six inches. All manner of devices have been invented for doing this, from big machines that remove small plugs of soil to spiked sandals. On small sections of ground a spading fork jabbed into the soil and worked back and forth slightly can create a regular pattern of small holes that will let air into the soil.

Irregularities in a lawn's surface can be filled with a topdressing of equal parts sand, loam, and compost sifted through a ¼-inch screen. This should be spread thinly and raked into the existing grass with an iron rake. It is better to spend two or three years filling a deep depression than to try to fill it all at once and kill the underlying grass.

It is a curious contradiction that we use so much water on lawns, when in nature grass is the result of not enough water. An inch of water a week, or enough to soak in five or six inches, is the usual prescription for keeping a lawn green. However, just as many lawns don't need fertilizer, many never need watering. A lawn that is not watered during a prolonged dry spell may turn brown, but it will revive once moisture returns. Grass was around long before we were.

Ignore all the advice about when to water; ignore the people who tell you not to water at night because you will cause fungus, or during the day because droplets of water will become tiny magnifying glasses and burn holes in the grass blades. It rains at all times of the day, doesn't it? I prefer not to water at midday for the simple reason that the sun evaporates some of the water before it gets to soak in. I don't water in the middle of the night because I am usually asleep.

Of Lawns and Barbers

ANYONE with a pair of scissors can cut hair. If all we wanted was shorter hair, then most of us would cut our own. To be sure, barbers are more deft, their scissors and comb working in swift synchrony over our scalp. But speed is not the only reason we have journeyed across town, relinquished our eyeglasses, and asked someone else to shear us for a price. The justification of time and expense occurs once the heavy cutting is over, when our ears are revealed and our forehead is bare once more. Now the barber reaches for his electric razor and, with a few vibration-filled strokes, trims the edges behind our ears and at the back of our neck. "Finishing," he calls it, and it is what separates barbers from the rest of us. As soon as the sheet covering our shoulders has been removed and the cut hairs dusted out from behind our collar, we get our glasses back and are asked for our opinion. We always say "Fine," but we are never sure until we have reached back and felt the close-cropped bristle at the nape of our neck, the distinguishing feature of a proper haircut.

So it is with cutting grass. We can all whack back the vegetation. If the grass is being cut with a scythe or a machete, skill is needed to control the height of the cut, but this isn't necessary with a lawn mower, either a gasoline-powered rotary or a hand-operated reel mower. With either of these, virtually anyone can convert even the rankest hayfield into a close approximation of a lawn. What distinguishes a truly well-mown lawn, however, is not the evenness of the cut in midfield but the condition of the grass at the edges. Edges are the hardest part of mowing any lawn. Not only is there usually a great deal of edge, but the grass that grows there is often hard to reach with the mower, being protected by various obstacles: here a rock, there a fence post or tree trunk. Often we end up leaving tufts of tall grass on the edges of the lawn, looking as out of place as isolated tufts of hair would at the borders of one's head.

Many people turn to professionals to mow their yards. But there isn't any reason that we can't all learn to do our own. It is, after all, a lot easier to see the back of one's lawn than the back of one's head. We simply have to reduce the problem to its component parts. Either (1) we find a way to prevent the grass from growing where the mower can't reach, or (2) we find a way to cut it even in these inaccessible locations.

Consider the grass that grows under trees. Even if there are no low-hanging branches of the sort that pluck at and tear the backs of shirts as you pass underneath, there is a limit to how close you can get to the trunk with a mower. Invariably, a small circle of tall grass remains at the base of the tree trunk. The only safe way to get rid of such a ragged edge is to prevent grass from growing there in the first place. Why? Because trees and sod are incompatible. When they are young, trees cannot compete with grass roots. Even a fair-sized sapling will be stunted if it is planted in the midst of a lawn without protection from grass and weeds. Once a tree becomes big enough to compete with grass, it usually does so to the latter's detriment, as anyone who has tried maintaining the lawn under a copper beech or a Norway maple can attest.

Even when grass will grow right up to the base of an established tree, it shouldn't be allowed to. Sooner or later, whoever is cutting the grass will bang into the trunk and injure the tree. You don't have to bang the trunk with something sharp; you don't even have to leave a mark. Simply bumping the housing of a power mower against the bark can bruise the tender cambium layer under the bark, causing it to die. Because the cambium is the originator of the tree's vascular system — the plumbing that transports water and food up and down the trunk — as the cambium goes, so goes the tree.

All tree trunks in a lawn should be surrounded by a grass-free zone so that you aren't even tempted to try mowing close. This is easier said than done. What keeps Kentucky bluegrass and other fine lawns dense are the underground stems (called rhizomes) that grass plants send out in all directions. In the middle of the lawn they are a welcome feature, but at the edge they are a nuisance, because the lawn keeps spreading.

One way to prevent this spread is to cut back the edge now and then: Slice into the soil to a depth of six inches or so to cut errant rhizomes, and uproot those that have been so severed. This job can be done with a spade, or even a shovel if a slightly scalloped edge isn't objectionable. Most people turn to the traditional half-moon edger, a tool some associate with brick sidewalks, anthills, and hot summer mornings. Whatever tool is used, the job needs to be done at least annually.

In theory, you can also erect an impermeable barrier at the edge of the flower bed, something that the grass rhizomes cannot penetrate. Among the possibilities are various materials buried in the ground: strips of aluminum or plastic, or bricks set on edge. In practice, the aluminum gets bent, the plastic becomes brittle, and wherever there is frost all three are heaved out of the ground each winter. The only solid edgings that can truly be relied upon are full-dimension granite curbing (the sort used to edge streets) and the expensive, heavy-gauge steel sheets used in arboretums. There is one nonsolid material that works admirably as a barrier, however, and that is air. A simple trench, a moat half a foot wide and no deeper, filled with nothing, will keep the grass rhizomes where you want them. The moat must be cleaned out now and then, but this is less work than slicing down through sod on a regular basis.

Finally, you can keep grass in its place by rendering the adjacent soil inhospitable. This is most easily done with a good layer of mulch, a layer that will at the same time provide attendant benefits to whatever plants are growing in its midst.

If you can maintain the lawn's edge at a sufficient distance from obstacles, then you can mow the grass at the edge with whatever you use to mow the rest of the lawn. But there will always be places where grass has grown out of the lawn mower's reach, up against a stone wall or under a chain-link fence, for instance.

This requires a means to cut the grass in inaccessible locations. One of the most basic tools for this task is a pair of sheep shears, a multipurpose tool that can be used to trim grass, cut hair, and, in a pinch, shear sheep. Other hand shears are mechanical variations of this tool, usually converting a vertical closing of the hand into a horizontal closing of two blades.

Trimming any sizable amount of grass this way, however, soon tires the hands. Even the electric models powered by rechargeable batteries are not much better. But fortunately there is a comparatively recent invention that makes short work of long edges — the string trimmer. This machine cuts grass and other vegetation with the tip of a whirling monofilament nylon line. The great virtue of using a nylon line to do the cutting is that when it hits something hard, like a brick wall, it does no damage to either the wall, the machine, or the operator. The line merely frays at the tip as tiny bits are broken off, and more line must be paid out from the spool on the string trimmer's head. By walking slowly and swinging the head of the string trimmer from side to side close to the ground, you can cut large stretches of difficult lawn edge with relative ease.

Battery-operated, electric, and gasoline-powered models of string trimmers are available. The gasoline-powered versions are the most mobile, but they weigh 10 to 20 pounds and generate the vibration, noise, and problems associated with two-cycle engines. Where the work to be done is within a hundred feet of an outlet, electric models are a better choice. For some, rechargeable battery models will provide a compromise.

Although string trimmers are relatively safe (far safer, say, than the prototype of a string trimmer invented in Texas in the 1940s, which used whirling flails made from coat hangers), they can still be hazardous. Sturdy shoes, long pants, gloves, and eye protection should be worn to ward off bits of flying debris. And because the whirling cord is invisible there is always a chance that you will strike something unintentionally. For this reason string trimmers should never be used in the vicinity of tree trunks. Of course, there will be no temptation to do so if the grass is kept away from the trunk in the first place. Don't give this tool a bad reputation by using it to kill trees and shrubs. Use it where it is needed, and then stand back and savor the close-cropped bristle at the lawn's edge.

High-Quality Harvest

HOMEGROWN VEGETABLES are supposed to taste better than the ones sold in the supermarket. Indeed, the promise of crisper lettuce and sweeter corn is the principal reason I engage in something that could otherwise be dismissed as a losing proposition — an activity that can consume more time and money than the end product is worth. However, if the promise of superiority is met in the form of a truly ripe tomato, say, or a muskmelon that slips freely from the vine, then all such economic arguments end up on the compost heap. Come fall, I can't remember why, during my spring struggles to get the soil dug and the seeds sown, I ever doubted that a vegetable garden was worth the effort. What convinces me are the carrots, the beans, the cucumbers, and turnips (yes, turnips!) — produce delectable enough that much is eaten before it even gets indoors.

What I have come to realize, however, is that superior taste is not a foregone conclusion. It is perfectly possible to raise your own vegetables and have them taste worse than the ones sold in the supermarket. Supermarkets, despite all the wisecracks about pistol-whipped bananas and pink-golfball tomatoes, offer remarkably fine produce, month in and month out. Their lettuce is as crisp as it is because it has been carefully picked at just the right time, quickly chilled to remove field heat, and rushed to retail markets, even though these may be several thousand miles away. A home gardener who picks a head of lettuce in the backyard about noon on a sunny day, and leaves it sitting in the sun on the patio for an hour, invariably ends up with salad greens that are inferior to what we can buy at the store. Pride in having grown something yourself adds to a vegetable's flavor, but it is no substitute for harvesting in a way that ensures the highest quality.

Most vegetables should be picked when they are young. I know a cook who insists that once the flower has fallen off a zucchini, the infant squash is on the verge of being too old. Baby carrots, petits pois, new potatoes — these delights are readily available in a home garden. With the exception of melons, tomatoes, and winter squash there is little risk in picking any vegetable prematurely. Supermarkets are not oblivious to the fact that smaller zucchinis taste better than those the size of softball bats. (Indeed, they never try to sell the latter, unlike home gardeners who are always trying to foist such specimens on friends and neighbors.) But supermarkets must contend with the fact that young vegetables, tasty as they may be, are incredibly fragile. They bruise easily, and their skins are so thin that the flesh inside quickly dries out, causing the vegetable to wilt and shrivel.

The home gardener must contend with this too, and vegetables are best picked the day that they are to be used, preferably in the cool of the morning. Handle them carefully so as not to bruise them. Refrain from piling things on top of one another. A used grape box, of the sort found in the trash behind fruit stands, will serve admirably as a broad, shallow garden basket, an inexpensive equivalent of an English trug. Once picked, vegetables should be kept cool. Put them in a cool cellar if possible; at the very least keep them in the shade. A light sprinkling of water will further cool the vegetables as it evaporates.

Some vegetables, like parsnips, carrots, and potatoes, remain tasty over a long period of time and can be stored safely in the row until they are needed. But most vegetables have only a short period of perfection, during which time they must be harvested. Corn, for example, is at its best for scarcely more than ten days. The season can be extended by successive sowings, or by planting a series of cultivars with different numbers of days to maturity. (Choose cultivars that differ by at least a week to prevent excessive overlap.) But one cannot pick sweet corn and expect it to last for a week or so in the bottom of the refrigerator. Leaving it in the garden isn't good either: the sugars continue to change to starch until the kernels are as inedible as field corn. One can, of course, set about freezing or canning extra produce that won't keep, but most home vegetable gardeners learn to eat lots of whatever is in season at the moment. Bingeing on any vegetable, be it asparagus or eggplant, can get tiresome, especially when the vegetable is unadorned. This is why a resource like *The Victory Garden Cookbook* by Marian Morash and Jane

Doerfer (Knopf, 1982) is a welcome addition to a gardener's library. When we are about to have boiled beans for the fourth night in a row, we open to the bean chapter and choose between salmagundi or stir-fried snap beans and beef.

Personal preference has a lot to do with when a vegetable is picked. Everyone seems to have a different opinion about when corn is just perfect. I like mine on the far side of ripe. The following are some general guidelines, suggestions that favor the palate more than the eye. Taste, not appearance, is what vegetable gardening should be about.

Beans   Green beans are best harvested before one can feel the outlines of the individual seeds in the pod. Invariably a few pods escape attention only to be found later, their skins yellowing, the beans inside bulging. Simply treat these as shell beans — shell out the seeds and discard the pod. These can be cooked separately or mixed in with the green beans.

Beets   The inner leaves make the tastiest beet greens. Discard those that are yellowed or disfigured by the tunneling of leaf miners. With the exception of 'Long Season', which retains its quality even when huge, beetroots should be picked when the roots are no bigger than a tangerine.

Broccoli   The edible portion of broccoli is the flower stalk and buds. The latter open quickly into yellow flowers (which can nonetheless be eaten) if not picked promptly. Most cultivars will continue to produce a succession of small shoots once the main flower head is cut, so there is no need to try to extend the season by putting off harvesting broccoli that is ready to eat.

Cabbage   Heads of this vegetable are ready to harvest when firm and heavy. You can get some idea of how dense the head is even though it is still on the plant by patting it on one side and noting how much inertia it has. Mature heads left in the garden will eventually split as pressure from developing leaves inside the head becomes too great. This does not ruin the cabbage, though the split outer leaves may die and rot if they have become detached from the stem. Split heads are, however, a nuisance to handle in the kitchen.

Carrots   These can be picked anytime. The largest ones are less tender, but it is nevertheless best to leave carrots in the garden until you need them, to prevent the roots from drying out.

Corn   Raccoons have an unerring way of knowing the exact moment when corn is ripe. Humans usually consider dry, brown silk the sign that picking should begin. You really ought to have the water boiling before you pick the corn, but you need not run from the garden to the pot, because the new super-sweet corn cultivars, like 'Early Xtra-Sweet', remain sweeter for a longer time after picking. Once kernels turn a golden color they are getting too old, and by the time a dent appears at the end of each kernel the corn is virtually inedible (nutritious yes, but inedible).

Cucumbers   Harvest these vegetables before the seeds inside swell up, well before the cucumber reaches full size. Once fully grown, cucumbers turn yellow, at which point they are suitable only for pickles. Keeping fruit picked assures additional cucumbers.

Lettuce   Even small seedlings are tasty; picking only the outer leaves of young plants prolongs the supply of greens. When the lettuce plant begins to expand upwards, the stem elongating between each leaf, it has begun to bolt and will shortly flower and set seed. The leaves of bolting lettuce are too bitter for most people to enjoy.

Muskmelon   When the stem slips readily from the melon, it is ready. Test by lifting up a melon. If the vine falls away, take the melon with you.

Onions   These are tasty at any age. Once the tops fall over, the onions should be pulled up, dried in the sun for a day, and braided. Large, mild onions like 'Sweet Spanish' should be eaten within a few weeks of harvest. 'Stuttgart', an authoritative onion, will keep many months.

Peas   Harvest as soon as the peas fill the pods. When peas are big enough to flatten each other in the pod, they taste starchy and bitter. Such overmature peas can be left on the vine, allowed to dry, shelled out, and used for soup.

Peppers   Harvest anytime. Left on the vine, peppers turn red and their flavor sweetens, producing a vegetable with an entirely different taste.

Potatoes   Young potatoes begin to form when the plants bloom. Anytime afterward, a little surreptitious digging with one's fingers near the base of the plants will yield pullet-egg-size new potatoes.

Summer Squash   The younger the better. Failure to remove mature squash inhibits future flowers. In the case of zucchini, this may be a preferable option.

Winter Squash   Butternut, buttercup, or acorn squash must be left on the vine until the underside of the squash is a different color from the top and the skin is hard. Generally, I wait until just before frost to harvest.

Tomatoes   More discussion has gone on about the ripening of tomatoes than any other vegetable. Tomatoes left on the vine until they are fully red (or yellow, or orange, as the case may be) taste different from the store-bought ones, no matter what the tomato-marketing lobby may tell you. That isn't to say you have to wait that long for them to taste better. When frost threatens, and you need to decide whether or not to pick, remember that most store tomatoes were picked at a stage called "mature green," when the tomato was full-size but not yet showing any color. Even the term "vine-ripened" means only that the tomato was beginning to show color before it was picked. If frost threatens, pick. Better a half-ripe tomato indoors than a frozen one on the vine. Any tomato showing color will ripen up to be superior to any you can buy in the supermarket.

Surplus Vegetables

At the time the garden was being planted, the extra tomato plants were too good to discard, so I transplanted them all. I also planted a few extra hills of squash as insurance, in case some of the plants died. To tidy things up indoors, I sowed what carrot, cucumber, and beet seed remained in the packets. And so, once again, my vegetable garden has become bigger and more productive than I intended.

As long as frugality, foresight, and order are virtues, these annual surpluses seem inevitable. Equally unavoidable, unfortunately, is the accompanying sense of obligation, the feeling that now something must be done with all that extra food. I cannot simply let the tomatoes rot, the cucumbers balloon, the corn go starchy.

No one else is willing to take the vegetables off my hands. All the neighboring gardens have gone into overdrive simultaneously. There is no sense in carrying a basketful next door. I would simply end up dueling zucchinis.

Our great-grandparents dealt with whatever vegetables they could not eat immediately by canning them. This made sense when a can of corn or tomatoes or peas from the store cost as much as a pound of roast beef. The home-canning habit, along with the jars themselves — heavy glass pints and quarts with stiff wire bails — were passed down from generation to generation. By the time I came along, pressure cookers were in use, and electric freezers, too, but the philosophy had not changed. When my mother wanted tomatoes or beans in the winter, we were sent down to the fruit room to get a quart jar. For corn, peas, broccoli, cauliflower, we went to get a container out of the freezer.

Now it is my turn to deal with the surplus, and I can't help noticing that the frozen peas from the supermarket are almost identical in flavor, and considerably cheaper, than the ones my wife and

I put up. The same is true for frozen corn and stewed tomatoes. What our ancestors did as a means of saving money is not economical anymore. And I am not enough of a purist to preserve the tradition for its own sake.

That is not to say, however, that I no longer preserve the surplus. But my motivation is better taste, not savings. One way to improve the flavor of a newly opened quart of home-canned tomatoes is to doctor up the contents. A little celery, onion, green pepper, and chopped herbs spruce up the taste. But why wait until midwinter to do this, at a time when those ingredients are more expensive, or perhaps unavailable? It is far easier, I have concluded, to take the time in the summer to assemble the ingredients when they are just outside the kitchen door. Canning or freezing a finished dish assures that the contents will be distinctive the moment the container is opened.

To save the bumper crop of tomatoes, we like the following fiery variant of a Mennonite community chili. Starting with a peck of surplus ripe tomatoes we add six green peppers, five jalapeño peppers, ten onions, one bunch of celery, two cups of sugar, two cups of vinegar, some cloves, and some cinnamon. We cook them all together in a large kettle, stirring frequently, and can them just as we would pure stewed tomatoes. When you are tired, or have unexpected guests, you need only fry up a pound of beef, open a quart of this sauce, add a can of store-bought horticultural beans, and another of corn (if you think the guests can't take the heat).

In a similar manner, any extra cucumbers will become jars of pickles, the eggplant will be transformed into frozen caponata, the zucchini (well, some of it anyway) into ratatouille. This technique is now working so well that in the future I intend to deal with each surplus as an ingredient, not as a raw material to be stockpiled.

It occurs to me that I could even design the vegetable garden around those dishes that the family likes eating. I already plant a mixture of salad greens and the herbs used to produce the herb vinegar for dressing the salad. Why not decide how much of what to grow according to the ingredients needed for the rest of the menu? It is an exciting idea, this meal-based plan for the vegetable garden. For a moment, in my zeal for the perfectly calculated garden, I forget that the best-laid plans for any vegetable garden always end in surplus.

Summer is also the season for bramble fruits: blackberries, raspberries, and their kin. It can be scratchy business picking these. Blackberry canes could double as concertina wire. The berries must not be piled too deeply in the basket or carried roughly back to the house, or the fragile fruits will be crushed under their own weight. Whether eaten fresh, frozen, or in jam, there is then the matter of the seeds. Small and hard, they are exasperatingly adapted to fit tightly in the spaces between a person's teeth. Jelly is a seedless preserve, but the work of straining the cooked pulp explains why most of us are content to make jam.

The following is a simple, seedless solution. In a large, clean glass jar, layer equal volumes of fruit and sugar. Start with an inch of fresh fruit pressed down, then add an inch of sugar, then more pressed fruit, and so on. You need not fill the jar at one time but can wait and add to it as the fruit is available. Cover the jar loosely and place it in a cool, dark cupboard or some comparable location. The sugar will draw moisture out of the fruit, and the resulting liquid will begin to ferment; cool temperatures prevent runaway fermentation. In a few months' time the contents will have stabilized. Whenever it is needed, some of the resulting clear, red, sweet, lightly alcoholic liquid can be poured off to use as a topping for meat, pudding, cake, or ice cream. The contents of the jar are supposed to keep forever. I can vouch that they are no less ambrosial after twenty years.

Vegetable Storage

THE TRUE NEW ENGLANDER, it is said, doesn't worry simply about the upcoming winter but about the winter after that. I offer this as an explanation for the hundreds of onions now hanging in heavy braids down in the cellar. Of course I don't expect anyone to accept this as an excuse, since there are far more onions down there than any one family could use in three years, even if the onions were to keep that long. I am forced, therefore, to admit that my real reason for housing such an excess of onions is that they make me sleep better. Going to bed amidst plenty, I find, brings with it an ancient reassurance that all is well — the lullaby of a full larder.

The origins of this response are probably deep in prehistory, but I can trace mine back to Mother's jelly. Batch after batch of paraffin-sealed jars, some as old as I, lined the shelves of our family's fruit room — red currant and raspberry, green mint, rose geranium, purple beach plum. It was more than the four of us could possibly eat. Not that we didn't try. Ours was the only family I ever knew of that regularly ate jelly on scrambled eggs. As we grew older, the jelly was joined by jars of applesauce, stewed tomatoes, canned string beans. We bought a second freezer and started filling it with containers of corn, broccoli, blueberries, and peaches. We began drying and threshing our own beans for baking. We grew all our own potatoes, and considered wheat.

Today, things have changed. We don't make tomato paste any-more. When we want soybeans, we buy them. We still do a little freezing, canning, and pickling, but it's mostly of specialized dishes we can't get at the supermarket more easily and cheaply, like chili or chutney. It is the combination of ingredients, all harvested in season, that adds value and makes these concoctions economical. We haven't stopped stockpiling plain vegetables altogether. The onions in the cellar are proof of that. But the surplus vegetables we grow and keep over the winter are now almost entirely the ones easiest to store. I find they give no less peace of mind.

Trundle boxes of winter squash live under our bed. Allowed to ripen fully, handled at harvest as though they were eggs, and stored at the correct temperature, many kinds of winter squash will keep for a year. From the vine, we move our squashes (and pumpkins) to shallow boxes, where they nestle a single layer deep in crumpled newspaper. These boxes spend several days in full sun, and the squashes are turned several times to allow all sides to dry and harden in the heat. From there the boxes go to the upstairs bedrooms. It is a mistaken notion that squashes need to be kept cool. They keep much better at a temperature of 65 degrees Fahrenheit. The only attention they get once they are put to bed is a periodic inspection to see that they haven't begun to spoil, and that can be done when cleaning the dust pussies from around the boxes.

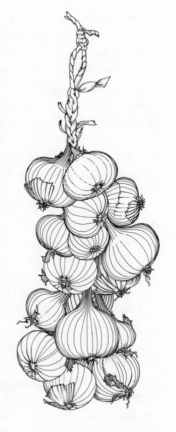

Onions are nearly as easy to store, but they do require cool temperature and dry air. In the cellar where I store mine it gets as cold as 45 degrees during the winter. Thirty-two degrees would be ideal. Onions can be piled two layers deep in slatted boxes or hung in a mesh bag, but the bulbs get the best ventilation when the stems have been braided. Let the onions mature in the garden until their tops fall over naturally and begin to shrivel. When a majority of the onion tops have fallen knock over any that remain standing. A week later all the onions will be ready to pull up and lay on the ground (or the floor if it is rainy) to dry out a bit. Braiding should begin about a day later, at a point where the tops are dead enough to be pliable but not so decayed that they break easily.

The braiding method is properly called a French braid, with new onion tops being laid into the braid periodically so that the resulting braid is much longer than any one top. If the tops are of ideal consistency they can simply be braided by themselves, but for safety's sake I like to secure a length of stout twine around the necks of the original three onions and carry it along with one of the lines as I braid. This makes a strong braid that will not break, no matter how brittle the onion stems may become. It also allows one to tie a neat loop at the end with which to hang up the onions. I try to make braids no longer than two feet, lest they become too heavy to lift or prone to snap under their own weight. I hang the newly completed braids in a warm place (70 to 80 degrees) to dry for a few weeks. This leaves them with papery skins. As brittle as these skins may be, resist the temptation to rub them off. The removal of just 20 percent of the skin will let the onion lose water and shrivel up. Rehang the braids in a cool location, and help yourself to an onion by cutting or twisting one from any point in the braid whenever you wish.

While onions like it cool and dry, root crops such as carrots, beets, and potatoes like it cool and damp. The higher the humidity, the better. We store ours in a makeshift root cellar created by insulating the undersides of the bulkhead doors that cover the outside cellar stairs. This keeps the space underneath at an even temperature; in the coldest part of the winter we can open the inside cellar door a crack and let in a bit of warmth from the furnace to keep the temperature from dropping below 32 degrees. To keep the humidity high around the vegetables, and to keep mice from gnawing them, we keep everything in covered galvanized trash cans. We have found that we can store the potatoes and beets loose. The carrots we pack in damp sand so that they are not touching one another. The sand separating them cuts down on the spread of rot should one carrot decay and allows the movement of air and water in and out of the roots. Stored this way the carrots are as sound and tasty (much more tasty than their supermarket counterparts) in May as when they were harvested in October. Both the carrot and beet tops are trimmed away before storage, leaving only a half-inch or so of stub. And as with all vegetables, only undamaged ones qualify for storage.

The only vegetable that we freeze a winter supply of is green peppers. The price of peppers shoots sky-high every winter, making it worthwhile to lay by a homegrown supply. Furthermore, they require no blanching before freezing. Consequently we simply slice up the end-of-the-season surplus into strips and pack them in small plastic bags (the kind with the built-in zipper), one pepper per bag. These bags take so little space in the freezer, and the contents are so welcome in stir-fried dishes, that they have become a family staple.

Of course some of the vegetables stored for the winter won't be eaten. Every year some of the produce goes the way of Mother's jelly. The squashes wither or liquefy and end up on the compost heap. The onions and potatoes sprout and follow suit. Beets usually keep the longest but at some point pass over into inedibility. Waste is never desirable, but if you haven't invested a lot of sugar or electricity or labor in preserving the food, it is a small loss. I consider it inconsequential compared to the comforts of weathering the winter well stocked.

On Trial

MORE THAN twenty years ago, I condemned 'Gold Nugget' squash unjustly. With the wisdom of hindsight I can see that inexperience played a role, and so did greed. My mistake was an easy one, one that any gardener could have made. But I am getting ahead of myself. First, a review of the facts.

Several things attracted me to 'Gold Nugget'. It was reputed to take only 85 days to reach maturity, an unusually swift schedule for a winter squash. Furthermore, the plants were described as being runnerless bushes that could be grown in a small space. I didn't pay much attention to the account of the fruit — small, slightly flattened, orange, about five inches in diameter, and weighing one and a half to two pounds. Where I was gardening in New Hampshire in newly broken ground, the days to maturity and space needs seemed more important.

We moved into the house so late in the fall that we could do little more than figure out where we wanted the vegetable garden before the snow fell. Very early in the spring — or, more accurately, late in the winter, since I was eager to start digging — I began spading up the still snow-covered ground. The soil wasn't frozen, a sign that I took to mean it had been a comparatively mild winter rather than the truth, which was that I was digging in an extraordinarily wet spot.

I remember well the plot that resulted. It was seven by eleven feet. And because of the sods that I had incompletely inverted, it looked like a badly shaved scalp. By the time I had sowed the peas, radishes, carrots, beets, onions, tomatoes, and corn, there wasn't any room for the squash. So I hastily spaded up an annex, a circle roughly four feet in diameter in the adjoining sod. Here I planted the 'Gold Nugget' seed.

The seed germinated fine. I think it all germinated, and I am pretty sure that I did some thinning. But you know how it is; you hate to pull up those promising seedlings. This is especially true when you have recently learned what woodchucks can do to peas and other young vegetables. I probably left six or seven squash plants in that four-foot circle.

Despite the high water in the spring, the garden dried out that summer and needed watering. I did this in the evening under the notion that less water would be lost to evaporation, or maybe I was worried about water droplets acting like lenses and burning holes in the leaves. I also did it by hand, but not very carefully — when you are waving one hand around your head constantly to keep away the mosquitoes you tend to quit long before the soil is adequately soaked.

I also remember that I had trouble with weeds, especially with that perennial grass we call witchgrass and that people in other parts of the country call quack grass. My spading up of the soil produced a nursery bed for this pernicious weed. The only way I could have gotten rid of it would have been to get down on my hands and knees and relentlessly pull up every last little bit. This I didn't do, in part because the chicken-wire fence I had hastily erected to keep out the woodchucks prevented me from getting close to the squash.

Not surprisingly, the harvest was a disaster. We got some squash, perhaps a half a dozen of them, in contrast to my vision of a wheelbarrowful. And for every squash that weighed a pound and a half, there were two more that could have doubled as tennis balls. I reread the catalog description and discovered that this squash was only supposed to yield four fruits per plant, but still I hadn't even come close.

The next year a lot of things changed. The garden tripled in size. I got on top of the witchgrass. I arranged with a local poultry farm for a load of decayed chicken manure. I bought a sprinkler. And I planted butternut squash instead. I had the space, and I knew I had the necessary 105 frost-free days.

The butternut squash was a great success. We grew so much that we put some away in straw-lined boxes under the bed and ate them all winter. I concluded, as anyone would have, that 'Gold Nugget' was grossly inferior in every way. I never planted it again. I even remember visiting someone years later who was growing 'Gold Nugget' and wondering to myself why. Hadn't he learned yet?

He had learned. He had, I suspect, learned to grow squash long before he ever planted 'Gold Nugget'. In his hands the squash was growing as its breeder had intended. When we fail as gardeners, it is all too easy to blame the plant we are growing rather than ourselves. Never having grown 'Gold Nugget' squash well, I am not in a position to say whether it is a good squash or not. But it was unfair of me to condemn it just because it was the victim of my own ignorance.

The way we learn to be better gardeners is by experimenting. At least that is what we call it. We try raised beds one year, a different petunia the next. These trials usually end up producing competent gardeners, but it would be a mistake to say they get at the truth. What the gardener is left with is a repertoire of prejudice rather than facts. The prejudices range from the benign to the beneficial. After all, the garden grows well under their guidance. But the information cannot be certified as fact until it has been checked by experiment. And few of us have the time or inclination to undertake the research.

The chief problem with garden-variety experimenting is the lack of a control group. In the never-ending quest for the best-tasting sweet corn, for example, you may well plant one kind of corn one year and another kind of corn the next. No matter which corn tastes better, you can't really conclude that it is a better-tasting corn because the variation might just as well be due to differences in the amount of sunlight or rainfall. Furthermore, gardeners seldom change just one variable at a time. Typically a new year will begin with a resolve to do more weeding and more watering and more fertilizing. Under those circumstances it is absolutely impossible to decide what deserves the credit for any improved performance.

To conduct a proper experiment, the kind that allows you to say with justification that a particular plant outperforms another, you must grow them both at the same time. Not only at the same time but in the same place. Since it is impossible for any two things to occupy the same place at precisely the same moment, this means growing them in close proximity. Precision actually requires that you grow more than one plant of each and that you array them randomly in relation to one another. It isn't correct to put all of one kind on the left, all of the other on the right. Growing multiple specimens of each kind of plant is also necessary to prevent individual variation from obscuring the true differences between the two populations as a whole.

You also have to worry about such things as edge effect, since plants growing at the perimeter of a garden are subject to different conditions than those in the middle. You have to be sure that all your experimental subjects are getting the same amounts of water, light, and fertilizer. In short, setting up and running a proper experiment demands a tremendous amount of work. It is no wonder that most of it is done at experiment stations and institutes of higher learning. (Those readers who are interested in how to do such research at home should consult Lois Levitan's *Improve Your Gardening with Backyard Research* [Rodale Press, 1980].)

What inhibits most of us amateur gardeners from performing such experiments isn't just the work, however. We are hampered by a reluctance to consign even part of our garden to less than optimal performance. For every winner in an experiment there is also a loser. It may be shortsighted of us, but most home gardeners are constantly reaching for the brass ring of perfection. We want all our plants to grow well. If we think that more fertilizer will improve the situation we apply more fertilizer to every plant in the row. Hang the controls, full speed ahead.

This isn't all that bad. But we must not mistake the conclusions of our own experimenting for absolute truths. If we recognize that what passes for wisdom may in fact just be acquired prejudice, we will be better gardeners. And it is a good idea, as painful as it may be, periodically to look over the list of our earlier failures. Some of them are sure to deserve a second chance.

Short Days

ONE OF THE INNATE PERVERSITIES of nature is that the longest day of the year occurs well before halftime in the growing season. The date of the summer solstice is around June 22, and although the date of the last spring frost is never precise here in New England, the two events are seldom separated by more than a couple of months. The heat waves that follow the solstice are mere distractions; sooner or later everyone notices that the days are steadily getting shorter. When some four months after the solstice the weather forecaster warns of a freeze, few gardeners are all that concerned. This far north, the days have become too short for things to grow well anyway. Not only are the days short, but the sunlight that reaches this latitude is less intense now, the result of the sun's crossing the sky close to the horizon. The lettuce and kale sown so eagerly in September in anticipation of a repeat of the spring performance are doing miserably. Even under cloches or inside cold frames, where temperatures are warmer than elsewhere, the seedlings limp along, putting out new leaves with decreasing frequency. Farther south, fall crops seem to grow just fine, but I don't know whether this is because the average temperature is higher, the days are longer, or the light is more intense. Here in our garden, no amount of fertilizer, water, or warmth seems to make up for the shortening days.

The only compensation offered us by these short days is that they prompt the blossoming of a number of plants. Decreasing day length is responsible for the appearance of diminutive yellow sunflowers atop the towering clumps of Jerusalem artichokes. Shorter days also bring on chrysanthemums in their many autumn hues of red and rust, bronze, magenta, and gold. Indoors, the Thanksgiving and Christmas cacti are both stimulated to bloom by decreasing day length, as are the most traditional of holiday decorations, the poinsettia, and those more recent additions, the kalanchoes with their clusters of star-shaped florets rising from pots of succulent foliage.

DAY LENGTH CYCLE AT VARIOUS LATITUDES NORTH of EQUATOR

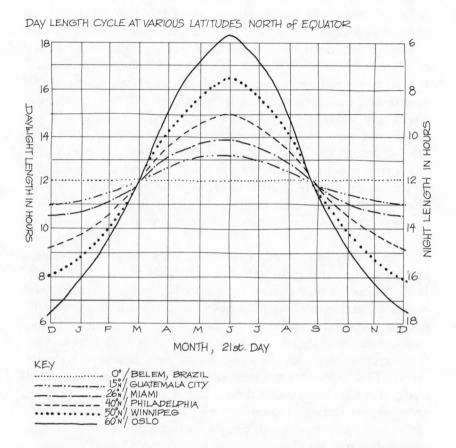

MONTH, 21st. DAY

KEY
.... 0° / BELEM, BRAZIL
—·—·—·—·... 15°N / GUATEMALA CITY
— · — · — · — 26°N / MIAMI
— — — — — 40°N / PHILADELPHIA
•••••••••• 50°N / WINNIPEG
————————— 60°N / OSLO

The dependence of flowering on day length exhibited by these plants is called photoperiodism. Two USDA researchers, W. W. Garner and H. A. Allard, discovered the phenomenon in Beltsville, Maryland, while working with 'Maryland Mammoth' tobacco from 1915 to 1920. A mutant of 'Maryland Narrowleaf', this strain of tobacco was of particular interest because it grew taller and had larger leaves, but it had the annoying habit of refusing to flower before the plants were killed by frost. The only way to ensure a supply of seed for next year's crop was to dig up plants in the field and transplant them into greenhouses, where they would eventually blossom and set seed.

The upshot of Garner and Allard's investigations was the discovery that 'Maryland Mammoth' initiated flower buds only when the day length was less than 12 hours. This occurs on the autumnal equinox, around September 23, but in Maryland that is too late for the flowers to finish developing, open, and set seed before the plants are killed.

Having discovered the importance of day length in the flowering of 'Maryland Mammoth' tobacco, Garner and Allard went on to divide all plants into three categories: short-day plants, which require days shorter than a critical length before they will flower; long-day plants, which flower when days are longer than a critical length; and day-neutral plants, which are unaffected by day length. There is no one day length that separates long-day from short-day plants. The distinction is between whether the plants respond to increasing or decreasing day lengths. Furthermore, flowering is not the only plant behavior influenced by day length; activities as diverse as the swelling of onion bulbs and the formation of strawberry runners are affected as well.

Since Garner and Allard's time, their three categories have been somewhat expanded to include cases in which plants are not absolutely dependent on a certain day length but will flower sooner if it is present, and even odder instances where a plant jumps from category to category depending on the temperature it is grown in. Christmas cactus, for example, is a short-day plant at high temperatures (85 degrees Fahrenheit) and a day-neutral plant at low ones (60 degrees). This explains what houseplant enthusiasts have known all along: that Christmas cactus flowers best if kept cool for the months of September through November. Such temperatures encourage the plants to flower, even though turning on lights in the house at night creates days that are longer than the plants' critical length.

Actually, to speak of the effects of day length on plants is to look at the subject from the wrong perspective. Plants don't measure the length of the day; they measure the length of the night. So-called short-day plants are actually long-night plants. Interrupting the night with a short stretch of artificial light will trick a plant into responding as though it had just been through two successive days each with short nights.

Many tropical plants are short-day plants, since at the equator days and nights are always about 12 hours long. Provided there is adequate moisture and warmth, these plants flower more or less year round. Trying to grow short-day plants in the temperate zone is often futile. The much publicized winged bean from New Guinea, for

LIGHT NEEDS of SHORT and LONG-DAY PLANTS

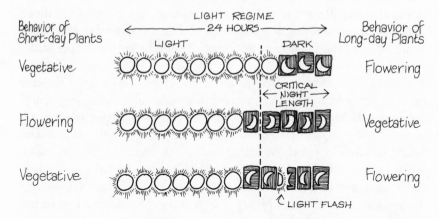

example, is certain not to flower early enough here to yield any pods. I have also had to give up hopes of ever growing any 'Cuzco Giant' corn, a short-day cultivar from Peru whose individual kernels are as big as a nickel.

We do, however, grow chrysanthemums. Chrysanthemums are short-day plants that require day lengths less than 14½ hours to initiate buds and day lengths less than 13½ to continue developing them. Though blossoms are initiated by the same day length, different chrysanthemums bloom at different times because the time from bud initiation to blossom opening varies from six to fifteen weeks depending on the cultivar.

Here in a heavily populated neighborhood we worry sometimes that the blossoming of our chrysanthemums is being delayed by light pollution, by streetlights, porch lights, passing cars, all of which can give off enough light to trick chrysanthemums into behaving as though the days were longer than they really are. Moonlight we don't have to worry about, but we try to place the chrysanthemums in as dark a part of our gardens as possible.

Forgoing outdoor lighting at night is one thing. Indoors is another matter. We can't go to bed when the sun sets, and so we have had to forgo growing our own poinsettias. Poinsettias are tropical plants that require 12 hours or more of uninterrupted dark at night. Friends who are more fastidious with their houseplants than we have successfully gotten last year's poinsettia to bloom again by moving it into a dark closet for 14 hours every night. But they have had to remember to do it every night for eight weeks and never open the closet accidentally while the poinsettia was in there. It seems much easier to buy new poinsettias every year — poinsettias grown by someone else who has taken the responsibility for keeping their plants in the dark.

Poinsettia growers and commercial flower growers in general have become adept at modifying day length to control blossoming. Chrysanthemums are now sold as both cut flowers and pot plants year round. A few hours of light in the middle of the night in a greenhouse simulates long days, and covering the plants in late afternoon with sheets of black polyethylene or black cloth simulates short ones. No longer are chrysanthemums the mark of an autumn bouquet. This is too bad. There are plenty of reasons to feel exuberant in spring and summer. Let's save the short-day plants to cheer us up in the fall.

Compost

THE SUBJECT hints of alchemy. Raw materials consisting of common wastes are transformed into something so sought-after that there is never enough. Although the metamorphosis is dramatic, there is no great secret to how compost is made. Nor is there any one correct way to do it, despite the impression that may have been given by the volumes of information on the subject. At the risk of adding to the aura of mystery and exactitude surrounding compost, I here add my advice to the heap.

Compost is nothing more than partially decomposed organic matter, made up primarily of the remains of leaves, stems, and other plant parts. It is a dark, crumbly, pleasant-smelling substance that resembles nothing more than what you would find were you to roll back a decaying log in the forest. Soil to which compost has been added can be worked more easily, holds more air and water, and is less likely to erode. The compost provides some nutrients directly and others indirectly, by increasing their availability. All in all, those who see compost as a kind of vegetable gold are not far from the mark.

Unfortunately, although you start with a large volume of raw material when you make compost, you invariably end up with a small amount of concentrated product. No matter how much there is of this, it never seems to stretch far enough. Somewhere between planting the rhubarb and top-dressing the hedge, you run out. When you have run out you can't just go out and buy more (although peat humus and composted cow manure will do in a pinch). No, you have to make it.

Most gardeners are in a hurry, and their impatience has led to the invention of numerous recipes for what I call fast compost. Fast compost takes advantage of human labor and attention to ensure an optimum environment for the growth of microbes, and hence rapid decomposition. How soon the compost is ready for use depends on (1) moisture, (2) temperature, (3) aeration, (4) the surface area of the organic matter, and (5) nitrogen supply. In the best of conditions, finished compost can be made in two weeks, though two months is a more reasonable goal.

The ingredients for quick compost must be assembled all at one time. Basically they are equal volumes of a carbon source (such as dry leaves, hay, straw, or seaweed) and a nitrogen source (such as grass clippings, fresh weeds, or manure). More concentrated nitrogen sources can also be used, ranging from ammonium sulfate to alfalfa meal, cottonseed meal, or blood meal, but lesser amounts of these are needed. Some recipes also recommend adding one part soil to the

compost to inoculate the organic matter with organisms. All the ingredients should be finely cut up. This can be done by hand with a machete and a chopping block, or by machine. Either mix all the ingredients beforehand, or build the pile in thin alternating layers, each only a couple of inches deep. As you build the pile, hose it down so that the contents are thoroughly moistened. The minimum size for a completed pile is roughly four feet in diameter and four feet high. So constructed, a pile should begin decomposing almost immediately. Rapid decomposition will generate heat: the pile may get as high as 160 degrees Fahrenheit. This is hot enough to kill weed seeds and disease organisms inside the pile.

It is necessary to turn a fast-compost pile now and then to keep the interior well aerated and to be sure it is uniformly moist. Turning also allows you to shift the undecayed matter on the outside of the pile into the interior. This is easiest to do by repiling the compost heap adjacent to the old. The more frequently the pile is turned (once a week is not too often), the faster the material will decay. If the pile fails to heat up, you need to add more nitrogen. Finally, when the pile is no longer generating heat, the compost is ready for use. The faster the compost, the coarser the finished product is likely to be, but it is perfectly reasonable to spread it in the garden and let it finish breaking down there.

I am an expert at what I call slow compost. I like slow compost because it takes so much less labor than fast compost. I don't have to assemble all the ingredients at once. Indeed, I can dispense with many of them altogether. The finished product may not be quite as rich, but in terms of nutrients gained for energy expended, it is probably more so. As a way of recycling materials, slow compost cannot be beat, regardless of the time it takes.

Every fall, huge quantities of leaves fall in this town. Overwhelmed by their abundance, the neighbors work hard getting rid of them. In the past this meant burning; today, it usually means entombing them in plastic body bags. This is outrageous. Not only is it an inexcusable waste of plastic bags, but it is compost lost. Dead leaves, and nothing more, make perfectly good slow compost if you pile them up, keep them moist, and wait. Minimum pile size again is at least four feet in diameter.

Because loose leaves tend to blow over into the neighbor's yard, I corral mine inside circular bins made from wooden snow-fencing. (A

50-foot section cut into three lengths will make three bins, each slightly more than 5 feet in diameter and 4 feet high.) It is surprising how many leaves one can put into a small volume. The leaves from this one-third-acre yard neatly fit into a single one of these bins.

There is not enough nitrogen in dried leaves for decomposition to be rapid, but there are enough microbes present for it to get under way without the addition of soil or other activators. The pile should be concave at the top to funnel rainwater into the interior. The aim is to keep the leaves moist enough that a drop or two of water will appear when a sample of leaves from the interior of the pile is squeezed hard. By spring, I find the pile has shrunk to half its height. I turn it once or twice during the summer to break up the lumps of leaves, mix in air, and speed the breakdown. A year after the pile is made, my slow compost is ready.

There is of course nothing wrong with adding grass clippings, weeds, or vegetable wastes from the kitchen to a slow-compost pile. When I have any organic matter to dispose of, I toss it on the heap. This gets mixed in when the pile is turned. A slow-compost pile usually does not heat up enough to kill weed seeds and other harmful organisms, so I refrain from adding them to the pile.

The result of either fast or slow compost-making is a dark, crumbly substance. I use mine without screening it, but it can be rubbed through a sieve made from ¾-inch hardware cloth. Any pieces that are undecayed simply get tossed into the next compost pile. There is never any danger of applying too much compost to a garden. If you have enough, add a layer an inch or two deep to the entire garden every year. In the case of a new garden, spread the compost and mix it into the top few inches of soil. Or else work a shovelful into the soil under each transplant as you put it in. For established plants, spread the compost on the surface of the soil around their bases. A new garden with poor soil deserves a couple of inches of compost spread over it in the fall or spring and dug in.

Whatever you do, do something with your compost. By definition, compost is only partially decayed, and the metabolic fires continue to smolder, ultimately resulting in carbon dioxide and ash. Many a miser has tried to hang on to compost only to discover that the pile grows smaller and smaller and eventually vanishes into thin air. Compost is only really valuable when it is put to use.

Getting the Car Back
into the Garage

SUMMER IS OVER and the weather forecast calls for snow. But before the car can be put in the garage, room must be made. Nature abhors a vacuum, and in the car's absence its space has been taken over by flower pots, bags of fertilizer, potting soil and peat moss, a lawn mower, a wheelbarrow, rakes, hoes, shovels, and a gasoline can — all the ingredients of an active garden. In the haste of spring planting, or getting ready for vacation, or just plain putting things away for the night, these have been unceremoniously dumped in the middle of the garage floor until now, and it is impossible to imagine how there could be room for an automobile. But room must be made, and the approach of winter weather is good enough reason to attack the mess.

What is needed is consolidation, packing stuff away until spring. The days are so short now that even the houseplants are not growing much, and there will be no call for most of this material for many months. On the other hand, when spring does come it will start with a rush, and it is important to be able to put your hands on the seed flats quickly, to have a lawn mower in working condition.

Start by throwing things out. Not all the containers that the annuals came in need to be saved. The fiber pots are particularly expendable, being impossible to clean.

Any plant labels or tags that turn up can be heaved too, but not before the information on them is safely copied down into a notebook, or whatever record is being kept of what was planted where and when.

All the planting containers that are being saved, from seed flats to pots, should be thoroughly cleaned in hot soapy water. Many of the smaller ones can be run through the dishwasher, but be careful to load the plastic ones into the top rack, where they won't melt. When everything is dry, stack them by size and store them upside down on a shelf where they will be easy to reach in the spring.

Any wooden flower boxes or other tubs that do not have plants growing in them should be emptied and brought in under cover. There is no reason to let wet soil decay them unnecessarily. Large terra-cotta pots kept outdoors will crack and scale if subjected to repeated freezing. Bring them in where it's dry.

The fertilizer now sitting in various bags on the floor should be put up where it will stay reasonably dry. Most chemical fertilizer is hygroscopic, which means it tends to absorb water, even from the air. Finely ground fertilizer can become rock-hard over time, and then must be crushed with a hammer before it can be used. Where the amounts are small, as in the case of starter fertilizer used for transplants, put the fertilizer in an airtight container. Larger amounts should at least be lifted up off the floor and stored where they won't get wet from the meltwater dripping off the car's undercarriage.

Ground limestone, rock phosphate, bonemeal, and other powdered substances are less apt to pick up water, but even these should be stored off the ground or else the bag will deteriorate, and the next time you try to lift the sack the contents will cascade onto your feet.

While fertilizer and lime should be kept dry, any remaining soilless mixes should be kept moist. If a planting mix that contains peat is allowed to become totally dry, it is extremely difficult to remoisten. Close up plastic bags. If the mix is being stored in a barrel, keep the cover on. Twenty-gallon trash barrels are inexpensive and convenient receptacles for potting ingredients. In addition to having one for prepared mix, it's nice to have one for vermiculite, another for perlite, and — depending on what you are growing — some for sand, sphagnum, or bark chips. Arrange these along one wall of the garage where the car won't run into them, but where it will be easy to help yourself to ingredients, supermarket style.

The tools should also be cleaned before they are put away. Scrape off clinging dirt or other debris. Lightly rub rusty metal with coarse steel wool, and then wipe the exposed surface with a rag moistened with household oil. This will protect the metal from moisture over the winter. Running the same rag up over wooden handles will also waterproof the wood somewhat. Ideally every tool has its own hook, but lacking that, lean each up against the wall out of the way. Push brooms and lawn rakes should be stood working end up, so that the bristles and tines don't get bent out of shape by the tools' weight. Hoes, bow rakes, and any other tools with a right-angle bend at the end should be positioned so that the back of the tool faces out. Otherwise it's all too easy to step on the tines or blade, and instantaneously whack yourself on the nose or the side of the head with the handle.

The power mower and any other piece of equipment with a gasoline engine also need to be readied for winter. If an owner's manual for the equipment is available, follow the directions therein. Otherwise the winterizing procedure is as follows. First disconnect the wire from the spark plug. Then remove caked grass from under the housing and around the wheels. On tillers, unwind vegetation wrapped around the tines. Then go over the engine itself, being sure that cooling fins are clear and wiping off caked oil and dirt.

Most small engines have a foam air filter. Remove this and dismantle it, being careful not to drop dirt down into the carburetor. The foam element inside the air filter should be thoroughly washed in hot soapy water, rinsed, and dried with a clean towel. Before reinstalling it, saturate the foam with a tablespoon or so of engine oil, working the oil into the foam with your hands.

Reconnect the spark plug, start the engine, and let it warm up for five minutes. Then turn it off, drain the gas tank, start the engine again, and run it until it stops. If you can reach into the gas tank, dry it with a clean towel.

Locate the oil plug on the underside of the engine, remove it, and let the crankcase oil drain out into a container for disposal. Refill with fresh 10W-30 motor oil, or whatever is specified.

Remove the spark plug, pour in two tablespoonfuls of motor oil, and crank the engine ten times to work it through the cylinder. Replace the spark plug, but not the ignition wire. In the spring remove the spark plug once more, pull the starter briskly to clear out the oil, clean and adjust the spark plug (or just as easily, install a brand-new one), and the engine will be ready for use.

This draining of the gas and running of the engine to dryness is necessary to prevent the gasoline in the engine from leaving gummy deposits over the winter. Winterizing can be reduced to a simple cleaning of the engine and air filter, however, if Amoco premium unleaded gasoline is used as fuel. This is almost pure toluene and does not leave gummy deposits in storage. The extra cost of this gasoline is more than offset by the convenience it confers.

When everything has been cleaned and neatly stacked away along the perimeter of the garage, there should be just enough room for the car. You will soon learn that the car must be pulled up all the way to the vermiculite can, so that the driver's door doesn't knock over the shovels on opening, and so that the passenger can get out past the flower boxes. It is always tight, but in the glare of the headlights is a daily reminder that no matter how bad the roads were driving home, spring isn't too far away.

Cover Crops

By OCTOBER the garden is closing down. Even if it hasn't frosted yet, the days are getting cool enough and short enough that plant growth has slowed dramatically. The remaining vegetables and other annuals will soon be dead, and when their remains have been added to the compost heap, the ground beneath them will be bare. More than six months will pass in this garden before the soil can be planted again. During that time it can succumb to erosion or to weeds, which are adept at growing in soil that is too cold and too wet for cultivated plants.

To prevent this, each fall I sow a crop of winter rye (*Secale cereale*) wherever there are more than a few square yards of soil that would otherwise be bare. This winter rye is a variety of the same grain that is used to make bread and rye whiskey. Because what I plant is intended not to nourish me but rather to prevent loss of soil, it constitutes a cover crop. Because I intend to dig it into the soil in the spring when it is still fresh and green, it also constitutes a green-manure crop, although I doubt it will add significantly to the soil's fertility. What makes winter rye so attractive for my purposes is that it will germinate in cold soil. The seed will sprout at temperatures only a couple of degrees above freezing, and the resulting plant will resume growing anytime the air temperature rises above 40 degrees Fahrenheit.

If I could sow the wintering-over crop earlier, I might choose something other than winter rye. One of the legumes, like alfalfa, clover, or vetch, would have the advantage of adding considerable nitrogen to the soil, but these are best sown in spring or summer. Were I going to fallow a bit of land, and had I a year to let the crop grow, I would certainly plant a legume. And if I were trying to eradicate some noxious perennial weed I would sow repeated crops of buckwheat, digging the plants in and reseeding every six weeks. The dense shade cast by a stand of buckwheat will kill even the most pestiferous weed. But buckwheat is extremely cold-sensitive, collapsing with the first frost, and so is of absolutely no use for winter cover.

Because I must wait for the annual flowers and vegetables to finish their season, I can't ordinarily begin sowing winter rye until sometime in September or early October. The earlier I sow, the more growth the individual rye plants will make. To compensate for the short season I simply increase the density of seeds. Whereas I ordinarily sow two or three pounds of winter-rye seed per thousand square feet, I increase this to four or five pounds for late sowings. The seed is so cheap that the expense of sowing it generously is insignificant. Rye can be sown until about three weeks prior to the ground's freezing up. It won't make much growth in that time, but the seed will germinate, and the plants usually get fairly well established during the warm spells of late fall.

If you have the chance to plant winter rye in late summer, perhaps following early corn or late peas, don't hesitate to sow a pound of hairy-vetch seed per thousand square feet along with the rye. This extremely hardy vetch grows well with winter rye and will contribute a good measure of nitrogen to the soil, but it needs a month and a half of warm weather to become well established.

Before I sow, I turn over the garden with a spading fork or a rotary tiller, digging under the weeds and any remaining refuse of flowers and vegetables that didn't make it to the compost pile. Then I like to level out the garden with a garden rake, flattening the ridges, filling in the holes. This step isn't necessary, but I'll be looking at the empty ground for half a year, so I'd like it to look its best. Every year the winter-rye patch becomes the best stretch of lawn I own.

Sowing rye seed is easy. It is

a big, coarse seed that originated as a weed in wheat and barley fields, and through the selection of threshing and winnowing came to resemble these grains in size and shape. Sowing winter-rye seed is like sowing grass seed with training wheels. The seed is inexpensive and easy to see on the ground. I broadcast it by hand, practicing my throw to make the seed fall as evenly as possible. By going back and forth over the area several times I can achieve a remarkably uniform distribution.

The only disadvantage of sowing such large seed is that it has to be covered with soil. I do this by hand with the same rake I used to level the garden. Gently push and pull the soil back and forth until the seed disappears beneath the surface. Just be careful that you don't rake all your carefully distributed seed together into one pile. Burying the seed is much easier if you have a tiller with a depth adjustment. Use the shallowest setting and the highest speed, and race back and forth across your plot, whipping the seed and the soil into an indistinguishable froth.

Newly sprouted rye is not conspicuous. In fact, it is virtually invisible. The reddish-purple shoots are a couple of inches high before they unfurl into green blades. The plants remain alive all winter and begin growing rapidly with the first warmth of spring, shading the soil enough to block the growth of early-spring weeds. By late spring each plant will have distinctly blue-green foliage and will be sending up a seed stalk that will be four or five feet high when the flowers open.

There are a couple of disadvantages to waiting this long to dig the winter rye back into the soil. First is the problem of trying to bury two- or three-foot stalks without getting them all wrapped up in the spading fork or around the tiller's axle. If for some reason you are faced with the task, use a rotary mower to chop up the aboveground portion of the plant before you begin digging. But there is a second disadvantage in waiting until the last minute to dig under the winter rye. When fresh organic matter is incorporated into the soil, it begins to decompose immediately, and the microorganisms involved in the decomposition use nitrogen to carry out the decay. Unless the crop is itself high in nitrogen, the microorganisms can temporarily tie up a good part of the nitrogen present in the soil, resulting in a temporary nitrogen shortage that will hinder the growth of any flowers or vegetables you plant at the time. It is best, therefore, to plan on tilling the cover crop into the soil at least three weeks in advance of planting, or as soon as the winter rye has reached a height of ten inches. This is the point at which the plants contain the greatest amount of nitrogen.

Try to incorporate the rye into the top eight inches of the soil. Unlike some weeds, it is relatively easy to kill. As the roots, stems, and leaves decay they will add organic matter to the soil, and a certain amount of nutrients as well, though nowhere near as much as would be gained from turning under an established sod. The real value of winter rye is the way it guards against the entry of weeds and, above all, the assurance it gives that the bare ground itself won't go somewhere else while you are waiting for next year's season to start.

Tulips

My EDUCATION as a gardener is full of holes. Few are as conspicuous as my lack of experience with tulips. You see, until last year I had never grown tulips. This gap had come to my attention before, but I had managed to dismiss it with a series of rationalizations. Tulips are expensive, I'd told myself; there is only a single flower per stalk; only one season of bloom; and mice eat the bulbs. But the fact is that in the fall I was usually too tired to think of planting much of anything.

Last fall, humbled into the matter by a gift, I planted tulip bulbs for the first time. This year I am planting them again. I cannot pretend to be a veteran tulip grower (nor do I ever expect to become one). But even after one season, I have had to refine my prejudices.

The greatest virtue of tulips is that they are committed to bloom when you buy them. Each flaky, brown bulb is like one of those Chinese shells — the ones that release a paper blossom when you drop them into water. Except that tulip bulbs must not be dropped in water, because flooding will kill them. But, as I know enough not to plant them under a downspout or where puddles of water stand in the spring, next year's blossoms are assured.

That is, if mice don't eat the bulbs. Moles get blamed for the loss of tulip bulbs, but moles are chiefly carnivores. Mice using mole burrows as subways are the true culprits. I am told that the deeper bulbs are planted, the more likely they are to avoid such trouble. But the deeper bulbs are planted, the more likely they are to be flooded during the winter. The only sure way I know to protect tulip bulbs is to bury them inside cages made from half-inch wire mesh. The cage should be roughly six inches deep and can be folded from a single piece of wire. Not everyone has mouse problems, however, so it seems quite reasonable to wait and see whether bulbs disappear before worrying about such protective measures.

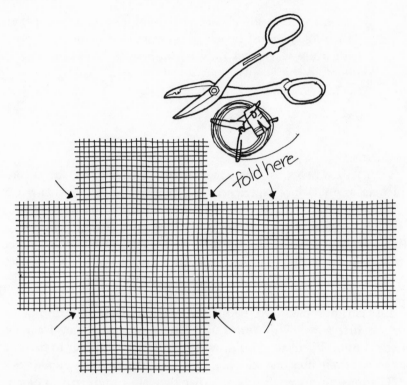

Because the tulip bulbs I buy already contain flower buds, the advice about proper planting depth — and spacing, and adding compost and bonemeal at planting time, and additional fertilizer when the ground thaws in the spring — all this has nothing to do with whether or not the tulips will bloom next spring. These directions will affect whether or not the tulips will produce blossoms year after year. If I were content with one season's bloom, then planting tulips would be no more complicated than buying bulbs in the fall, digging holes the depth of a trowel, dropping in the bulbs pointed-end up, filling the holes, and waiting. After petal-fall in the spring, I would treat the tulips the way the city's public-works people do — pulling them up and chucking them to make room for other plants.

Growing tulips this way, as winter annuals, isn't such a bad idea. Tulips are almost certain not to bloom as well their second spring, no matter what provisions you make for their well-being. At best you get fewer, and smaller, blossoms, on stems of uneven height. At worst, nothing emerges from the ground again but leaves. And for tulips to have any chance of making a second flower bud, their foliage must be left to grow and die naturally. Maturing tulip leaves not only take up space, they are ugly to boot. Some people try to hide the dying leaves by transplanting annuals into their midst, while others dig up the bulbs as soon as the flowers are gone and replant them at the same depth in an unused corner of the garden. The latter strikes me as too much work and presupposes that I have an unused corner in my garden.

As much as I would like to grow tulips as annuals, frugality prevents me from heeding my own advice, and instead I have been following the wisdom of others. Books state explicitly that I must not plant tulips too soon, or they will start growing prematurely and be damaged by winter. (In hardiness Zones 4 and 5, plant in September or early October; in Zones 6 and 7, October or early November.) Last fall I waited, as I was told, carefully storing the bulbs at a temperature of less than 65 degrees in the meantime. However, since then I have had time to think about the importance of late planting, and it doesn't make sense to me. What is preventing the bulbs I planted last fall from sprouting prematurely this year? They, after all, have been in the ground all summer. Tulips may not make very good

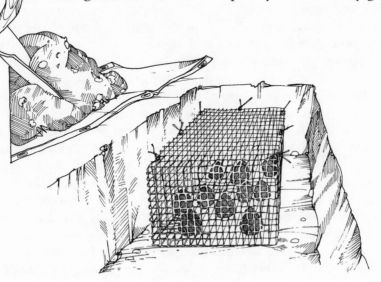

perennials, but I know some that have bloomed year after year. Why aren't they equally at risk of injury from premature planting? I suspect that late planting is a piece of advice that has been passed on without a second thought, and unless someone can convince me not to, I intend to plant my next tulip bulbs as soon as I get them home.

Deep planting is recommended, but how deep depends on whom you consult. Advice ranges from four inches to a whole foot. Apparently, the deeper the bulbs are, the less likely they are to produce nonflowering daughter bulbs, an important consideration if the tulips are being grown as perennials. (Some authorities measure depth from the top of the bulb, which strikes me as ridiculous, since the hole must be dug to the bottom of the bulb.) Planting the bulbs eight inches deep seems a safe compromise; and it's a convenient depth, too, because the average adult's hand measures about that from the tip of an outstretched thumb to the tip of the little finger, making a handy ruler.

Because roots will be growing out of the bottom of the bulb, the quality of the soil used to cover the bulb is less important than what is underneath it. Work in the equivalent of a cup of compost, or a handful of composted sewage sludge under each bulb. Bonemeal is a traditional bulb food, but modern-day bonemeal is so sanitized that most tulips will long since have disappeared by the time its nutrients become available. Add a little if you wish, as a ritual blessing for the bulb's well-being.

It is hard to improve the soil at the bottom of one of the small holes made with a bulb-planter or trowel. I prefer to excavate the whole area where I am planting bulbs, piling the soil to one side on a piece of canvas so that it can be returned neatly and completely.

When the soil is ready, I press each bulb down firmly so that there are no air pockets underneath, and then fill the hole. Here in the North, where the ground freezes solid, a layer of a mulch such as compost or old horse manure gives the bulbs time to develop a good root system before the ground sets up. No fertilizer is needed until spring, and then a sprinkling of balanced fertilizer before the tulip foliage even appears may improve the tulips' chances as perennials.

How far apart to space tulip bulbs is something that I have not quite worked out. For long-term culture, the farther apart the better. A foot is the distance recommended for tulips to be grown as true perennials. On the other hand, unless you are planting lots of bulbs this spacing is going to appear spotty. Six inches apart is the more

commonly recommended spacing, but even this leaves big gaps between the plants the first year. This spring I found myself wanting
to shove my tulips closer together, to resemble more the tulips grown
in pots, where the bulbs are nearly touching one another. This fall I
am experimenting with bulbs four inches apart, at the risk of reducing their long-term survival, which, as I keep pointing out, isn't
guaranteed anyway.

The basic difficulty with arranging tulips in the garden is that
they are extremely formal flowers. For years I have criticized plantings in which a single tulip, a single daffodil, and a single grape
hyacinth were lined up in succession around the edge of a lawn, a
design with all the grace of a border of whitewashed rocks. I was sure
that I could create a more naturalistic look, given the chance. I
couldn't. With only a dozen bulbs of each kind of tulip, it was impossible to create a drift of varied hues, and instead I got vivid lumps
of color here and there. This year I am putting eight tulips together
in one spot, three of the same kind nearby, and a single one at a
slight distance. But I don't hold out too much hope for this scheme.
Those of us who can't plant tulips by the hundred probably will
always end up with flowers that appear somewhat unnatural. The
moral is to plant them where they can be enjoyed, out the kitchen
window, where the car door opens, where you stoop to pick up the
morning paper.

The vivid color of tulips in early spring is what makes them worth
planting. And this is just as true indoors, so I save a few bulbs for
forcing. Certain tulip hybrids force better than others, but the differences are usually in how long the flowers last. Unlike paper-white
narcissus, tulips require a cold period before they will bloom (which
is why they must be planted outdoors in the fall, and why they
cannot be grown in the South [Zones 8 and 9] without being artificially chilled before planting). For forcing, tulips need at least twelve
weeks in the dark at 40 to 45 degrees. It matters absolutely not at
all what soil the tulips are potted in for forcing, because forced tulips
are unlikely ever to bloom again and are best discarded. Six or eight
bulbs can be put in a six-inch pot, close enough together that they
are almost touching one another. Since the bulbs are planted shallowly, their tips just sticking out of the soil, the pot does not have
to be a deep one. I use a special pot called a bulb pan, whose depth
is half the pot's diameter.

Finding a place that has a consistent temperature that is correct for forcing can be a problem. Our kitchen refrigerator is much too crowded, and buying a second refrigerator just for forcing bulbs would be too much of a luxury. I could place the pots in my cold frame, filling up the space around and over them with perlite, and finally covering the frame with some opaque material like tar paper to keep out the light. Last year, instead, I put the pots on the steps under the cellar bulkhead. A maximum–minimum thermometer assured me that the temperature was in the range I wanted, and when night temperatures in this space got close to freezing I moved the pots to an unheated crawl space. All I had to do during the three months of waiting was keep the soil in the pots moist.

By the time the chilling period is completed, the pots are filled with roots, and shoots are projecting from the tips of the bulbs. At my convenience, I bring the pots into the light, putting them first in a north-facing window out of direct sunlight until the pale foliage turns green. Then the pots are moved to full sunlight, preferably where the air temperature doesn't exceed 60 degrees. When the flowers show color, the pots go where they will be enjoyed the most, but the flowers will last longer if this also happens to be a cool location. How long it takes between when you first bring the bulbs into the light and when flowers appear depends on the time of year. The pots forced the earliest take the longest; later in spring the bulbs are ready to jump into bloom given light and warmth. My first batch of forced tulips didn't look exactly like the ones sold by florists. But it didn't matter. Tulips grown indoors, as I have discovered, come with their own guarantee of beauty.

Outdoors, tulips are subject to a host of natural and seminatural disasters; late snow that breaks down flowers and foliage, wind storms, rainstorms, dogs, and thieves (a friend this spring lost her entire planting one night, each sliced off neatly at the base). But these are no more than the usual plight of plants.

Flowers that survive to maturity should be snapped or cut off before the seed head develops anyway, to avoid depleting the bulb of energy. Tourists in Holland during tulip season are always aghast at the sight of whole barges filled with decapitated tulip flowers, each cut off in its prime so that the bulb will be as large as possible when it is eventually sold. The foliage, however, must be left to manufacture food for next year's flower. As unattractive as old tulip leaves may seem, resist the temptation to bury them under a mass of annuals or other plants. The tulips do not welcome the competition.

The season of tulip bloom depends on the cultivar. Last to bloom are the orchid-flowered and parrot tulips. But as showy as these tulips may be, I find them wanting, simply because they are so late. Late tulips are like late crocuses. By the end of May enough other things are in bloom that tulips are not half as welcome as they are a month earlier.

The earliest tulips to bloom are the species tulips, sometimes called botanicals. These are smaller, shorter-flowered tulips than the more familiar hybrids, but they have several advantages in addition to their earliness. First, because they are short and stocky they are resistant to abuse from weather. Second, some of them are multiflowered. Third, the bulbs are smaller and can be planted closer together and less deeply. And finally, of all the tulips, the species have the best reputation for flowering year after year. They aren't the most common, or the sort of tulips one can expect to be given. But most bulb companies offer them, usually on a back page or two. I have gone out and bought a couple dozen, and I won't be a bit surprised if by next fall they have revised my perceptions of tulips still further.

Hardiness Zones

IF GARDENERS were content to cultivate locally native plants, the issue of hardiness would never arise. But gardeners are inveterate collectors of exotic flora; the plants we grow come from all eight corners of the world. Snowdrop and scabiosa originated in Europe, pelargonium and gladiolus in Africa. The tulip hails from Turkey, rhubarb from Manchuria. Hollyhocks, peonies, and forsythia are native to China. Bleeding heart and Japanese iris come from Japan. Australia has provided strawflowers and bottlebrushes. Petunias and fuchsias are South American. Dahlias are Mexican. Gardeners in the eastern United States grow California poppies while those in the West grow New England asters.

Whether we do this globetrotting ourselves or let catalogs and nurseries bring the plants to us, the first question that comes to mind when we encounter a foreign plant is: Can I grow this? By that we mean: Will this survive more than a year in *my* garden? Here in the North the issue of hardiness is most often decided one way or the other by the winter.

Winter, of course, isn't the only barrier to survival. Plants can succumb to a shortage of water, or a surplus. High temperatures can kill plants, as can the lack of a cold spell if one is needed for dormancy. Pollution, the wrong soil pH, and too much or too little light can all contribute to a plant's demise. But the principal architect of temperate landscapes is the minimum temperature. How cold it gets is a better predictor of what will grow than any other single measure.

Not surprisingly then, most plant-hardiness-zone maps take only minimum temperatures into account. These maps are isotherm maps showing the locations of areas that have the same low temperatures. Of the several such maps in current use in this country, the two most common are the Arnold Arboretum map and the USDA map. Both

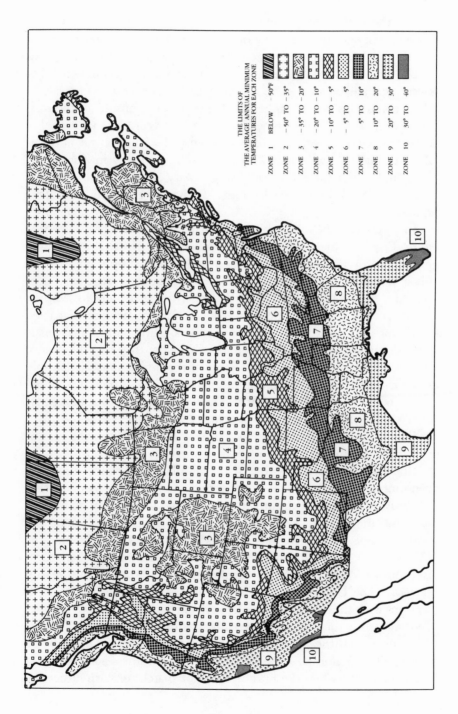

THE LIMITS OF
THE AVERAGE ANNUAL MINIMUM
TEMPERATURES FOR EACH ZONE

ZONE 1   BELOW   −50°F
ZONE 2   −50° TO −35°
ZONE 3   −35° TO −20°
ZONE 4   −20° TO −10°
ZONE 5   −10° TO −5°
ZONE 6   −5° TO   5°
ZONE 7   5° TO 10°
ZONE 8   10° TO 20°
ZONE 9   20° TO 30°
ZONE 10   30° TO 40°

divide the United States and Canada into 10 hardiness zones, each zone corresponding to a range of average minimum winter temperatures. The USDA map, for example, labels as Zone 6 those regions of the country where, on average, the temperature gets down to between zero and − 10 degrees Fahrenheit. A gardener who knows that these conditions prevail in her garden (either by consulting the map or, preferably, by keeping her own weather records) can reasonably expect to succeed with any plant known to be hardy as far north as Zone 6. She can, of course, also plant anything hardy in Zone 5, 4, 3, 2, and 1, but should be increasingly wary of plants that are hardy only to 7, 8, 9, or 10. At least that is the theory behind hardiness zones.

In practice, there are problems. First of all, it isn't always possible to find the hardiness-zone data for a given plant. Instead of saying a plant is hardy to a particular zone, a catalog may simply say that the plant is hardy in Canada, or that it is extremely hardy, as if "extremely" were a useful adjective. You can't get smart and look up on the map to find the hardiness zone of the nursery, because that is no predictor of the hardiness of the stock it is selling. Most perennials were dug and put in cold storage for sale before they had the chance to experience a winter outdoors. Some of the bigger nurseries simply serve as bookkeepers, transshipping plants to the customer from nurseries in other parts of the country. The best advice on hardiness zones comes from those books, like *Wyman's Gardening Encyclopedia* (Macmillan, 1986), that make a point of listing for every entry the coldest hardiness zone in which the plant will survive.

But there is another problem: the numbering systems differ depending on which hardiness-zone system you are using. A plant that is hardy in Zone 4 according to the Arnold Arboretum map may succumb if you plant it in Zone 4 of the USDA map, because the Arnold Zone 4 goes to only − 20 degrees Fahrenheit, while the USDA Zone 4 goes down to − 30 degrees. The table on page 170 is a comparison of the USDA and the Arnold Arboretum numbering systems. The USDA system further divides each zone into a and b sections with the a being the cooler half, the b the warmer. Whenever you are using zone data to determine hardiness, you must be sure that you match the published references with the right map. Some states, like California, have more detailed hardiness-zone maps of their own. But when the numbers do not match up with either the

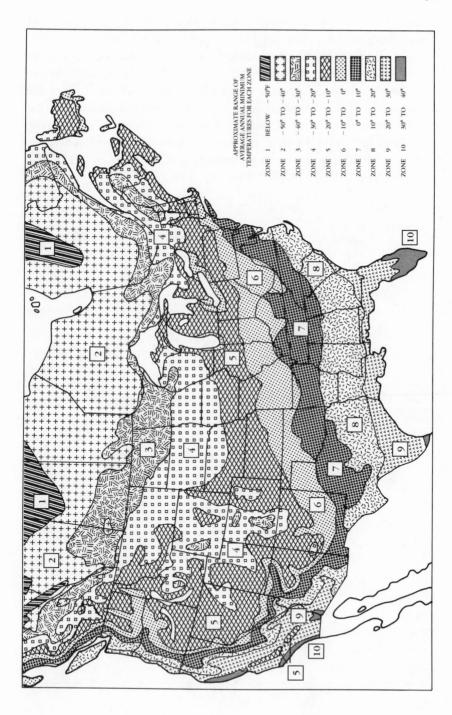

ZONE 1   BELOW   −50°F
ZONE 2   −50° TO −40°
ZONE 3   −40° TO −30°
ZONE 4   −30° TO −20°
ZONE 5   −20° TO −10°
ZONE 6   −10° TO   0°
ZONE 7   0° TO 10°
ZONE 8   10° TO 20°
ZONE 9   20° TO 30°
ZONE 10   30° TO 40°

APPROXIMATE RANGE OF
AVERAGE ANNUAL MINIMUM
TEMPERATURES FOR EACH ZONE

Arnold or the USDA system these maps are principally useful only for moving plants around within the region covered by the map.

The third problem with hardiness-zone maps is that, in putting sole emphasis on minimum temperatures, they say little about the southern extremes of species. Tulips don't grow in Texas, or sugar maples in Mississippi, not because of the cold but because of the heat. Nowhere is the importance of summer temperature clearer than in efforts to import English gardening practices to this country. In terms of minimum temperatures most of England is Zone 7 (USDA), roughly what is found in Washington, D.C. Yet we have great dif-

Relationship Between the Arnold Arboretum and USDA Hardiness-Zone Number Systems

Arnold Arboretum Hardiness Zone	Range of Average Annual Minimum Temperature F	U.S. Dept. of Agriculture Hardiness Zone
1	Below −50	1
2	−50 to −45	2a
	−45 to −40	2b
	−40 to −35	3a
3	−35 to −30	3b
	−30 to −25	4a
	−25 to −20	4b
4	−20 to −15	5a
	−15 to −10	5b
5	−10 to −5	6a
6	−5 to 0	6b
	0 to 5	7a
7	5 to 10	7b
8	10 to 15	8a
	15 to 20	8b
9	20 to 25	9a
	25 to 30	9b
10	30 to 35	10a
	35 to 40	10b

ficulty growing even such staples of the English garden as the common wallflower. If the plants don't freeze out during the winter they're killed by summer heat. Even in the Pacific Northwest where winters are mild and summers are cool, wallflowers can be grown only by watering to compensate for the summer drought. Southern gardeners particularly need statistics on summer hardiness as complete as those we currently have for winter hardiness. If nothing else, it would forewarn northerners who, moving to warmer climates, find that they aren't able to take many of their favorite plants with them.

But even if we had complete northern and southern limits to hardiness for every cultivated plant, gardeners would still persist in trying to grow things that they technically can't. It is our nature to continually test the limits of the possible. Those who live in Zone 5 think nothing of trying something said to be hardy to Zone 6 and are only slightly more reluctant to try plants from Zone 7.

Some of the time we get away with it. The fact that hardiness zones are based on average minimum winter temperatures means that some winters will be warmer than the mean. After two or three winters with above-average temperatures, a shortsighted gardener might conclude that camellias are hardy in Boston. But then, of course, along comes a winter with below-average temperatures to balance things up. No sooner are we lulled into a subtropical complacence by the sight of bamboos in Connecticut or citrus in Georgia than the coldest winter in a century wipes out hundreds of species, reminds us of our geography, and clears the slate for yet another round of optimistic gambling.

This is not to say that because the zone map assigns a particular number to a region, the reasonable gardener must give up trying to grow more tender material. The climate data on which the zone maps are based comes from a limited number of weather stations. There are, for example, only 243 National Weather Service Stations. Delaware, Maryland, and Vermont have a single station apiece. Arkansas, Connecticut, the District of Columbia, Kentucky, Maine, Mississippi, New Hampshire, Oklahoma, Rhode Island, and Utah have two each. The climate in your garden may differ considerably from the data gathered at the nearest weather station. The Grand Canyon, for example, contains four hardiness zones as you travel from the rim to the valley floor. On an even smaller scale, the temperatures on a sunny slope up against the foundation of the house may differ dramatically from those in a hollow at the low end of the garden. The term for this sort of small-scale climatic variation is *microclimate*. Depending on the location of your garden, its microclimate can easily be a whole zone milder or more severe than the region in general. Don't rely too much, therefore, on the experiences of other gardeners who purportedly share the same hardiness zone.

A change in elevation of a thousand feet will on average add or subtract three degrees to your minimum winter temperature, depending on whether you are going down or up. A garden on a south-facing slope may be a full zone warmer, one on a north slope a zone colder. Gardens within five miles of a large body of water enjoy a significant increase in plant hardiness, as do those gardens with an ample snow cover or those that are protected from the wind.

All of these corrections to the basic hardiness-zone data are refinements. But we will never be able to predict completely whether a particular plant will survive in a particular location. In the end the only sure answer to the question comes from trying. Gardening, like painting, can only be done roughly by the numbers.

Cold Facts

THE LONGER THE WINTER, the more time there is to worry about the plants outside. Will they survive the cold? For the phlox, the bee balm, the asters, and other perennials purchased by mail last spring, this is the first winter outdoors. They spent last winter in cold storage waiting for spring shipment. The newly planted cherries and azaleas have been through winters outdoors, but they were in nurseries to the south of here. Will they survive this far north?

The winters aren't any worse than they used to be — they just sound that way. When I was growing up, the weather forecast reported only the temperature; now it includes windchill, an excuse to subtract another twenty or thirty degrees. I have to stop and remind myself periodically that plants aren't warm-blooded, and that both they and my car battery will never feel any colder than what the thermometer says. This is reassuring.

Less reassuring is the knowledge that for every warmer than usual winter there will come a colder than usual one to compensate. That is, after all, what average minimum winter temperatures are all about. Gardeners who like gambling, and that includes a great many indeed, bet that the mercury will stay up, and set out plants that are ordinarily grown one or two hardiness zones farther south. Sooner or later, however, a normal or below-normal winter comes along and weeds out all the tender stock.

I prefer not to have to replant every few years, so I grow mostly those plants that have proved to be hardy in this zone. But just because a plant is hardy doesn't mean that it will survive the winter. This could be an unusually cold winter, or one with wildly fluctuating temperatures. Most cold-hardy plants become so only after a long exposure to gradually cooler and cooler weather. Temperatures well above what a plant is capable of withstanding may nevertheless kill it if these temperatures occur all of a sudden in the fall, before the plant has become accustomed to cold. Equally dangerous can be a sudden drop in the temperature after a midwinter warm spell.

What is more, not all parts of a plant are equally cold-hardy. Roots, for example, are typically much less resistant to cold than overwintering stems. For plants growing in the ground this is not a problem, because the soil is usually warmer than the air. But it can be a problem for plants growing in containers, because the root ball is relatively unprotected.

There is nothing gardeners can do to change winter temperatures, but we can do a few things to help prepare plants for the worst.

Much of the damage from cold, if it occurs, will not be due to the low temperature itself, but to the drought it induces. Frozen water is unavailable water, and if a branch loses water that it cannot replace, it will die. Evergreen foliage killed by drying out looks as though it has been scorched; hence the term *winter burn* for such injury. The best way to prevent winter burn is to keep the soil well watered in the fall until the ground freezes, and to prevent it from freezing deeply by mulching it heavily. Some people erect screens of burlap around tender plants to ward off drying winds, or spray the stems and foliage with one of the commercially available antidesiccants. But these are gamblers' attempts to save plants that they probably shouldn't be trying to grow anyway.

Another kind of cold damage may come from repeated freezing and thawing of the soil. This breaks roots and heaves plants out of the ground, where they die. A layer of mulch over the whole garden that keeps the soil at a more or less constant temperature is the best way to stop the freeze–thaw cycle. Traditional advice is not to apply mulch until the ground freezes. But when you stop and think about it, that isn't how mulch is applied naturally. Leaves fall off trees long before the ground freezes. Straw, salt-marsh hay, pine boughs, and oak leaves make good mulches when put on at least four inches deep. Maple leaves should be chopped up; you can do this by running a rotary mower over them. Otherwise they pack down too tightly, preventing air from reaching roots beneath, and can smother some plants.

The best mulch of all, of course, is a good deep snowfall. When snow comes early and stays, there is no reason to worry about applying any other mulch. I have gone so far as to pile snow shoveled from the driveway around rosebushes when the snow cover was thin.

Plants aren't the only living things that take advantage of the milder temperatures under mulch. So do meadow voles, which feed on roots and bark, and often girdle young fruit trees. Keeping mulch away from the trunk of a tree helps prevent such damage. But since this is hard to do with snow, every winter I wrap the trunks of young trees I think are rodent bait with a hardware-cloth cage or a spiral strip of heavy plastic designed for the purpose.

Bark can also be damaged by a precipitous drop in temperature, causing it to freeze quicker than the wood beneath and split away from the trunk. It is even possible to hear this happening sometimes on a bitter-cold night — a sound like a rifle shot. Nothing can be done to prevent this, but tacking the bark back as soon as one discovers it may prevent the underlying living cells of the cambium from drying out and dying. Another form of bark injury that sometimes occurs during winter is sunscald. This happens when bark warmed by the sun suddenly cools to a critical temperature, killing cells on that side of the trunk and ultimately resulting in a dead patch, or frost canker. Sunscald is only a problem on young smooth-barked deciduous trees, such as sycamores, and can usually be prevented by wrapping the trunk with a strip of paper or burlap tree-wrap to keep it shaded. Young beech trees do this naturally by holding on to their dead leaves all winter.

In general, older plants are hardier than young ones of the same kind. This means that I need not worry about winter veterans. For the newcomers, having provided water and mulch, I simply hope for the best. If they are going to make it to spring unscathed, they will do so on their own strengths. I find it surprisingly comforting that there isn't a whole lot I can do for them now.

Trees as Houseguests

WHEN I WAS GROWING UP we always waited until Christmas Eve to buy our tree. By dusk most of the vendors had become desperate enough that they were happy to sell their remaining stock for next to nothing, an annual savings that I suspect my father enjoyed more than the holiday itself. Of course, by that point the selection of trees wasn't the best. What remained were trees missing all the limbs on one side, trees with bare midriffs, trees with broken tops — the sort of trees no one wanted to buy. But my father had long ago devised a solution to all this. He never bought just one tree. He bought several. Four for a dollar was his opening bid, though he would settle for three. One of the trees had to be taller than the other two, and it had to have a nicely shaped top, a spire suitable for topping off with an aluminum-foil star.

When he got the trees home the first thing my father did was saw three inches off the butt of each trunk, as though they were carnations bought from a florist. Then he would have one of us hold the tallest tree upright while he set about fitting the second tree in against it. This was a matter of trial and error that involved a lot of bending of branches this way and that, but in the end the second tree's trunk lay right alongside the first. Then he did the same with the third tree. When he was done there were so many side branches radiating out from the three-in-one trunk at the center that his artifice was completely obscured. Ours was always the fullest, the bushiest, the best-formed Christmas tree in the neighborhood.

If we were the last people in the neighborhood to put our Christmas tree up, we were also the last to take ours down. Other people's trees scarcely made it through the twelve days of Christmas. Ours usually lasted through Easter. Oh, we took off the lights and ornaments within a month, replacing them some years with handcut, white paper snowflakes. But most often we just left the tree, which was always a fir balsam, clothed only in its fragrant needles, a bit of boreal forest north of the living-room rug. One year our Christmas tree rewarded us with three inches of new growth when spring came, and we half expected to find roots sprouting from the base when we finally and reluctantly carried it outside.

The secret to our trees' longevity was that we never let them dry out. Instead of a conventional stand, we held the tree up with clamps and a ring stand brought home from my father's chemistry laboratory. The great virtue of this homemade stand was that it allowed us to put a large bucket under the ends of the trunks, one that held four or five gallons of water. If the water level in the bucket dropped below the cut end of a trunk, the tree was a goner. Its needles would soon begin drying and dropping, and it would have to be banished as a nuisance and a fire hazard.

There are some people who think it more ecologically sound to buy a Christmas tree that still has roots, a so-called living Christmas tree. The trouble is that unless you have planned ahead, such a tree frequently ends up drying out too. Because the ground is too frozen or too snowy for the tree to be transplanted outdoors, it often ends up waiting for spring in the garage, where, unwatered, it slowly dies of drought. If you are determined to have a living Christmas tree, you should dig a hole in the fall, fill it with dry leaves, cover it with something waterproof so the ground underneath doesn't freeze, and put a supply of soil for backfilling indoors where it won't freeze either. Then after Christmas you can reasonably expect to plant the ex–Christmas tree outdoors. I have never, however, been remotely tempted to do this. It is far easier to recognize that Christmas trees were grown to be such than it is to go to the trouble of adding an evergreen every year to the backyard landscape, trees that the backyard probably doesn't need and, even if it did, that would be far more pleasant to plant at any other time of year.

Cut trees, even in our house, never last forever. Eventually they must be carried back outdoors. But if you have procrastinated long enough, the departure of one tree can be offset by the appearance of branches from another. Many spring-blooming trees and shrubs can be persuaded to bloom weeks earlier than normal if the cut branches are brought indoors to a heated room and put in water. The closer it is to the time that the plant normally blooms outdoors, the sooner the branches will flower indoors. If you wait until the first of February to cut the branches you should have to wait no more than six weeks, and as little as three, for such early bloomers as forsythia and Japanese witch hazel. Wherever you get your branches, cut them again when you get them home, just like you did with the Christmas tree, and be sure they always have ample water.

Many people have the mistaken notion that crushing the ends of branches will permit the stems to take up more water. Somehow, the same people who suggest hammering the ends of forsythia branches never recommend hammering the ends of Christmas tree trunks. Just because it is more practical to hammer forsythia doesn't make it more desirable. Think of a woody stem as a fistful of drinking straws. Crushing their ends is unlikely to improve the flow of water. A clean, angled cut, made with a sharp knife, is all that is necessary.

In the case of branches that are slow to come into bloom, it may be necessary to change the water in the containers periodically to keep it fresh. Within limits, the warmer the room the branches are stored in, the more rapidly they will come into flower. Once the branches are in bloom, however, the bloom will last longer in a cooler room than in a warmer one.

Forcing branches is so straightforward there isn't a whole lot more to say, except that, just as with Christmas trees, you shouldn't be in a rush to discard the branches once they have bloomed. We always kept our pussy willows long after the blossoms had opened fully, spilled their yellow pollen, and fallen off. We kept them until they put out green leaves and a mass of new roots. Plant one of these branches outdoors when the ground thaws and you will soon have a domestic supply of willow from which you can cut your own branches year after year. If you really want to be frugal you can even save the water the willow branches stood in and use it to root cuttings of other plants. Willow water isn't as good as commercial rooting hormones, but it does contain substances that promote root formation, and some people soak easy-to-root cuttings in it before putting them in a propagating bed.

Cherry, plum, and peach all force well, as do flowering dogwood, forsythia, bridal wreath, red maple, shadbush, Japanese quince, spicebush, and pussy willow. You shouldn't content yourself with these, however, when it is so easy to experiment. In March a single flowering branch on the hall table is worth a dozen on the bush in May.

There is something about a spray of forsythia, or the needled boughs of Christmas trees, that can't be matched by regular house-plants. Perhaps it is because the dieffenbachias and jade plants and schleffleras come and stay forever. We end up treating them as members of the family at best or, in the case of the fig tree at the end of the sofa, as part of the furniture.

The woody plants from outdoors, however, are altogether different. They aren't capable of remaining indoors indefinitely, and as such they always carry an air of foreignness. (Sometimes they carry more than that. I remember the year that a family taking down their Christmas tree discovered a live screech owl still sitting on one of its branches — a very patient and somewhat worried screech owl that had spent the entire holiday season eyeballing the family's cat.) Thickets of dogwood branches or fir-balsam boughs will never join the family. They can only be guests, and as such command special attention. They are a proof that there is something other than snow and ice beyond the storm door. They are always welcome because they bring news of greener times ahead.

A Christmas
Cold Frame

IT MAY BE DIFFICULT to gift wrap, but a homemade cold frame makes a fine Christmas present — practical, impressive, and original. Like all homemade gifts, it will bestow not only itself but the thoughts about the recipient that went into its construction. A willingness to share should be among this person's many virtues, because even if the donor already has a cold frame of his own, one never knows when it will overflow and extra space will suddenly be needed.

A cold frame is a simple shelter, a bottomless box with a transparent or translucent sloping lid. Think of it as a poor man's greenhouse: inside, the climate is moderated enough to add a month or more to each end of the growing season. (The adjective "cold" refers to the fact that these structures have no internal heat source, as contrasted to, say, hotbeds, which are identical in appearance but warmed by an underlying layer of fermenting horse manure.) Cold frames have innumerable uses, but chief among them are encouraging early and late plantings of cold-tolerant greens and serving as halfway houses for seedlings on their way from windowsill to garden.

There are no absolute dimensions for a cold frame any more than there are for a garden, but it is best not to build one so broad that you must climb in to tend the plants. Similarly, though the sides are usually low, six inches is a minimum for the front side — the lowest. Otherwise there isn't enough headroom for plants.

A cold frame should be situated in full sun when in use, and the slope of the cover should face due south. The angle of this slope is again something of a personal decision. Solar architects point out that as a rule of thumb the slope in degrees should roughly approximate the latitude at which the cold frame is to be used. Sunlight will strike the cover perpendicularly in spring and fall and will warm the interior as much as is possible. The steeper the cover, however, the higher the sides and the back, and the smaller the square footage inside the cold frame. If I followed these guidelines here at 42 degrees North latitude, my cold-frame cover would have to be as steep as a slate roof.

I prefer to give up some of the sunlight-gathering ability of my cold frame in favor of capacity and an economical use of materials. The design I use is a modification of a cold frame built by James Underwood Crockett. The cover slopes at a mere 7 degrees, but it performs so well that thus far I haven't wished for more.

Just as the dimensions of a cold frame are a matter of choice, so are the materials. Those who are sure of where they want their cold frame can make its walls of stone, concrete, or brick. I move my cold frame around occasionally and disassemble it some winters, and hence it is made of wood. I decided to use plywood, realizing that even

Materials

4x4-foot panel of ½-inch or thicker exterior plywood

Two 15-inch and two 9-inch lengths of 2x2-inch construction lumber

Four 4-foot lengths of 1x3-inch common pine

Two 1-foot lengths of 1x1-inch common pine

Three 4-foot lengths of corrugated redwood molding

Three 4-foot lengths of 1½-inch round redwood molding

Two 4-foot lengths of 26-inch-wide corrugated clear fiberglass

Twenty 2-inch #12 brass screws (for corners)

Twenty 1½-inch #8 flatheaded wood screws (for cover)

Sixteen ¾-inch #8 roundheaded screws with washers (for fiberglass)

Two 2-inch bolts with washers, lock washers, and wing nuts (for cover props)

One pair 4-inch strap hinges with screws or bolts

1 quart glossy white latex paint

Copper naphthenate (Cuprinol) wood preservative

exterior-grade plywood eventually delaminates; but plywood is readily available, convenient, and cheap. Those who can afford redwood might as well dispense with cold frames altogether and build a greenhouse instead.

My cold frame can be built for about $50 worth of materials and several evenings-after-supper's worth of labor. The table lists the necessary materials.

Cut the sides of the cold frame from half a sheet of plywood, as shown. Once the four panels are cut, paint them liberally with copper naphthenate (Cuprinol). Unlike creosote or pentachlorophenol, this wood preservative is not harmful to plants.

Assemble the box using a 2x2-inch block in each corner and brass screws. The brass, though more expensive than galvanized screws, won't corrode, thereby facilitating disassembly. If you never intend to take your cold frame apart, use galvanized screws or even nails. Once the box is assembled, paint the interior with glossy white latex to increase the reflectance. Don't worry if the copper naphthenate bleeds through the paint, turning it from white to aqua; when you repaint next year, the wood preservative will have faded enough that you can mask it.

Assemble the cover as shown. I use a lap joint to join the 1x3-inch boards, though Crockett simply used angle irons. The redwood molding is attached with 1½-inch screws. The center strip of half-round redwood is not strictly necessary, although it helps support the fiberglass if the cold frame is left outdoors under snow. Where I bought my fiberglass, the redwood strips being sold were six feet long, not eight, and I was thus obligated to buy an extra four feet of redwood, which I wanted to use up.

Fiberglass never transmits as much sunlight as glass does, and it won't last as long either, but it does withstand baseballs and bicycles that may inadvertently fall on it. Buy the heaviest grade you can find and attach it with ¾-inch roundheaded screws and washers.

The strap hinges for attaching the cover will have to be bent 90 degrees in a vise and the extra metal cut off with a hacksaw. In addition, I ground one end off each pin, removed them, and inserted a nail instead. This allows me to remove the cover without having to unscrew the hinges.

Attach the cover props to the sides so they can be adjusted to hold the cover ajar, and the cold frame is complete. Its 16-square-foot

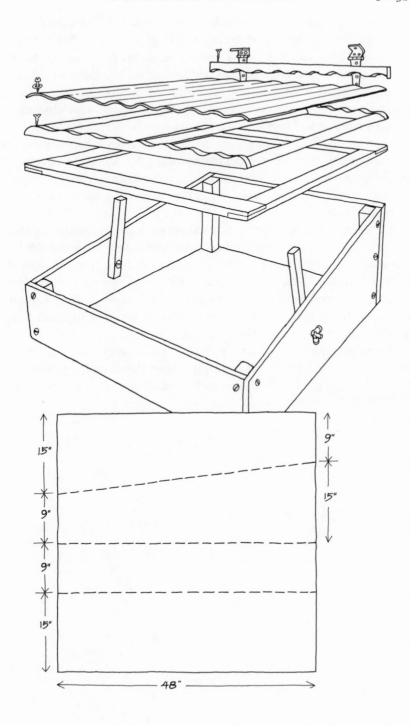

expanse will seem huge in the cellar and even larger under the Christmas tree, but outdoors next spring it will appear barely big enough.

Having been frugal so far, I now recommend one addition to the cold frame — an automatic opener for the cover. Because of their relatively small inside volume, cold frames tend to overheat if one doesn't ventilate them on sunny days. If you spend your days close enough to your cold frame that you can prop the cover open six inches every time the temperature goes above 40 degrees Fahrenheit, open it still farther when the temperature reaches 60 degrees, and close it gradually as the temperature drops in the evening, then you don't need an automatic vent. But I do. These automatic vents screwed to the inner edge of the front side of a cold frame have a cylinder that when warmed by sunlight puts pressure on a piston, which in turn raises a lever arm attached to the cold-frame cover. Mine, which has the trademark Thermofor, exerts 15 pounds of force (meaning it will open a 30-pound cover hinged on one side), can open the cover a full 12 inches, adjusts to begin opening from 55 to 85 degrees Fahrenheit, and has a built-in return spring that helps prevent wind from getting under and lifting the cover accidentally.

These automatic vents aren't cheap. In fact they can double the expense of a cold frame. But consider how much money was saved by building the cold frame oneself. And besides, it's Christmas, isn't it?

Gifts from the Cellar

THE COLD FRAME that I built for Christmas last year was really too large to fit beneath the tree. This year's gifts — a pair of them — are of more manageable dimensions.

The first is a collapsible potting bench. Last spring I filled my seed flats, sowed the seed, and later transplanted the small seedlings into separate pots all on the kitchen counter. While there was nothing unsanitary in this, the ingredients being more or less sterile, it was not particularly neat. Fine bits of peat tended to linger even after I had cleaned up, and some opinions were expressed that this sort of work might better be done elsewhere. In the ensuing months, I decided to build a full-size, proper potting bench with containers underneath to hold the various things needed for sowing and potting. That I was too busy to get started had one advantage: it allowed me to think a bit more, which led to my concluding that only the garage was roomy enough to accommodate such a piece of furniture. And March nights in the garage are both dark and cold. Not the sort of place I want to change a tire, let alone handle the dust specks that constitute petunia seed. I want to do that sort of thing where it is warm, and well-lit, and friendly — back in the kitchen. And so I designed and built instead a simple collapsible potting bench that can be set up when needed and then taken down and put away in the garage, alongside the stacks of pots and the galvanized trashcans filled with peat, vermiculite, and milled sphagnum moss. And when the bench leaves, the mess goes with it.

The bench's dimensions can be changed to suit individual preferences. Mine makes full use of a 3x4-foot piece of plywood. I used ¾-inch plywood; ⅝-inch would be lighter and probably just as good. Additional materials are listed in the table on page 186.

Begin by cutting the plywood into four pieces with the dimensions shown. The two dark strips are waste. The largest piece will be the working surface. Using glue and finishing nails, secure one of the

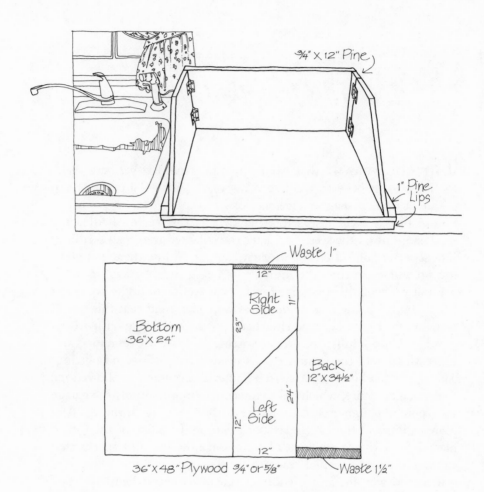

Materials

3x4-foot panel of ¾- or ⅝-inch plywood

Two 36-inch lengths and two 23¼-inch lengths
of 1-inch-wide pine board

Two pairs of 2-inch hinges with screws

1½-inch finishing nails

Glue

36-inch pieces of 1-inch pine to the underside of the front edge. This will serve as a cleat to prevent the whole bench from sliding around. The remaining three pieces are set on edge and secured similarly to the top surface of the other three sides, forming a 1-inch raised lip that will hold the three walls in place.

Hinge the left-hand wall directly to the back as shown, but hinge the right-hand wall to the ¾-inch piece of pine that is in turn attached to the back with nails and glue. This allows the right wall to fold flat on top of the left wall, making a sandwich three layers thick. When the back and sides have been hinged together they should fit neatly inside the lip on the base. The tips of the two side walls will project just a bit and should be sawed off flush with the front edge.

Sand all the surfaces, and round the edges and corners of the plywood slightly to prevent splintering. Two coats of polyurethane will seal the wood and make cleaning up easier.

The three walls serve as a backstop against which potting soil can be mixed and piled. When the work is done, any soil that remains can be swept off the front edge into a container. The walls can then be folded and, along with the base, put away.

My second present is a berry-basket basket. My family was blessed with an abundance of berries this year. Gallons of blueberries, strawberries, and raspberries. The trouble with berries is that if you pick them by the gallon, you seldom have a gallon when you reach the house. This is especially true of raspberries, fruits so delicate that they are crushed to death if piled more than a few deep. The solution, of course, is pint berry baskets, which were invented to protect the fruit (not simply as a means of selling a few berries for an exorbitant price). But spreading a gallon into pints means dealing with eight separate containers. Try to carry these all at once and you risk doing as much damage as when the berries were all in one container.

And so, my berry-basket basket, a carrier designed to safely transport a gallon's worth of pints. Its inside dimensions are 18x9¼ inches. The table on page 188 is a list of materials needed.

Cut the ends from 10-inch wide pine boards (which measure an actual 9¼ inches wide). The sides and bottom are made of ½-inch-thick pine; the thinner wood is used simply to make the unit lighter. Attach the slats with box nails, spacing the slats so as to leave a gap between adjacent ones, allowing ventilation. An old section of broomstick or some other dowel serves as a handle, and the holes

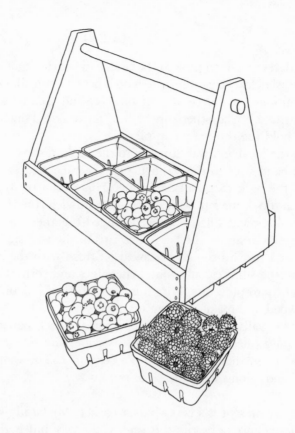

Materials

Two 16-inch lengths of 9¼-inch-wide pine board

Five 19½-inch lengths of 2¾-inch-wide,
½-inch-thick pine board

21-inch length of ⅞-inch-diameter dowel

Box nails

drilled in the side pieces should be of a diameter to match. Other than sanding the edges, no further finishing is necessary.

Some will say that I can't use the term "gift" for either the bench or the basket, since I will be using them as well in the months to come. But the evenings spent downstairs building them have been special ones, working with warm, dry, clean wood, listening to the family's footsteps overhead. I feel entirely justified in applying the term to anything associated with the pleasure.

A Christmas Goose

GARDEN SCULPTURE should mirror its environs. There is nothing wrong with pink flamingos or plaster gnomes, provided the garden is located in flamingo or gnome country. Here at Columbus Street, however, granite benches and bronze toad water faucets are the mode. For years I had coveted a lead rabbit, the sort that can be left among the lilies with impunity. Last Christmas Elisabeth gave me one. It is made not of lead but of terra-cotta and cement and has spent the summer under a rosebush, its round gray nose and big eyes just visible among the leaves of violets. This Christmas, in return for the gift of the rabbit, I am giving Elisabeth a goose.

Every fall flocks of geese fly overhead on their way south. At night, the sound of their honking signals the passage of wilderness over this city. By day, I can see the birds, the Canada geese flying in tight formation (regular Vs high overhead) or, less commonly, snow geese flying in the irregular crescents that contribute to their nickname, wavies. This is usually as close as I get to geese. But early one day, while fetching the morning paper from the sidewalk, I watched a dozen Canada geese fly down Columbus Street, lower than the telephone wires. What they were doing at that altitude I don't know, but it was close enough to leave me with the conviction that at least one belongs among our alpine strawberries.

My goose is made of wood and doubles as a support for two flowerpots. Flowering potted plants can be positioned where the additional color is most welcome. Unfortunately, they tend to be top-heavy, tipping over in the slightest breeze. This can be rectified in the border by sinking the pots into the soil, but not so on a porch or terrace. Hence I have hollowed out the back of my goose to hold a pair of standard 7-inch pots.

The bird's dimensions were of my own choosing, based loosely on those of a Canada goose. My intention was to build something that would suggest the spirit of a goose, not serve as a decoy. For the body

I used three short pine boards. The ends are six-sided polygons, and the top has holes cut to hold the flowerpots. These holes must be of a diameter that will support the pots by their rims, and it is best to have the pots in hand while cutting the holes to make sure they fit. I screwed the three pieces of lumber together with drywall screws, producing something that looked like a step stool.

For siding I used old lath. Renovating a house built in the days of horsehair plaster generates a large quantity of this rough wood, which is normally thrown out. However, its texture is perfect for mimicking goose feathers. If lath is unavailable, thin strips of any rough wood will do. It is easier to start with something rough than to distress a new board. I cut the lath to fit around the holes in the back and tapered the tail ends of some to simulate feathers. Leaving a space between each piece of lath, I attached the lath to the wooden framework with 4-penny galvanized box nails. The result resembled a cross between a lobster pot and an outhouse seat for two.

Carving the head and neck required the most effort and artistry. I sketched the

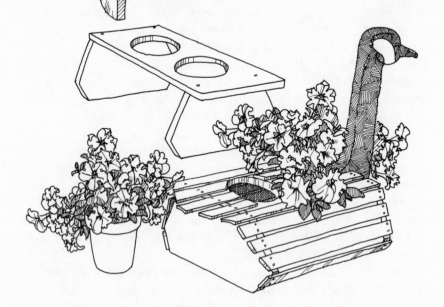

outline on a relatively knot-free section of two-by-six, omitting the bill. I roughed out the head and neck with a saw and finished it with a knife and chisel. The bill was carved separately out of a scrap of wood and fitted into a notch cut into the head. I did not bother to sand the head and neck, preferring to leave some texture there as well. A pair of 2½-inch drywall screws, extending out from inside the body, secured the neck in position.

Finally, I painted the completed bird to resemble a Canada goose — a black neck with a white throat patch, gray-brown wings, and a white belly and rear. It is an unusual bird, my goose, quite apart from the petunias that will be cascading over its back next summer. Judging from the way it carries its head, there is a bit of a swan in its ancestry. On the other hand, thus far no one has mistaken it for a duck. Someday I may carve a more realistic specimen. But no subsequent bird will ever be quite as memorable as this one, the very first goose to alight in our garden.

A Good Twenty-five-Dollar
Garden Bench

FOR A GARDENER, the greatest luxury is often nothing more than the chance to sit down. The more tired you are, the less it matters where you sit. The wheelbarrow, the compost heap, the ground at the end of the row all serve about as well when your legs have given out. But by midwinter, most of us have forgotten the simple pleasure of resting atop an upturned bucket, and as we turn the pages of mail-order catalogs many of us begin seriously contemplating the purchase of a garden bench.

A bench in a garden, even in a deserted garden, is a sign that people are welcome. Well built and well placed, a garden bench is more than just a place to sit; it is an invitation to sit. Mail-order benches are some of the most persuasive invitations ever issued. There is, for example, a bench designed by the Edwardian architect Edwin Lutyens — eight and a half feet long, with curved arms and a high, scrolled back.

Despite the lure of such a bench, I haven't taken any catalog up on its offer. I might claim that my reluctance stems from the fact that most fine garden benches are made of teak. At a time when there is so much concern over the disappearance of tropical forests, who wants to contribute to the problem by encouraging the loggers? But the fact is that teak (*Tectona grandis*) is a second-growth species, a tree that springs up after the primary forest is cut. India, Burma, Thailand, and Vietnam are the sources of most commercial supplies of teak, and much of it is plantation grown. What threatens teak forests in these regions is not an excessive demand for the teak but the expansion of agriculture. So it might be argued that a strong market for teak, rather than a boycott of the wood, is the best way to preserve the tree's natural habitat.

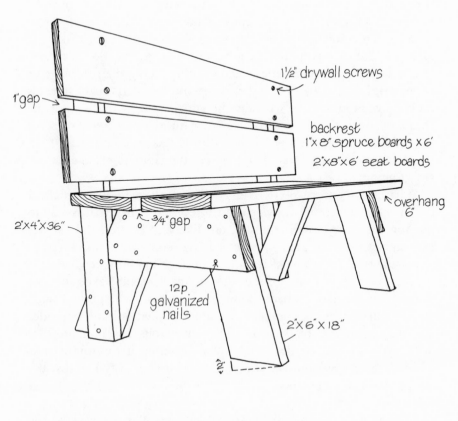

1½" drywall screws

1" gap

backrest
1"x 8" spruce boards x 6'

2"x 8"x 6' seat boards

overhang
6"

2"x 4"x 36"

¾" gap

12 p.
galvanized
nails

2"x 6"x 18"

2"

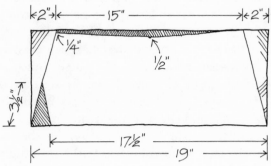

2" — 15" — 2"

¼"

½"

3½"

17½"

19"

To be honest, what keeps me from acquiring one of these benches is not its tropical origin, or even its lofty price, but its permanence. Barring a forest fire or a lightning strike, a teak bench will last a lifetime. Thoroughly resistant to rain, snow, ice, and sun, teakwood ages gracefully, weathering to a silvery gray as the decades pass. While such longevity has the advantage of reducing the per-year cost of the original purchase, I find the guarantee of perpetual sameness unsettling. Nothing else will stay the same in the garden — not the shrubs, the trees, not even the gardener himself. I'd like to reserve the right to change my seat, if not with the seasons then at least with the decades, the same way that I reserve the right to change what I am growing.

What this country needs is a good twenty-five-dollar bench, a bench that is perennial yet won't last forever. A bench that is easy to put together, easy to replace, and not likely to be stolen. In short, this year's Christmas gift, a homemade six-footer with a backrest.

I made this bench out of common construction lumber. The seat, the legs, and the support for the back are made of 2x8, 2x6, and 2x4 stock. The backrest is made from two pieces of 1x8 spruce board, which comes from the lumberyard lightly planed only on one side. The accompanying table is a slightly generous list of materials. When you are buying the wood, take the time, if the lumberyard will let you, to pick out the straightest and least knotty lengths. Let the professional carpenters contend with the rest.

The pitch of the legs, the curve of the seat, and the angle of the back are all determined by two short lengths of 2x8 that connect everything together. If you cut the two 6-foot-long seat pieces out of each of the 2x8s, you will have plenty left over to make these two pieces according to the measurements shown. (These dimensions yield a bench that is perfectly suited to my body. Readers are certainly invited to change things around to suit theirs.) When these two connectors have been cut, use them to mark the angles for the top and bottom of each of the 18-inch-long legs and cut them out of 2x6 stock. Note that the tops of the front legs will have a slightly different angle of cut than the tops of the rear legs, because the cutaway portion of the top of each connector is not quite symmetrical. The bottoms of all four legs are cut at yet another angle, an angle that is the same for all four bottoms. Use the bottom front edge of the connector as a guide.

Next, nail each connector to two legs, with four 12-penny galvanized nails per leg, as shown. Then fit the 36-inch lengths of 2x4 that will serve as supports for the backrest. The bottom front edge of these supports should be flush with the bottom front edge of the rear legs. Mark and trim each so that it has the same angle as the bottom of the legs, and secure with four more nails. Position these nails as far up and down the leg as you can without cracking the wood. (If you are afraid the back is not secure enough, you can later nail an additional length of wood across the connector and the backrest support, just under the seat boards.)

At this point you have constructed a pair of lowercase *h*'s. Set these upright and nail the two seat pieces in place, allowing each piece to overlap 6 inches at each end. The front half of the seat should be flush with the front edge of each connector. Leave a ¾-inch gap between the front piece and the rear. Although the bench is now taking shape, resist the temptation to throw yourself down on your new seat, because until the back is in place the bench is likely to fold up on you. Attach the first backboard flush with the top of the backrest supports, using four drywall screws on each side. I left a gap of an inch between the bottom of this board and the one below it. Once the backrest boards are screwed in place, the bench is as stable as ever it will be.

There are several things you can do to extend the life of this bench. I set each bottom leg in a pie pan full of Cuprinol (copper naphthenate) for half an hour to let it soak up the wood preservative in the part that will be in contact with the ground (and so will rot the

---

Materials

Two 10-foot (8 foot if available) lengths of 2x8
construction lumber

One 8-foot length of 2x6 construction lumber

One 8-foot length of 2x4 construction lumber

One 12-foot length of 1x8 spruce board

1 pound 12-penny galvanized nails

Sixteen 1½-inch drywall screws

soonest). You could also stain or paint the bench, and you could decide to let your bench winter-over in the garage.

But bear in mind that the whole purpose of a twenty-five-dollar bench is that it is easy to replace. Don't exhaust yourself finding ways to make a perishable object last forever. You might better take the time to build half a dozen benches. That way, whenever the urge to sit comes over you, you'll have a place to do it in style.

Humidity

WHAT SEPARATES houseplants growing on a windowsill from those in a greenhouse is not so much a difference in the amount of light they receive as a difference in the humidity. One of the chief delights of stepping into a greenhouse in midwinter is the warm, moist air that fills your lungs. This is a far cry from the desert-dry air one encounters inside most homes in midwinter — air so parched that it desiccates nose and throat, shrinks furniture joints, sends sparks jumping from fingertips to metal doorknobs, and leaves everyone with the impression that the house is chillier than it actually is. Plants, too, show the signs of dry air: leaf tips turn brown, the edges turn yellow, buds fall, and in extreme cases the leaves follow suit. Adding moisture to the air is clearly a desirable thing to do. But the choice of how to go about it, and how far to go, needs some discussion.

The moisture content of air can be expressed in two ways. *Absolute humidity* refers to the amount of water vapor (usually expressed in grains, there being 7000 grains per pound) in a cubic foot of air. A more common measure, however, is *relative humidity,* which is the ratio of the amount of water vapor present in the air to the maximum amount of moisture that the air is capable of holding at that temperature. When a weatherman reports that the relative humidity is 50 percent, he means that the air is holding one-half of the moisture that it is capable of holding.

The first fact to know about relative humidity is that warm air can hold more moisture than cold. When fully saturated air is cooled it can no longer hold all its water vapor, and some condenses out as liquid. This explains why clouds rising over a mountain range dump rain on the windward side, and why air conditioners drip. At 80 degrees Fahrenheit a cubic foot of air can hold about 11 grains, at 70 degrees only 8 grains, and at 60 only 6.

There are two ways to increase the relative humidity of air in a room. The first is to increase the moisture content, and the second is to lower the temperature. The increase in relative humidity that comes with a decrease in temperature explains why the air inside most homes is so dry during the winter. Outdoors, there is little difference in relative humidity from summer to winter, at least in those parts of the country where rainfall is evenly distributed over the calendar. Here the average relative humidity in July is the same as in January — roughly 65 percent. But although the relative humidity outdoors stays the same, the absolute humidity, the actual moisture content, is lower during the winter because cool air holds less moisture than warm. Indoors, the furnace warms the air without adding any additional moisture. As a result the warm air inside the house has a much lower relative humidity than the air outdoors. If the air outdoors has a relative humidity of 50 percent at 30 degrees and the furnace raises the temperature to 70 degrees indoors, the relative humidity drops to 11 percent, a condition not found outdoors except in places like the Mojave Desert.

Air this dry is injurious to many plants. They simply cannot replace water lost through evaporation fast enough, no matter how moist the soil in their pots. Epiphytes, those plants which commonly grow above ground without much soil around their roots, such as cattleya orchids, many ferns, and philodendrons and their kin, are especially sensitive to dry air. One can water the roots until they rot without compensating for the effects of dry air on the foliage.

At the other extreme are the plants that flourish in dry air, for example cacti and other succulents, *Sansevieria,* the snake plant, *Aspidistra,* the cast-iron plant, and the various *Dracaena.* I think of these as barbershop plants, because that has become the adopted home of many. But these plants originally evolved in deserts and similarly arid landscapes.

Most indoor foliage plants need a relative humidity of 40 to 50 percent, an intermediate state between the foot of a waterfall and a desert. The problem is how to achieve this condition.

There is no shortage of opinions. Spraying a light mist of water on the foliage is a great favorite, although everyone agrees one must do it often. Three times a day is good, ten times a day is better. Gardeners who are rooting cuttings apply mist every fifteen minutes, which suggests that ninety-six times a day may be best. Most of us, however, don't have the patience or the automation to pull it off.

Another way to increase humidity is to set the pots on a tray filled with water and pebbles so that the pots are dry but water vapor rises up past the leaves. Simply clustering plants together increases humidity somewhat, because water evaporating from one plant's leaves moistens the air of its neighbors.

All the same, I cannot help wondering how effective these techniques really are. What does it take to raise the humidity from 20 to 40 percent in a room 15 by 15 feet with an 8-foot-high ceiling when the air temperature is 65 degrees? I did the arithmetic and discovered that theoretically it takes the evaporation of only 2880 grains of water, or roughly half a cup. But once again Nature defeats theory. I was forgetting that the air in the room changes regularly, as often as twenty times a day in a house as drafty as this. That means that I would have to evaporate about a cup of water an hour, or six quarts a day. And this would humidify only a medium-sized room.

Gardeners who are serious about increasing the humidity of the air in their homes won't rely on misting or water-filled trays. They will get a humidifier, a big one with a reservoir that holds several gallons of water, one that will give off a steady stream of moisture into the air. With a good humidifier one can raise the humidity as high as one pleases. But how high should that be?

For the plants, saturation is the limit, but the limit for the house is much lower. The problem with high humidity indoors during the winter is the differential in temperature between the inside and the outside. When moist warm air hits a cold wall or window, the air cools and loses some of its water. If the surface that the water condenses on is a windowpane, the water will run down and wet the sill. If it is inside the walls, and there is not a tight vapor barrier just under the plaster, it may wet the sheathing of the house, cause paint to peel, dramatically reduce the effectiveness of insulation, and prematurely rot studs and other structural members. Experimenters at the University of Minnesota concluded that if the outside air temperature is −20 degrees or colder, the relative humidity inside should not be over 20 percent for the house's sake. From −20 to −10 degrees, humidity should not be over 25 percent. From zero to 10 degrees, it can be as high as 35 percent. And from 20 to 40 degrees, not above 40 percent.

Obviously, there are times when the ranges of humidity suitable to the house and to the houseplants do not overlap. These are the times when you want a greenhouse with its condensation-immune frame of cypress, redwood, or aluminum. Lacking that, there is nothing to be done but grow those houseplants that can tolerate relatively low relative humidity. When the days become longer and brighter, humid air will return, and the plants will make up for lost time, and lost leaves. Until then, plants and plantsmen are both like dry seeds, waiting for the right conditions to begin again.

Maple Syrup

MAKING MAPLE SYRUP is magic. It doesn't matter whether you set out to make a single tablespoonful or a whole gallon. And even when you have made syrup repeatedly and think you understand everything, it is still magic. I have made maple syrup for so many years that the trick ought to be old hat. But each February I find myself just as excited about the upcoming show, a show in which I will always be both performer and audience. When the steam begins to rise from the pan, people come to watch, and stay to help. While I am glad to have the company, I never quite understand why they aren't making their own syrup. It is so simple.

All you need is a maple tree and a winter with temperatures below freezing. All maple trees produce sap that can be boiled down to make syrup. Maple syrup is usually made from the sap of the sugar maple (*Acer saccharum*) because its sap has the highest sugar content, averaging about 2 percent. But you can make syrup from box elder (*A. negundo*), silver maple (*A. saccharinum*), big-leaf maple (*A. macrophyllum*) and even red maple (*A. rubrum*) and Norway maple (*A. platanoides*). However, the sap of these maples has a lower sugar content (1 percent or less), and thus it takes much longer to make syrup. Also, the syrup that results will have a different taste, though it will be just as sweet. My advice is to find a sugar maple. You need only one. If you don't live in a part of the country where they grow naturally, look for one that has been planted for its bright-orange fall foliage — a street tree perhaps, or one on a golf course, or one in someone's backyard.

The season for making maple syrup is late winter, when the daytime temperature begins to rise consistently above freezing but the nighttime temperature still drops below freezing. Maple-syrup season usually lasts several weeks, until the buds on the trees begin to swell. During this period sap will drip from any recent wound on a maple

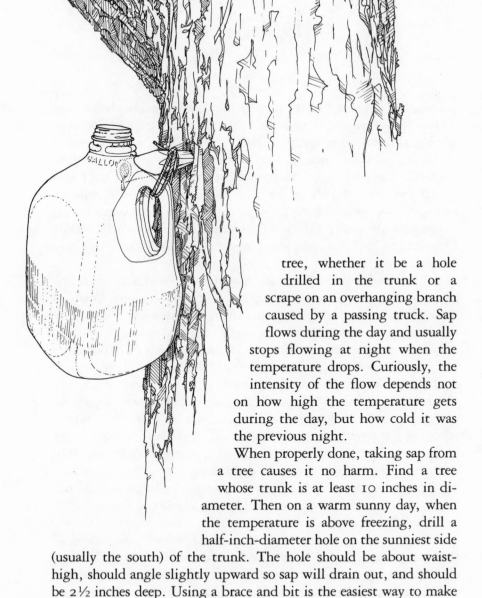

tree, whether it be a hole drilled in the trunk or a scrape on an overhanging branch caused by a passing truck. Sap flows during the day and usually stops flowing at night when the temperature drops. Curiously, the intensity of the flow depends not on how high the temperature gets during the day, but how cold it was the previous night.

When properly done, taking sap from a tree causes it no harm. Find a tree whose trunk is at least 10 inches in diameter. Then on a warm sunny day, when the temperature is above freezing, drill a half-inch-diameter hole on the sunniest side (usually the south) of the trunk. The hole should be about waist-high, should angle slightly upward so sap will drain out, and should be 2½ inches deep. Using a brace and bit is the easiest way to make the hole. If the tree is larger than 18 inches in diameter you can drill a second hole on the east side. Trees 24 inches or more in diameter will allow a third hole on the west side. No tree should ever have more than three holes drilled in a single year. (You can, of course, drill holes year after year, but the most recent ones should be at least 6 inches away from the old ones.)

Sap should begin dripping out of the holes almost immediately. To collect the sap you will need some sort of spout to guide the sap out of the hole and into a container. Traditionally, metal spouts are used, and these can be purchased for less than a dollar at hardware stores in regions where people make maple syrup. Not everyone, however, lives in one of those regions or has the foresight to order the spouts from a supplier. It is just as easy to make your own spouts anyway.

My first spouts were whittled from staghorn sumac branches. These branches have a large, soft pith that is easy to ream out with a piece of stiff wire. They were used by the Indians to make the stems for their peace pipes. Staghorn sumac grows like a weed along highways, in abandoned fields, and in other waste places. Select branches that are about an inch in diameter and cut them into 3-inch lengths with a handsaw. Ream out the pith, peel off the bark, and taper one end so that it is small enough to fit smoothly and snugly into a half-inch-diameter taphole. When gently hammered into the trunk these should conduct the sap a couple of inches out from the side of the tree, where it can drip into a container.

Any clean bucket with a cover to keep out rain and dirt will do. The cheapest and simplest one I have ever used is a one-gallon plastic milk jug. Since they hold only a gallon of sap they may have to be emptied after a good day's run, but no one is going to make off with one. Metal spouts come with a hook to hang the bucket on. I tie the handles of my milk jugs to my wooden spouts so the spout sticks directly through a hole cut into the top of the jug.

Sap doesn't run every day in maple-syrup season; it runs only on those days when the temperature is that peculiar blend of freezing and thawing. If the temperature doesn't get above 32 degrees the sap doesn't begin to flow, and if it rises above freezing and stays there for days it will stop running. To make a cup of syrup you will need two and a half gallons of sap, which may take a week to collect from a single tree. Consequently you have to wait to accumulate enough sap before you start boiling, especially if you have tapped only one tree.

Because sap contains sugar it will spoil, especially if the weather is warm, though if the snow is deep enough you can bury containers of sap in a shaded snowbank. When buried in snow it will keep outdoors for a week. Otherwise store it in the refrigerator.

For every cup of finished syrup you must boil off roughly 39 cups of water. I collect sap all week and boil on the weekends. If you are planning to make only a few cups there is no reason not to do the boiling indoors. The amount of water vapor the syrup-making will add to the air will be no greater than that given off by a good humidifier.

However, if you are going to be making a quart or more (and therefore boiling off 10 gallons of water), it is probably best to do at least the initial boiling outside — over a fire built between walls of concrete block or on the barbecue grill. Plan on burning up a good deal of firewood. Syrup-making, even in the most efficient commercial evaporators, consumes nearly ten times as many calories in fuel as the resulting syrup contains. Backyard syrup-making is even more inefficient.

Wherever you do your boiling you will need a broad-bottomed pan with sides at least 6 inches high. Pour a couple of inches of sap into the pan and bring it to a boil. Add additional sap as necessary to keep the level of the boiling liquid constant. Adding additional sap gradually rather than all at once is less likely to interrupt the boil. When you run out of sap continue boiling but begin sampling the liquid in the pan, being careful not to burn your tongue. You will find that the sweetness increases steadily as you reduce the liquid.

Be careful never to let the bottom of the pan go dry, either; the syrup will scorch and darken. If you are making a little bit of syrup in a large pan you may have to transfer the nearly completed syrup to a smaller pan for finishing. Or if you do your initial boiling outdoors you may decide to finish it on the kitchen stove. As the syrup gets closer to finished it begins to foam and can boil up over the sides of a shallow pan, making an awful mess. Watch the heat or keep a dab of butter handy. The tiniest bit of grease will quickly flatten the foam (the old oil on troubled waters). Finished syrup is a saturated sugar solution that is about 67 percent sugar. If you boil beyond that point sugar crystals will appear when the liquid cools. If you stop boiling before that point you will have watery syrup. As you taste the about-to-be syrup you will find that the viscosity increases suddenly just before it is done. Watch for the point at which the syrup sheets, rather than drips, off the spoon. Another way to tell when syrup is done is to use a candy thermometer. The temperature should read 7 degrees above the boiling point of water. (Water officially boils at 212 degrees, but the value varies with altitude and barometric pressure. If you plan on using a thermometer, boil some water by itself and measure its boiling temperature.)

There isn't any reason that your syrup has to be of legal density. Whatever thickness you make the syrup, it won't take up much space in the refrigerator, and it won't last long.

When the weather warms up for good the trees will stop dripping, and what sap does come out will be cloudy in the buckets — a sign that bacteria are already at work in the tapholes and in the buckets. Pull out the taps and ignore anything you have heard about sealing up or plugging the holes you have made. They will close themselves in a year or two, and the wood adjacent to the cavity inside the trunk will be sealed off by the tree so that the decay cannot spread to the rest of the tree's interior. The dangers of drilling too many holes in a tree come not from removing too much sap but from creating overlapping areas of decay that weaken the tree trunk. Watch as the summer progresses, and you will see the cambium start to grow in from the sides of the taphole. A few years later all that will remain to show the tree was tapped will be a circular hole in the bark, and that too will flake off eventually. But the taste in your mouth, the marvelous sense of accomplishment that comes with having made your own syrup, will remain indefinitely.

The Best-Laid Plans

GARDENS are not still lifes. A good design must look good not only when it is first planted but also later, when the plants have grown and changed their sizes, shapes, and colors. Only those rare people who are able to visualize what an entire garden will look like over time can safely plant a landscape all at once. The rest of us mere mortals must add plants to our gardens bit by bit, watching how each plant behaves. Year by year, we learn from our mistakes, and our successes, until we achieve some semblance of skill in the matter of where to plant things.

There is one way to speed things up and that is to learn from the experience of others. This is especially useful in the case of slow-growing trees and shrubs, because most of us can't anticipate living long enough to learn everything by our own trials and errors. It's good to develop the habit of looking into other people's yards, not so much to see what the current gardeners are doing but to see what their predecessors did. Mine is a good neighborhood for this sort of study because many of the gardens have been tended for three or more generations.

From my wanderings around the neighborhood I have come up with a handful of principles, most of which concern the effects of time on a landscape. These are not hard-and-fast rules, obviously, but they are the sort of truisms in which most of us put great stock and by which we are generally well served.

My first rule concerns the risk involved in planting long rows of anything. Gardeners may wish to take the chance in the case of annuals or other short-lived plants. But rows of trees, or allées, as they are called, have understandably fallen from favor. Should disease or some other virulent pest attack one plant in such a row it is likely to attack the others. This doesn't happen very often, but the skeletons of American elms along roadsides are a grim reminder that it can.

Even if no general disaster strikes, individual plants in a row frequently succumb for one reason or another, leaving gaps. Missing
teeth look cute on a child, less so in a hedge. Whenever you admire
a long border of evenly spaced marigolds or chrysanthemums, recognize that either the owner has been lucky or, more likely, has a
supply of extras growing out of sight. This is, of course, easier to do
with alyssum than with arborvitae.

My second rule concerns maintaining adequate distance between
the outside wall of a house and the nearest vegetation. Foundation
plants should never touch the foundation. It isn't good for the house
because trapped moisture will hasten decay, and it is even worse for
the plants. Here in the North the most dramatic problems occur
during winter, when gutters freeze and overflow, causing water and
ice alternately to rain down upon the plants beneath, flooding the
roots and crushing the tops. On the other hand, if the house has
particularly wide eaves, plants too close to the foundation may be
deprived of adequate moisture because they may be inside the roof-
line. As a rule, you should always be able to walk between the foundation planting and the house. This means knowing in advance the
ultimate size of your plants, so they won't encroach on the very structure you are trying to enhance.

Third, evergreens eat walks. The yews, rhododendrons, junipers,
and hemlocks planted on each side of the path to your front door will
look terrific for a number of years. But they will keep growing, and
eventually you will have to decide between radical, mutilating sur-
gery and meeting the mailman at the curb. Conscientious pruners,
or those gardeners with the courage to saw down a pair of adolescent
Colorado spruces for Christmas trees, can edge their front walks with
evergreens. The rest of us are best off with something deciduous,
preferably herbaceous.

My fourth rule is a reminder not to block the view. This means
don't plant trees in front of windows. Or tall plants in front of short
plants. Consider the vantage from which you will be looking at the
garden. And when you erect a screen of vegetation be sure you know
everything that it is eventually going to screen out. A previous owner
of this property planted a row of white pines on the boundary between this house and the next with the intention, I was told, of never
having to look at his neighbor again. By the time I moved here the
trees, being on the south side of the house, had grown so tall that

they were blocking out most of the winter sun. Gardening encyclo-
pedias give the ultimate sizes for plants. Your specimens may never
reach full size, but don't count on it.

Fifth, avoid what I called the painted-rock syndrome. There's
nothing wrong with the way painted rocks look, if that's what you
like. What's wrong with them is that if they are placed on the lawn,
which is what usually happens, each rock must be either moved —
or laboriously trimmed around — to mow the grass. The same occurs
with lots of little islands of vegetation in the middle of a lawn — a
rose here, some daylilies there, another rose there, and so on. Only
plants can't be as easily moved as rocks. Unless you want to spend
much of your time keeping the grass from growing into your garden,
consolidate the plants into a few larger beds with perimeters that are
short enough to be defensible.

My sixth and final rule is not to accept volunteers. I don't mean
the plants that other people volunteer to give you free of charge. I
mean those plants that appear in the garden of their own accord.
Unintentional seedlings, especially those of woody plants, are not the
welcome bonus they may at first appear to be. Consider seedling
maple trees: the seedlings are too numerous to pull up when they
first appear and too difficult to pull up when they are bigger. And it
is difficult to transplant them, except when they are leafless, a time
when they are inconspicuous and less troubling. Even though the
location of a young seedling is seldom propitious, most people conclude that it isn't doing any harm just yet. But the next time the
gardener looks up, the tree has a trunk six inches in diameter and
the shade from its leaves and the competition from its roots has killed
off much of what was originally in the garden. As a general rule,
eradicate chance seedlings. If you want to propagate something, do
it intentionally in a nursery bed or buy a plant from a nursery.

These, then, are a half-dozen thoughts about design. Those planning to plant a bare lot can take this advice to heart before starting
out. But what about those of us who began with an existing landscape, a landscape left by a predecessor who was still learning? The
only solution may be to cut down trees and dig out misplaced shrubs.
Such drastic revisions to the landscape are painful but in the end
rewarding. At the very least, the hours spent grunting and sweating
over a stump give us opportunity to reflect on the future of our own
best-laid plans.

Will It Grow
in the Shade?

WE WOULD LIKE ANOTHER BEDROOM, but sunlight topped our list of priorities when we went house-hunting. For us, the cost of an unrestricted garden has been a succession of people sleeping on the couch in the living room. All around us the yards are much shadier than ours, the shadows cast by mature sugar maples, copper beeches, board fences, and the houses themselves. Not surprisingly, the most frequent question our neighbors ask us is "Will it grow in the shade?"

Shade is an oasis from summer heat, a cool and inviting addition to any landscape. Had we not already had several mature trees on this property — a cherry, an elm, a white pine — we would most certainly have planted saplings at once. However, because less light means less photosynthesis, gardeners tend to be less enthusiastic about shade than are desert travelers.

One of the first things we did when we started gardening here was to saw down some adolescent white pines, and some overgrown yews and arborvitae, to give the ground along the south side of the house unrestricted exposure. I'm not saying that we have changed our mind in retrospect, but since then I have become somewhat more tolerant of shade. Shade does limit what you can grow, but not all that much. For every plant like corn that requires full sun, there is one like tuberous begonia that needs some shade. The vast majority of plants will grow with less than full sunlight. In nature many of them are shaded by their neighbors. Shaded gardens typically have fewer blossoms than those in full sun, but they invite greater appreciation of the forms of plants, the pattern of branches, the hues and textures of leaves.

Shade comes in many forms, from the light screen cast by the feathery leaves of overarching honey locust branches, to the dense, dark shadow of hemlock boughs sweeping the ground. Every shade gardener is an inveterate experimenter, testing plants out in different locations to see how they perform. Failures are almost always outnumbered by successes, leading to the entirely justified conclusion that the authors of gardening books don't know what they are talking about.

I have found that it helps to distinguish between shade cast by inanimate objects, like buildings or stone walls, and shade created by trees and shrubs. In the former case, the problem is simply reduced light. In the latter case, however, you must contend with the roots of the trees and shrubs. These often cast more of a shadow than the crowns, as they snatch water and nutrients away from lesser plants.

Sometimes the solution to shade is simply to grow lesser plants in their own containers where their root systems are free from competition. The Botanical Garden in Florence, Italy, has some nine thousand different species of plants growing on scarcely more than five acres of land that is heavily shaded by huge trees. The key feature seems to be that most of the collection is growing in individual terracotta pots. Some of these are small, of the sort used for geraniums, others are huge pots four or five feet in diameter. But large or small, the individual pots offer each plant's root system sanctuary from its more aggressive neighbors.

Growing plants in containers has its drawbacks. Unable to forage freely for water and nutrients, the gardener must see that both are always available. The best soil for plants growing in shade can be made by mixing two parts of organic matter (compost, leaf mold, peat moss) with one part of sand (river sand or builder's sand), and one part of loam. The result should be a slightly acid, loose soil that holds moisture. A well-constructed soil will need no additional fertilizer, but an annual application of any balanced fertilizer in the spring will result in taller plants with more robust flowers and leaves.

Sometimes all that the new plants need is temporary respite from the roots of larger plants. This can be accomplished by digging out the roots in a section of ground, or by spreading a few inches of new soil on top of the ground and planting in it. (Be careful not to cover the entire root zone of a tree with new soil, or you risk smothering it.) In a year or more you will discover that your root-free soil has been invaded by new roots, but by that time the transplants have built up their own root systems and can fight back for what they need.

Roots aren't the only barrier to growth, of course. The intensity of light is also an issue. The most dramatic way to increase the amount of light is to cut down the tree or dig up the shrub. Barring this, you can at least limb-up the trunks, pruning off the lower branches. This will give the plants a high crown that casts a diffuse, dappled shade. Many of the finest wild-flower gardens have been created by taking a piece of woodland and trimming out all the lower branches of the trees, a compromise that allows a green canopy and a green carpet to coexist.

George Schenk's *The Complete Shade Gardener* (Houghton Mifflin, 1984) is the best guide I know to the shade tolerances and preferences of various plants. It is appropriately dedicated "to leaves," but it contains suggestions for a great many flowering plants as well, from the obvious azaleas and rhododendrons to the less-familiar snowberry and highbush blueberry. Impatiens are the most famous shade-tolerant annual, though they bloom more prolifically in full sun. Browallia, coleus, wax begonia, lobelia, and heliotrope all flourish in partial shade.

Leafy vegetables do better than flowering and fruiting ones with reduced light. Leaf lettuce, beet greens, spinach, and scallions are worth trying in any circumstances. So too are raspberries, blackberries, currants, and gooseberries. Alpine strawberries will fruit all summer long in partial shade. Blueberries will produce some fruit with as little as four hours of direct sunlight a day.

The brighter and hotter the climate you live in, the more shade that a given plant will tolerate. Our houseplants that go outside for a vacation every summer always go to the shadiest part of this yard, under the branches of a Norway maple. Here they may still get more sun than they would indoors, under the eaves, behind the glass. Because they are in the shade, rather than in full sunlight, they are less likely to lose their leaves from the shock of coming back indoors in the fall to relative darkness. Our collection, which includes a split-leaf philodendron vine, a fruiting coffee shrub, a variegated screw-pine, a tub of ornamental ginger, and a large grapefruit tree, is an arresting addition to the backyard. The exotic effect is one more reminder of how much even the darkest corner has to offer.

Pruning Practice

LEARNING TO PRUNE TREES and shrubs is basically a matter of learning what happens as a result. No cut is without consequence, and misunderstanding the latter can make a shambles of the former. Consider the caller who telephoned an agricultural extension agent, asked how to make a windowsill avocado seedling branch, and was told to pinch out the top bud. A couple of months later the same person was back on the line complaining, "I took your advice. I have been pinching my avocado every day, and it looks terrible."

What makes this story funny is that most of us are secretly afraid of making some equally terrible mistake. Who has not hesitated to cut something back for fear that the plant might never recover? But no gardener is ever born pruning-proficient. We get that way only through years of practice. Practice, however, means making mistakes, and it is always easier to take one's first cuts, at least, in private.

I learned to prune on apple trees, and I still practice on them, early in the spring out behind the country house when no one is watching. I could prune the apple trees at any time of the year, and there are those who say the best time to prune is when you have a sharp tool in your hand. But I welcome the chance to get outdoors. The ground may be frozen or too wet to plow, but the sun is higher in the sky and warms me as I work among the trees' leafless branches.

Because I have been pruning these trees every year, I do not need to remove much. But when I began they had been neglected for more than a decade. When it comes to acquiring a feel for pruning, an understanding of what it means to cut a branch off here instead of there, I can think of no better practice range than an old apple tree. They are resilient plants: witness the way they withstand neglect, surviving long after the rest of the garden has disappeared. And practicing one's pruning on an overgrown specimen is much less fright-

ening than addressing a sapling: With an old tree you don't risk
ruining its future. Rather, your pruning might give it one.

Not that pruning will guarantee a crop of tasty apples. The tree
may never have been cared for because its apples tasted awful. Even
if they taste delicious, much more goes into a blemish-free bushel
than a well-pruned tree. The beginning pruner should approach the
tree intent on learning to prune, not on becoming a fruit grower.
Skills are the reward. As a lagniappe, you can expect blossoms on a
shapely bough.

Other than a ladder, pruning requires only two tools — a pair of
pruning shears for branches less than a finger's diameter and a sharp
pruning saw for anything larger. The saw can be straight or curved
or bowed, so long as it is sharp and comfortable to use. The shears
can be bypass or anvil, with short handles or long.

When you are done you will have:

(1) removed dead wood, preventing its decay from invading the
    rest of the tree;
(2) thinned out the branches to let in needed light and air;
(3) kept the tree's size within bounds, consistently favoring
    younger branches so as to rejuvenate all the bearing wood every
    six or eight years.

This, however, is only where you are headed; how you get there
is by pruning. The first cuts should remove dead or damaged
branches. Cut each back to healthy wood, just
above the promising side branch or the main
trunk. The larger the branch the more important it is that it be removed in stages, the final
cut being made when the piece of tree to
be removed is light enough
that you can hold it with your
free hand to prevent it from
tearing the bark as it
comes off.

The bark adjacent to
a cut must be carefully protected, for under it
is the cambium that will gradually grow out
over the cut surface, healing it over with a protective layer of new wood. The healing will

proceed faster, and decay will be less likely to get into the main trunk, if the side branches are not cut quite flush with the trunk. Leave the branch collar, the swelling directly adjacent to the trunk. If you cut this off in eagerness not to leave a stub that will fail to heal over at all, you not only make a larger scar than necessary but also remove a barrier to decay. There is no need to coat the cut surface with the tree paint sold to prevent decay; studies have shown that these compounds do no particular good. But neither do they do any particular harm. If you mind people noticing the wounds resulting from your pruning, put some on as a cosmetic.

With the dead wood removed you can begin to see the framework of the tree and decide which of the larger living branches need to be removed or shortened. Look for any that grow straight up, or precipitously downward, or that cross or double back on themselves. The goal in this is to thin out the crown of the tree, letting in a lot of light and air. I use two rules of thumb, depending on my mood. Early in the day I prune leaving enough open space so that a robin could fly through the tree without stooping; later in the afternoon I switch to the maxim that a cat thrown through the tree shouldn't hit anything. Both approaches work.

If there are many large branches that need to be cut, don't try to remove them all in one year, or at least save some until late summer or fall. Too severe a pruning causes the tree simply to bounce back with a great flush of new growth, giving you nearly as much to cut off again next spring. The experts try to do as little pruning as necessary so that later they have as little pruning to do as possible. But as a beginner your purpose is to learn how to prune rather than how not to.

When you have finished with the saw, pick up the shears. Cut off any suckers that have sprung up around the base of the tree. Farther up the trunk, these fast-growing shoots are called watersprouts. A watersprout here and there can be left if you need a replacement branch to fill up an overlarge gap left by removing some larger limb, but most of them should go.

Finally, move about the tree, shortening up the terminal shoots to keep the tree within bounds. Pay attention to which way the outermost remaining bud faces. Cutting the tip off the end of a shoot will cause the buds left below the cut to send out branches. The uppermost bud will do the most growing, because it is always dominant.

In general, cut to an outside bud; otherwise the resulting branch will be growing back into the tree.

When you are finished and standing under the tree up to your knees in prunings, you may well fear that you have overdone it. But drive by a commercial orchard and you will be reassured to see how sparse those trees are. What looks terribly thin now will look a lot less so once the buds have leafed out.

Stop and examine the tree you have pruned in the months ahead to see the results of your cuts. Note which buds are becoming branches; watch to see how open wood heals over. Next year prune some more. It will take several years for the larger scars to disappear, but the smaller twigs will respond to your cuts almost immediately. Over the course of several years, you will gradually come to feel that you are in command of the situation. Not only can you cut with confidence, but you know how the tree will answer. Many people have apple trees in their backyards. But only those who have learned how to prune them have the right to call themselves apple-keepers.

Pruning a Grapevine

I HAVE JUST volunteered to prune my neighbor's grapevine. Secretly, I am looking forward to the expression on her face when she finds 90 percent of the vine gone. I may even have to remove more than that, since the grapevine hasn't been properly pruned in years. The sight of nothing but short stubs where there was once a luxuriant tangle of vine will probably horrify her. It used to alarm me, too. But I will explain that such heavy pruning is all for the good, and a year from now she will agree.

Grapevines don't have to be pruned to produce grapes. That the country is full of wild vines growing up tree trunks and over stone walls is certain proof of that. But pruning is the single most important thing one can do to a cultivated vine to assure getting high-quality fruit year after year. You just have to get used to the notion that something so drastic can be so beneficial.

The purpose of pruning grapevines is to limit the number of buds on wood formed the preceding year. These are the buds that will produce fruit. Each of them already contains rudimentary leaves and the flower clusters that will result in from one to four bunches of fruit. How many fruit buds remain after pruning determines not only the number of bunches of grapes the vine produces that year but also the vine's growth and fruiting capacity for the next year. Leaving too many buds will prompt the vine to try to bear more fruit than it can. The overcropping will weaken the vine, delay the ripening of the grapes, reduce the vine's winter hardiness, and result in poor fruit-bud formation for next year. Viticulturists (serious grape growers) say one should always prune with an eye toward next year's crop. That way this year's crop takes care of itself.

It is easy to confuse the pruning of a grapevine with its training. Training refers to giving the vine a particular shape, not the process of limiting the number of fruiting buds. Obviously the two activities are connected. Where you choose to leave buds will determine how the vine grows, but training is secondary to pruning. If it is to bear well, a grapevine sprawled across an arbor above a patio needs annual pruning just as much as a vine confined to a short section of fence.

Grapevines can be pruned any time of year that they are leafless. Here in the North, I like to wait until March, when the worst of the winter is over and I can be sure that the buds I am leaving are on live wood. Later in the spring, the ends of every cut drip like leaky faucets. It looks awful, and I used to worry that the vine might bleed to death. But the liquid is even more dilute than maple sap, and its loss causes no harm whatsoever.

Before you make your first cut, it is important to be able to identify the various parts of the grapevine. The trunk is the main stem of the vine that emerges from the ground. If it is more than a few years old it will have dark-brown, flaky bark. The branches where the trunk divides are called arms. Branching off the arms are numerous canes, the preceding summer's growth. Canes vary in diameter — the largest can be as thick as your little finger — but all have a smooth, yellowish-brown bark. The buds on these canes are the important ones.

Deciding how many of these buds to leave depends on how vigorously the vine grew last year. An experienced grape grower can look at the vine and do the calculation in his head. The novice will find it easier and more reassuring to use what is called the "balanced pruning system," in which you weigh the canes that have been cut off and then determine how many buds to leave, a process that is much easier than it sounds.

On an established vine you should leave roughly 25 buds for the first pound of canes pruned off and 10 additional buds for each additional pound. Thus if you remove a total of 2½ pounds of cane prunings you should leave 40 buds. Of course you have to be careful not to overdo your initial pruning. If you hack away like mad and then weigh your cuttings, it is possible that you may have already pruned off the buds you were supposed to leave. Eyeball the vine and leave an extra couple dozen buds until you have weighed the prunings and determined just how many buds you ultimately want. Weighing the canes is easier if you first cut them into 2-foot lengths. Don't weigh any wood older than a year. It doesn't count.

Try to leave canes that are at least the diameter of a pencil and

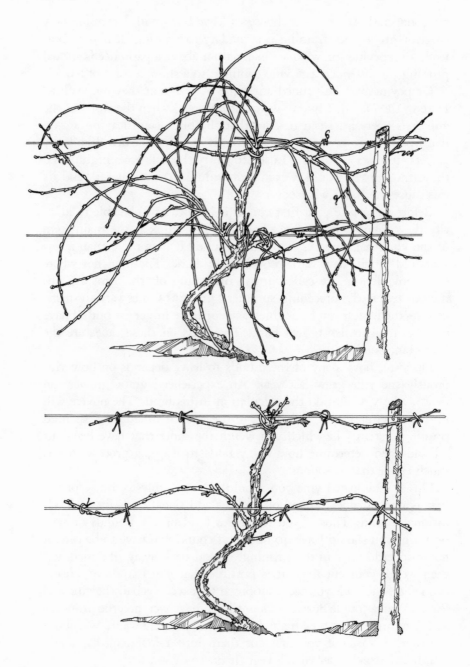

were exposed to the most light when they were growing. These will be the most productive. At this point you also have to take into account how the vine is being trained, since the location of this year's remaining canes will affect the location of next year's.

Commercial vineyards use dozens of different training methods. The home gardener, freed from the constraints of machinery and the necessity of making a profit, can embrace even more. I am going to train my neighbor's vine using the so-called four-arm Kniffen system. It is not the fanciest system of training, nor the most productive, but it is one of the easiest to understand and maintain. I have used it for years on my own grapes, and we are awash with fruit every fall.

A four-arm Kniffen vine is usually tied up to a pair of wires, the top one at five feet above ground, the bottom at two and a half. But you can train the vine on a chain-link or rail fence just as well. The object is to have four equal-sized canes after pruning, each bearing roughly one-quarter of the vine's remaining buds. At the base of each cane you should also leave a spur. A spur is a cane that has been cut back to only two buds. These buds will produce replacement canes during the summer, canes that can be tied down in place of this year's canes when you prune next spring.

The four-arm Kniffen system is easy to picture, but like all training systems it has the disadvantage that the illustration never looks quite like the real vine you see before you. I know my neighbor's vines won't have four arms conveniently placed in the right positions. I will just have to make do, looking ahead, leaving buds where they can grow into canes that will be where I want them next year.

I expect I will have to shorten the arms drastically to encourage canes to develop near the trunk. Sometimes, in extreme cases of vine neglect, there is such a long, thick trunk that the only pruning cut worth making is a few inches above ground. This causes dormant buds in the trunk to sprout, giving you an abundance of canes to choose from when you prune next year. Other times you can fashion a replacement trunk from a sucker growing from the base of an older vine. In colder areas it is common practice to encourage a cane or two to grow from the base as insurance against the trunk's being injured during the winter.

It may be a couple of years before my neighbor's grapevines achieve a recognizable shape. But it will only take me a morning to prune it so that it begins bearing healthy clusters of grapes right away. What more could she ask for?

Transplanting Trees

EARLY SPRING is the season that trees go around bare-rooted. Clad only in packing material (sometimes nothing more than a layer of plastic and a handful of damp excelsior), fruit and shade trees are being moved hundreds and even thousands of miles. Such interstate shipment of bare-rooted stock is an old custom.

Bare-rooted trees are dormant when they are shipped. Having been dug the previous fall and held in cold storage all winter, they are very dormant — they are sometimes so dormant, in fact, that they never leaf out. Delays in shipping may result in the stock's drying out fatally. Buying bare-rooted stock is a gamble. Most of it grows just fine, but losses of 20 percent or more are not unusual. Some grows poorly, and some not at all. Bare-rooted trees continue to be a common offering, in large part because they don't take up much space in storage, and because, being soilless, they're light enough to mail easily. These factors help keep the price down, and if a tree is young enough and of the right species, you can get away with stripping all the soil off its roots. But if a tree doesn't survive the bare-rooting, it never seems much of a bargain.

Buying either balled-and-burlapped ("B & B") stock or potted stock is a better way to ensure a successful transplant. Not that these trees are without problems of their own. Digging up a root ball and wrapping it in burlap or some other material discards 90 percent of the root system. But the roots that remain are safely ensconced in soil. When you buy stock growing in a pot you get all the roots, but these may be wrapped around each other in the bottom of the pot. Unless you take care to straighten them out when you plant the tree, they may continue to grow that way. And note that potted stock is sometimes nothing more than bare-rooted stock that the nursery has purchased in the spring and planted in a container. So wait until midsummer to buy your tree, when you can be sure that you are buying one that has successfully emerged from dormancy. Balled-

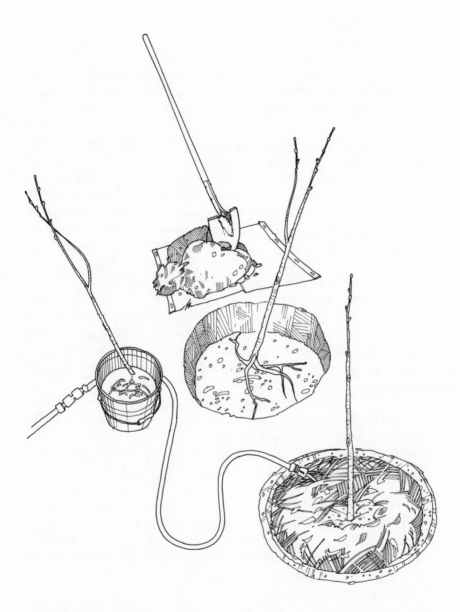

and-burlapped and potted stock can both be transplanted any time of year that the ground can be worked. Buying a tree that is in leaf may be a bit more expensive, but it is a guarantee that the tree isn't in a terminal coma.

Unfortunately, I can't always find a nursery that sells balled-and-burlapped or potted specimens of the particular dwarf quince or antique apple that I want — for any price. And so every spring I order some trees bare-rooted. I do so with the full understanding that I may have to order some of the same plants again next year. Forced to gamble, I can nevertheless do some things that improve the odds. The following precautions give bare-rooted trees the best chance of survival.

Order the youngest stock available. The younger the tree, the larger and longer it will grow. If it is a choice between a three- or four-foot-tall seedling or a five- to six-foot-tall one, select the former. The smaller plant will get a surer start and soon outstrip the larger.

Specify that the tree be shipped as early in the spring as it can be planted. This means as early as the soil can be worked. The later a tree is shipped, the longer it remains dormant and the less likely it is to revive.

When the tree arrives, unpack it and prune any roots that appear damaged. Because the roots will be dry, you should soak them in a bucket of water for at least two hours prior to planting (much longer than overnight, however, and there is a risk of drowning the tree). After soaking, be sure to keep the roots moist while you are busy planting it. A bare-rooted tree is like a fish out of water.

Ideally, the tree should then be planted at once. If you can't do that, heel it in outdoors by laying the tree on its side and heaping good garden soil over the roots. The sooner you plant it properly, however, the better off it will be.

When the planting hole is dug it should be much wider than seems necessary, wider even than the roots extend when spread out to their maximum. The purpose of such a spacious hole is to give the tree a vegetation-free zone of soil into which its roots can grow. The roots of young trees cannot compete with grass roots. Failure to provide a planting hole large enough in diameter will result in a stunted tree. Width is more important than depth. The hole need only be deep enough to accommodate the roots.

Don't worry about the quality of the subsoil in the bottom of the hole. The only roots that will be growing down will be support roots. The feeder roots are all located near the surface. Therefore, don't enrich the soil in the bottom of the hole with a lot of organic matter; this will only cause trouble years later when the organic matter rots, causing the soil to subside and the tree to sink so deep in the hole that it may suffer from oxygen shortage. (If the topsoil is thin and the subsoil impermeable, plan on building a raised bed, in effect piling good soil around the tree set on the surface.)

Position the tree in the hole so that it is at the same level that it grew in the nursery, or slightly higher. (You can determine the original soil level by finding the point on the trunk where the bark changes color.) Fill in around the roots with soil, putting the soil back in the hole in the same sequence it came out (save the best soil for last). When the hole is partially filled, stop and tamp the soil down firmly around the roots. Don't hesitate to walk on the soil to pack it down, but don't step on the roots themselves. Packing eliminates air pockets in the soil. Adding water to the hole at this stage and letting it drain out is another way to eliminate air pockets.

Finish filling the hole with topsoil. The need for adding organic matter to the topsoil, either in the form of compost or well-rotted manure (never fresh) depends on the condition of the soil. Creating a pocket of high-nutrient soil may simply encourage roots to stay in one place and never spread out. On the other hand, if the topsoil is terribly infertile there may be no choice but to enrich the planting hole. As long as the soil is at least moderately fertile, though, save organic matter to use as a mulch around the newly planted tree. Maintaining a grass- and weed-free zone around a young tree is the best way to improve its chances of thriving.

Use extra soil to create a low dike encircling the tree, to hold water, and fill the dike with water several times. Don't plant the tree in a depression to accomplish the same effect. In subsequent weeks and months keep the soil around the tree moist. But don't overdo it, say, by leaving a hose running, or the tree will drown.

If you follow these instructions, a bare-rooted tree should survive transplanting. (Remember that most bare-rooted trees were top-pruned before they were sold and need no further pruning until next year.) Eventually it will leaf out, weeks after its peers, but more or less intact. Perhaps only a few branches will die back. If, however, the tree never leafs out, or does so only partially and then dies despite the most assiduous care, don't blame yourself. It may not be your fault. Write or visit the seller and explain that the tree died. Many sellers will offer you a replacement. You might also encourage them to sell container-grown or balled-and-burlapped trees. I am considering writing my congressional representative and asking for an extension of the Mann Act, something that would declare the interstate transport of bare-rooted trees to be immoral.

Annual Heroes

SUMMER AFTER SUMMER, annuals rescue gardeners. No matter how many plants die back, don't come up, or are mysteriously consumed, the luxuriance of petunias thick with night-scented blossoms is enough to restore one's self-confidence. In the vegetable garden, zucchinis save the season. Who has time to mourn the watermelons when there are so many fat squashes to give away? These successes are so certain that some gardeners snub petunias, marigolds, and zinnias as "gas station plants" or quip that it is dangerous to leave a parked car with its windows down in August because one will return and find it filled with abandoned zucchini. Such critics are forgetting how many times they have been saved by annuals. What's more, they are missing the point: The real beauty of petunias and zucchinis is not their flowers or fruit, though these are fine enough, but the sheer persistence of the plants.

Annuals grow rapidly and flower quickly because, as their name implies, they must complete their life cycle, going from seed to seed in a single season. Annuals don't have the option of putting anything off until next year. When they die down in the fall, they are gone for good. Biennials, on the other hand, take two years to complete their life cycles. The first year is generally spent growing stems, leaves, and roots, the second producing flowers and seeds. After that, biennials, too, die back for good. Anything that comes up a third season is classed as perennial, though "perennial" doesn't guarantee the plant will last forever.

Vegetable gardens are surprisingly full of biennials: beets, carrots, cabbage, kale, parsnips, rutabagas, and turnips. The fact isn't obvious, or of much concern, to gardeners because the first year's growth is the edible part. Seed company employees are the only ones who regularly get to see the cream-yellow flowers of cabbage or the purple ones of salsify. Canterbury bells, foxglove, and sweet William

are grown for their flowers, however, and most gardeners must wait patiently until the second summer for these to bloom. Most aren't very patient at all, especially when they find that their biennials failed to survive the first winter.

Perennials are capable of blooming year after year. But it often takes a year or more for them to reach blooming size, and the blossoms then last only a few weeks. What's more, the plants are not immortal. The humorist's definition of perennial, from Henry Beard and Roy McKie, authors of *Gardening: A Gardener's Dictionary* (Workman Publishing, 1982), is "any plant which, had it lived, would have bloomed year after year."

There are good reasons to grow perennials, even biennials, but any plant that begins blooming the first year and blooms heavily that first year deserves a special place of honor. Most such plants are true annuals — cleomes, marigolds, zinnias. What is confusing is that some are biennials or perennials masquerading as annuals. The new foxglove cultivar 'Foxy', for example, does not wait for the second summer to bloom, but flowers five months after sowing. Whether such a plant should be called an annual is a moot point. It behaves like one.

Not only do some biennials act like annuals, but some perennials do too. In our garden, snapdragons bloom from June until October of their first year and then die. To us, snapdragons are annuals. But they die only because the temperature drops below 10 degrees Fahrenheit during the winter in these parts. Farther south snapdragons don't die of cold during the winter, and by spring they are realizing their true nature as perennials, albeit tender ones.

Recognizing the impatience of gardeners, plant breeders have been hard at work speeding up the flowering of plants such as hollyhocks. Hollyhocks are tender perennials that are usually grown as biennials. The plants form a clump of leaves the first year, send up a flower stalk the second. Perhaps it is the effort of producing flowers that then causes them to die; perhaps it has something to do with the rust disease that attacks the leaves. But thanks to plant breeding, gardeners no longer have to wait a year for hollyhocks to bloom. Several cultivars — 'Powderpuff', 'Majorette', 'Summer Carnival' — flower the first summer.

Some biennials can also be tricked into blooming the first year. English stock and globe artichokes can be grown as annuals if the young seedlings are exposed to a few weeks of near-freezing temperatures after they have produced a few leaves. Persuaded that they have already been through winter, they obligingly bloom.

In the South, the seeds of annuals (or plants to be grown as annuals) can be sown directly in the ground at an early date, but in the North, where growing seasons are short, seed must be started indoors and transplanted outdoors when the weather is warm enough. Many northerners prefer to buy young seedlings that someone else has raised from seed, and this has given rise to something called the bedding-plant industry, which grows nearly four billion seedlings each year — roughly one billion vegetable seedlings, three billion flowers. With each new season, the price seems to go up and the number of seedlings in a flat seems to go down — from twelve, to nine, to eight, to six. But in most respects the quality of the plants is excellent, with one exception. Too many of the plants being sold are already in bloom. Plants that flower while still in the flat tend to be stunted, never growing to quite the same fullness as those that were transplanted into the garden as younger seedlings. The growers know this, but they claim the customer won't buy bedding plants unless the plants are in bloom. They claim they have tried labels with color photographs and illustrations of the plants, without success. The only way to ensure that one's purchases realize their full potential is to hunt around for seedlings that are not yet in bloom.

In most nurseries and garden centers, all of the flats are sold for the same price, whether one is buying ageratums or zinnias. This in spite of the fact that the ageratum seedlings have been growing at least twice as long as the zinnias. That's twice as much watering, twice as much fertilizer, twice as much sunlight and heat. If you are planning to raise some of your own annuals, and buy others, then it makes a great deal of sense to buy the ones that have taken the most time to raise. The accompanying table gives the number of weeks from sowing to sale for a range of common bedding plants.

Time Needed (in Weeks) from Seed to Sale for Common Bedding Plants

Cosmos 4–6	Marigold, dwarf 8–10
Zinnias, tall 4–6	Salvia, tall 8–10
Marigold, tall 5–6	Snapdragon, tall 8–10
Cabbage 5–6	Verbena 8–10
Tomato 5–7	Impatiens 9–10
Zinnia, dwarf 6–8	Nicotiana 9–11
Bachelor buttons 6–8	Salvia, dwarf 10–12
Calendula 6–8	Ageratum 10–12
Pepper 6–8	Petunias 11–15
Celosia 7–9	Snapdragon, dwarf 12–14
Eggplant 7–9	Portulaca 12–14
Aster 8–10	Geranium 13–18
Cleome 8–10	

Annual gardens don't have to be vibrantly hot landscapes, even though the palette is loaded with yellow, orange, and red. By choosing plants in shades of pink, cream, and blue, and by resisting the temptation to plant them in rigid alternation, it is possible to create drifts as gentle and pleasing as any perennial border. What's more, they'll bloom.

Lettuce First

MOST RESTAURANT salad bars and most home vegetable gardens begin with lettuce. But not the same lettuce. The restaurant usually serves the crisphead, or iceberg, type. The lettuce in the home garden is likely to be either leaf lettuce or the semiheading Bibb, or Boston, lettuce.

Most of us grew up eating iceberg lettuce, not because it was served in restaurants but because it was the only lettuce commonly sold in stores. I don't remember anybody objecting to it until people began to raise lettuce themselves. Then I started hearing disparaging comments about iceberg lettuce — about how it was nothing but expensive water. Leaf lettuce, on the other hand, was said to be a fount of good taste and nutrition.

Head lettuce and leaf lettuce do differ, but the differences have little to do with one being tastier or more nutritious than the other. The real differences are that head lettuce is more difficult for the home gardener to raise and leaf lettuce is harder for stores and restaurants to keep. Home gardeners who think iceberg lettuce is truly inferior should try raising their own. The heads of iceberg lettuce that I have grown have been unparalleled horticultural and Epicurean triumphs.

Most years, however, I am content to grow the easier lettuces. My favorite is a leaf lettuce called 'Black Seeded Simpson', a very old cultivar with crumpled, juicy, light-green leaves. One of the earliest of all lettuces, it is ready to eat only six weeks after sowing. I also like 'Saladbowl', with its large, lime green rosettes of wavy, deeply notched leaves. And for a contrasting color, the best of the red lettuces is a new one called 'Red Sails', whose leaves have deep burgundy-red color overlying a green background.

Lettuce grows so quickly that there really is no need to start plants indoors. Seed will actually germinate on ice, and plants will survive temperatures as low as 20 degrees Fahrenheit. Lettuce seeds, however, do need light and moisture to germinate. As soon as the soil is thawed and dry enough to be worked, sow the seeds thinly, spacing them about an inch apart. Cover them only one-eighth to one-quarter inch deep and firm the soil lightly. Then be sure that the soil is kept moist until the seeds germinate, which may take a week or more if the soil is cold.

The first seedlings to appear in my garden are never the ones I have sown intentionally but rather volunteer seedlings, the offspring of plants I let go to seed the summer before. My neighbor across the street relies entirely on a self-sown crop. This makes for an extremely early if somewhat disorderly harvest.

You can, of course, start your lettuce plants indoors a month before conditions are suitable for transplanting into the garden. I can think of two reasons to do this. First, it does give you a two-week jump on a crop sown directly outdoors. Second, and perhaps more important to many gardeners, it gives you a picture-perfect planting with lettuces all in a row.

Seeds sown indoors will germinate rapidly. At a temperature of 70 degrees the seeds should sprout in two or three days provided the seed flat gets plenty of light. Ten days after the seeds have germinated transplant the seedlings into individual containers filled with a soilless mix. Lettuce plants at this stage do not need much room. I use the one-and-a-half-inch-square plastic pots that come in sets of six. The plants will spend only another two or three weeks in these containers before being moved outdoors.

Before they are transplanted to the garden, however, the two- or three-inch-high plants should be hardened off, a term that refers to accustoming them to outdoor conditions. To do this put the tray of young plants outside for a few hours the first day and then bring them back indoors. The next day they can stay out for longer. By the fifth day or so they should be tough enough to stay outdoors for good. During this time let the plants dry out a bit, but don't let them run out of water altogether. Outdoors in the sun and wind the plants use up water much more rapidly than they do indoors. Fortunately, even a seedling that has wilted to the point of lying flat on its side can usually be revived with a drink of water and a few hours in the shade. A cold frame, if you have one, is a perfect halfway station for lettuce seedlings on their way from house to garden.

When the plants are sufficiently hardened off, transplant them to their permanent locations in the garden. If individual plants are to grow to their fullest size they should be 8 to 12 inches apart. If you have extra plants and you promise yourself to rip out intervening plants shortly, you can jam them in more thickly. But I advise you to eat the extra transplants now. Many of them look good enough to eat, and are.

Lettuce requires abundant water, for that is the principal ingredient of all lettuce, even leaf lettuce. The plants also need a reasonably fertile soil, though it need not be any richer than that for most other annuals. And finally, lettuce likes cool weather, but not too cool. Plants make their best growth at temperatures between 60 and 65 degrees.

Anything that you can do to raise the air temperature in the vicinity of your lettuce plants early in the season will speed their development. The easiest way to do this is with a cloche. Whether you use a plastic gallon milk jug with the bottom cut out and the cap removed or one of the more elaborate water-walled polyethylene teepees, the lettuce plants under cover will grow faster than their companions out in the cold.

The speed with which lettuce grows and has to be eaten presents a problem of its own. In a row of lettuce of the same age, every plant will be ready to eat more or less at the same time. You have to eat the lettuce when it is ready, because within a couple of weeks the lettuce plants will begin to bolt, or go to seed. The first sign of this is that the center of the plant begins to form a stalk that gradually gets taller and eventually forms a mass of small yellow flowers. These in turn will make the seed that, if allowed to fall to the ground, will produce a crop of volunteer seedlings next spring.

Much of lettuce breeding has concentrated on producing cultivars that are resistant to bolting. But that only means that the inevitable is postponed for a short while. No lettuce is boltproof. Since lettuce must be eaten shortly after it is mature, it is wise to eat part of the crop early. One of the chief advantages of leaf lettuce is that individual leaves can be harvested without killing the whole plant. Pulling off outside leaves allows the center ones to go on growing.

Some gardeners are not content with leaf lettuce and want the crunchy, pale-stemmed inner leaves that can only be enjoyed by eat-

ing the heart of a lettuce plant. Hence the popularity of the so-called
Bibb, or Boston, lettuces. The best of this type is 'Buttercrunch', a
lettuce of such high quality that it is appearing in grocery stores,
which go to some effort to keep it from wilting, even selling hydro-
ponically grown specimens with the root ball encased in plastic.

Bibb lettuce (and its upright cousin, Cos, or romaine, lettuce) is
considered by some to be a kind of head lettuce. But in terms of ease
of culture these lettuces are closer to leaf lettuces. The only difference
is that you need to give the Bibb-lettuce plants more space than leaf
lettuce. A foot apart is a good measure. If you are sowing the seed
directly in the garden you must be zealous about thinning to give
the plants enough space to develop properly. Harvested at its peak,
the lettuce will be better than anything you can buy in the store.
But once again you will have the problem of producing more than
you can eat.

Ideally, you should sow only a couple feet of lettuce at a time and
make repeated plantings. If you sow a new section of lettuce row in
the garden every time the seedlings from the preceding planting are
up and growing, you will end up with a steady supply of lettuce. It
is difficult to get lettuce to germinate in midsummer because high
soil temperatures cause something called summer dormancy. (For
Bibb lettuce the critical temperature is 77 degrees.) But the determined gardener can find ways around this, such as sowing the seed
in the shade, or under a lattice. Or simply waiting until the soil cools
down and resuming lettuce planting in the fall.

I tell myself that some year I am going to get organized and do
this, but I haven't yet. I find that as the season progresses there are
things I would much rather eat than lettuce — peas, beans, cucumbers, tomatoes, carrots, onions, peppers. In this sense, the backyard
vegetable garden is exactly like the restaurant salad bar.

Cucumber Cover-up

BEGINNER'S LUCK is all right; it just doesn't last long enough. Take cucumbers, for instance. The first couple of years they are a snap to grow. A handful of plants produces in the course of a summer so many more cucumbers than any one family can possibly consume raw that you are virtually forced to make pickles. Oh, it's so easy.

But almost as soon as you discover that there is a limit to the number of pickles you can eat, your luck suddenly runs out. In these parts trouble always comes in the form of a little black-and-yellow-striped beetle. Looking no more dangerous than a slender ladybug, this beetle appears out of nowhere just as the new crop of cucumber seedlings stick their first two seed leaves out of the soil, and it attacks them with astonishing single-mindedness. There isn't much to one of these beetles, but there isn't much to a young cucumber seedling either. In a couple days of feeding, one or two of these insects can wipe out an entire summer's supply of sliced-cucumber-with-onion-and-sour-cream salad.

If your vegetable garden is close at hand, you might have the time to go out a couple times a day and attack the cucumber beetles your-self. They are so busy feeding that it is easy to sneak up on them and mash them. If you do this regularly enough, you will probably get the impression that you have been victorious. The cucumbers will appear to be growing well, the vines coiling their tendrils around whatever they touch, the flowers beginning to open.

But you haven't been victorious at all. The enemy has simply gone underground. If you took note during your mashings, those two bee-tles that you so proudly wiped out in a single blow were mating. Any fertilized females that you missed promptly laid their little or-ange eggs at the base of the seedlings. And now their offspring, tiny wormlike white larvae, are eating the cucumber vine's roots. The first you know of this is when the leaves begin wilting. If the larvae have eaten most of the roots off, the plants will soon die. But even if the vines survive, the cucumber harvest is done for.

If feeding by adults and larvae were the only two ways that striped cucumber beetles could ruin a cucumber crop, it would be bad enough. But there is a third and even more insidious avenue of attack. Many of the adult beetles carry in their gut a disease called bacterial wilt, which they inadvertently pass on to the cucumber plants on which they feed. An infected plant acts much like one that has had its roots eaten off — the leaves wilt on sunny days, appear to recover somewhat at night, and eventually die. To confirm the presence of the disease, cut a wilted stem and squeeze the sap out of it while watching for white exudate. Then touch a clean knife blade to the cut surface and slowly pull it away. If you see a white ooze that strings out in a fine thread between the cut surface and the knife blade, you have diagnosed bacterial wilt. There is nothing you can do but administer last rites.

I would not be recounting this sad tale if it did not have a happy ending. After years of protracted warfare with many casualties on both sides, I have at last found a way to restore a measure of peace in the cucumber patch. Because I lack the time to kill beetles myself, or the inclination to do it by proxy with poisons, I have devised a totally nonlethal solution. I simply cover the vines up so that the beetles can't get to them.

The idea is as old as screen doors. But the material is new — a sheet of spunbonded polypropylene. This fabric isn't woven; the long fibers are thinly matted together. The result is a soft, lightweight, durable white cloth that lets light and water pass through but not cucumber beetles. The principal use of this material in the garden is as a row cover to raise the air temperature underneath and thus hasten the growth of plants in spring. The great advantage of this fabric over other materials is that it requires no hoops or other support to hold the material up. If you lay it loosely over the seedlings, the plants simply lift up the cloth as they grow, like bread dough rising.

Cucumbers are heat-loving plants, and they benefit from the warmer temperatures underneath these floating row covers. But this benefit, in my experience, is nothing like the benefit of being protected from their archnemesis. To work, the fabric must be in place as early as the cucumber seedlings are. If you are using transplants cover the patch as soon as you put down your trowel. If you are sowing seed directly do not wait for the first sprout to appear. Cucumber beetles keep a more vigilant watch on your garden than you ever will.

The fabric comes in sheets as wide as 20 feet. But unless you have a very large cucumber patch use a piece of the more common width of 64 or 67 inches depending on the brand. Lay the fabric over the ground loosely, leaving plenty of generous wrinkles; the vines will need the space to grow. But be sure to seal the edges to the ground, or determined beetles will get in. Either use a lot of rocks to hold it down tightly, or, better yet, cover the edges of the fabric with dirt.

In the best of all possible worlds you could leave the row cover on all season, reaching under it only to pick cucumbers. But if you do this you will discover that your plants are bare. The fabric, as it screens out cucumber beetles, also screens out the insects needed for pollination. Most cucumbers are *monoecious*, which means that they have male and female reproductive organs in separate flowers on the same plant. Getting the pollen from the stamens of the male flower to the stigma of the female flower requires an insect like a bee.

Some kinds of cucumbers are described in seed catalogs as *gynoecious,* but this only means that they produce all female blossoms. These still require pollination. The pollen in this case must come from a nongynoecious plant, the seeds of which are usually dyed a different color and included in the same seed packet so you will be sure to plant some alongside the gynoecious seeds.

Whether you are growing monoecious or gynoecious cucumbers, if you want your plants to bear you have to let the pollinating insects get at them. The first flowers to appear are usually male, the first female ones coming a few days later. It is easy to recognize the female ones because they already have a miniature cucumber subtending the blossom. (Complaints about plants not bearing are sometimes from gardeners who simply have not waited long enough.) I wait until the first female flowers appear on my plants before I take the covers off. This far north, cucumber beetles have only a single generation a year, so by the time I uncover my plants they are in the clear. Farther south the beetles go through multiple generations. But I suspect that an adolescent seedling with a month of sheltered growth is in a much better position to survive than one that is attacked in its infancy.

Cucumber fanciers will point out that there is such a thing as a *parthenocarpic* cucumber, which does not need pollination. These cucumbers, sometimes called European or greenhouse cucumbers because they were developed for culture in a greenhouse, where insect pollination is difficult, produce fruit without fertilization. As a result the fruit has no seeds. Most parthenocarpic cucumbers are too thin-skinned to be grown outdoors. Recently, however, a parthenocarpic cucumber for outdoor culture has been bred and is now widely available. Named 'Sweet Success', and an All-America Selections winner in 1983, this cucumber can be grown indoors and out. Unlike other parthenocarpic cultivars, which must not be pollinated, the fruit of 'Sweet Success' becomes only slightly misshapen if the flowers are fertilized.

Even parthenocarpic cucumbers, however, are susceptible to extremely high temperatures, the kind found under row covers in midsummer. When the thermometer gets into the 90s flowers do not become fruit. This imposes another limit on how long you can leave the row covers over the cucumber vines. Where summers are cool you might get away with it. But in such a climate there are probably no cucumber beetles in midsummer to worry about.

For most of us the four to six weeks of peace that a floating row cover offers ordinary varieties of cucumbers is enough difference. It offers us a chance to grow cucumbers like beginners again.

True Tomato Taste

WITH A FEW BRUSH STROKES the Japanese artist evokes a landscape of mountains, wind, and bamboo. With a few tomato plants, the American gardener produces a vegetable garden. Tomatoes are the soul of backyard gardening. New gardeners begin with tomatoes; the old grow them to the end. And in between, like the Japanese artist, the gardener searches for ever-greater perfection. Our goal is not greener plants, or yellower flowers, or even redder fruit but rather a mysterious blending of some 118 different chemicals that compose tomato taste. To be sure, there is a premium put on earliness and bigness, but these are only preludes to the main event: the flavor of the ripe fruit. One of the central tenets of vegetable gardening is that home-grown produce tastes better than store-bought, and tomatoes more than any other crop are expected to bear out that claim.

Fortunately, home-grown tomatoes almost always *do* taste better, largely because the home gardener waits until they are ripe before picking them. Cooks and government economists notwithstanding, tomatoes are fruits not vegetables. Each tomato goes through a series of maturity stages. By the time the tomato flower is pollinated the incipient fruit already has its full complement of cells. Growth from that point involves expanding these cells to produce a full-sized tomato — a stage termed mature green. Generally this is 9 to 13 days away from the final stage of table ripe. The first color change, called breaker, occurs a few days later, when a slight yellow or pinkish blush appears at the blossom end. Over the next week the green color gradually disappears as chlorophyll breaks down, and the fruit turns yellow as B-carotene pigment is synthesized. A third pigment, a red carotenoid called lycopene, turns the ripening tomato first orange and finally red, as the tomato passes through the stages of turning pink, light red, and firm ripe. Variations on this theme produce tomatoes of other hues. White tomatoes, with a gene termed gh for ghost, break down the chlorophyll but never synthesize any carotenes. Inhibiting lycopene synthesis yields tomatoes that are orange and yellow when ripe.

Any tomato that is allowed to reach maturity on the vine will taste better than one that was picked at mature green and artificially ripened by treating it with ethylene gas as commercial shippers do. The so-called vine-ripened tomatoes you see advertised in stores are often merely tomatoes that were allowed to stay on the plant only until the breaker stage. But even in the select company of home-grown, some tomatoes taste better than others. The differences have to do with genetics and culture, both of which contribute to the blend of sugars, organic acids, and volatile chemical compounds that make up flavor.

Some gardeners grow the same kind of tomatoes year after year, content that they have found the best match for their site, and turn their attention to perfecting the flavor through better care. Most of the gardeners I know, however, try growing a new tomato or two every year. The very diversity of catalog offerings is proof that there is no one tomato for every garden or one tomato taste for every palate. The quest for perfection depends on the individual, but there are some things on which tomatophiles agree.

First, big tomatoes don't always have big taste. Some of the best flavor is to be found in the so-called cherry tomatoes. The fruits may be red or yellow, round, oval, or pear-shaped. Pickers may complain that the smaller fruit are a nuisance to harvest, but there is no denying the magnitude of the flavor.

Second, earliness is often gained at the expense of taste. In the far north, gardeners may have no choice, but in more moderate climes the later-maturing types should be grown for the main crop. Although there are exceptions, I think that determinate, or bush tomatoes, have poorer flavor than the indeterminate, or climbing tomatoes. Many people like growing determinate tomatoes because the compact, early ripening plants are well adapted to container culture on decks and patios. But I try to check to be sure that the tomatoes I'm ordering each spring are indeterminate.

For those who are confused by the distinction between determinate and indeterminate, the following may help. All tomato plants produce flower clusters at the tips of their stems, but in indeterminate plants the flower cluster is forced into a lateral position by the apical

bud, which continues to grow upward. In determinate plants this
bud does not develop. Each stem ends in a flower cluster and side
shoots develop, rapidly producing compact, bush-type plants. Because there is a limit to the amount of growth, determinate plants
tend to have early and concentrated ripening. There are degrees of
determinate with some being called semidetermi-
nate and other vigorous determinate depending
how many leaves the plants form between flower
clusters. Part of the cause of determinate
tomatoes' poor taste may be that there
simply isn't enough leaf surface per fruit
for full flavor to develop.

   Indeterminate tomato vines will grow
indefinitely, and if allowed to grow
without restriction they will take
up a huge amount of ground and
yield a huge number of tomatoes. If you aren't going to do
anything to train your tomatoes,
space your plants at least
three feet apart each way.

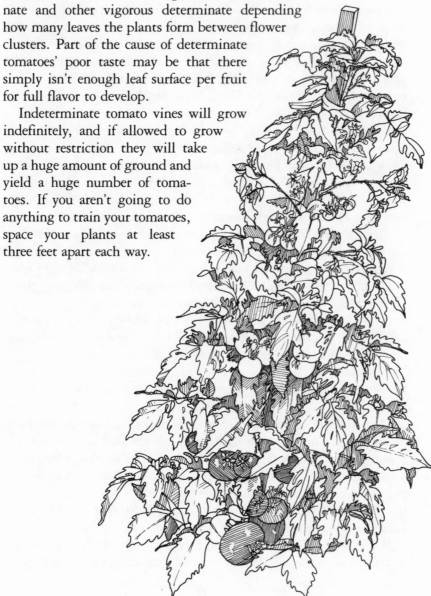

The problem is that it will be hard to pick the fruit in the thick tangle of vines, and some of the fruit will be dirty, and damaged by rot from contact with the soil. The best quality fruit comes from indeterminate vines that are somehow supported.

Tomato cages are cylinders of heavy wire. These can be made from leftover concrete reinforcing mesh if that is available. Otherwise any heavy-duty galvanized wire with a coarse mesh will do, if it can be shaped into cylinders 18 to 24 inches in diameter and 4 to 5 feet high. The cages can be tied to short stakes driven into the ground on each side so that there is no danger of their toppling over. As the young tomato plant grows and branches, keep tucking its shoots inside the cage. When the fruit ripens, reach through the mesh to harvest it.

Caged tomatoes probably give the highest yield of clean fruit per square foot, but each plant requires lots of room. Because I want to grow many different kinds of tomatoes every summer, I space mine closer together, prune the vines, and tie them to stakes. This reduces the yield per plant. But since the plants are closer together — as close as a foot — the yield per area does not drop significantly.

The simplest method of pruning is to remove all the suckers — the shoot that forms in the axils of each leaf — as the plant grows. If you pinch these out every week, they never get ahead of you. Wait two weeks, and you will feel that you are amputating major limbs. Alternatively, you can leave one of these suckers to grow and end up with two stems. While single-stem plants can be planted as close as a foot apart, two-stem plants need twice that. There is some evidence that a second stem reduces the incidence of fruit-cracking.

However you choose to pinch your tomatoes — to one stem or two — you will always be rewarded with a telltale yellow-green foam on the bar of soap as you wash up afterwards.

Once pruned, the tomato vines need support. Some people hold theirs up by weaving them back and forth through a series of horizontal strings. Others wrap them around ropes that hang down from a horizontal wire. I give each of my plants its own six-foot wooden pole set into the ground when I set out the transplant. As I prune the plants each week, I tie them to the pole with strips of old sheets. Other people swear by pieces of nylon stockings.

If people only raise one kind of annual from seed, it is almost certain to be tomatoes. If they seek to explore the full diversity of the group, they have to grow their own plants. Either way, tomato seedlings on the windowsill are a sure sign of spring. However, it is important not to rush the season and sow your seeds too early. Eight weeks before the last frost is soon enough, and if you procrastinate until six, you will be fine.

Tomato seed germinates best at 75 to 80 degrees Fahrenheit. I like to sow in a community flat and then transplant the seedlings to individual pots when they have their first true leaves. For years we have used plastic foam cups, many of them salvaged and rinsed out after church socials. These hold about the right amount of soil. It doesn't pay to be stingy with soil and risk stunting the growth of tomato plants. Give your tomatoes as much light as you can to keep them from getting leggy. Water only enough to keep the soil from drying out. You cannot transplant your tomatoes out until after danger of frost, and it is best to wait until night temperatures are consistently above 45 degrees.

All too often planting is delayed, by wet weather, by cold, by other appointments. And even though you have set the pots outdoors to harden them off, you discover that you have plants that are a foot or more tall and very leggy. One of the greatest virtues of tomatoes is that unlike nearly every other garden plant, the transplant can be set deeper in the garden than it grew in the pot. It doesn't have to be buried vertically. You can dig a horizontal trench, lay the plant in it so that just the terminal cluster of leaves sticks above the surface, and cover the root ball and stem with soil. The young plant will produce roots all along the buried stem, a generous foundation for future top-growth.

Tomatoes like it hot, but too much heat can cause flowers to fail as does too much cold. Even Texans have to start their tomatoes indoors, racing against the onset of summer's heat to get a crop. Tomato plants should be kept evenly moist. This will reduce fruit-cracking and blossom end rot. Common pests include flea beetles and Colorado potato beetles. But the most dramatic of all is the tomato hornworm, a four-inch-long green caterpillar that is all but impossible to see even when you are looking right at it. When you do find one, dispatch it at once, but not if it has white cocoons sticking out of its back. Any such caterpillar has already been attacked by a parasitic wasp whose young are about to hatch.

The one disadvantage of staking your tomatoes is that they cannot be covered with bedspreads and drop cloths when frost threatens in the fall (although I know some people who cut their plants off the stakes and lay them down when September comes). The rest of us pick the mature green and nearly ripe fruit and take them indoors to ripen, although we know they will never match the summer's best. True tomato taste is an elusive delight that many gardeners spend their life pursuing. What can be said for sure about this quest is that it is certain to end in your own backyard.

The First Word
on Herbs

THIS MORNING'S MAIL brought another book about herbs, a beautifully illustrated compendium on the culinary, medicinal, and cosmetic uses of these plants. Although unsolicited it is not unwelcome, and I have wedged it in between a book about narcotic plants and one about herbs in the medieval household. As my bookshelf attests, a staggering amount has already been written about herbs. So much, in fact, that a beginning gardener, looking to the printed page for advice, can be put off planting herbs altogether. When verbiage is laid down this thickly it quashes incipient efforts as surely as a heavy mulch.

To find a way through this herbal expertise you must realize that as a beginner you can hardly be expected to embrace all branches of the subject. The very word *herb* is so vague — a flowering plant whose aboveground portion does not become woody or persistent, and such a plant when valued for its medicinal properties, flavor, scent, or the like — that it can be applied to most denizens of the garden. To bring the subject within reach you need to ask yourself what it is about herbs that makes you want to grow them.

The answer, I wager, will not be that you intend to practice apothecary. Foxglove may be a source of digitalis, but the amateur application of cardiac glycosides is much too likely to result in homicide. You are not likely to dye your own fabric either, or to concoct your own shampoo. No, what makes most people want to grow their own herbs is the prospect of having a steady supply of fresh seasonings for food and drink.

Toward this end, the following is a starter set of culinary herbs. A couple are tender annuals that must be replanted year after year; several are the hardiest of perennials. All are easy to grow, and all have earned a place at our table. Perhaps the best measure of any herb garden's utility is the number of neighbors who appear at the back door with scissors.

No matter what a plant is called, if you don't like the way it smells, don't grow it. Gardeners desiring to grow their own oregano are invariably disappointed when they plant *Origanum vulgare* subsp. *vulgare,* a plant that most books call oregano but that has virtually none of the flavor of the commercial herb. Oregano is not any one plant but a flavor found in a number of plants. Gardeners who have a greater appetite for this herb than I report that the best source of oregano taste in the home garden is *O. vulgare* subsp. *hirtum* (sometimes called *O. heracleoticum*), a plant with the common name winter marjoram. Follow your nose and you will safely skirt all the morasses of controversy over which cultivar or which species is the "true" herb.

Most herbs need full sun. Certain ones, especially those native to arid lands, can tolerate drought, but even these are not averse to watering. Some people advise against fertilizing herbs because they will grow too lush and lack flavor. At the other extreme is great flavor but no plant at all. So apply fertilizer to your herbs with the same moderate hand that you will later use to apply the herbs to your food.

Whatever you do, refrain from spraying poison on anything that you are going to put into your mouth afterwards. Sprays may be unnecessary, since many of the chemical compounds that give herbs their fragrances are used by the plants to repel insects. However, insects are continually evolving ways to get around these repellents, and some pests now use the fragrance as guides to feeding and egg laying. Pests rarely become a cause for concern because herbs are used as seasonings and not as staples. There is usually enough of the plant for both two-legged and six-legged consumers.

The herbs described below are grouped into three categories: first, the hardy perennials, which you will purchase once and have for years; second, tender annuals, which must be resown; and third, a tender perennial that will keep as long as you are willing to carry it indoors in the fall before freezing weather comes and back outdoors in the spring.

The first of the hardy perennials is chives, an herb that I love only slightly less than onions. Still, I confess I don't grow chives. I don't have to. My neighbor does. He has been trying to give me some of

his chive plants as long as I have lived here. Get the picture? Chives are ridiculously prolific. Have a block party, and if no one is already growing chives, agree on who will. But don't everybody plant chives. The world doesn't need that many.

Mint is an herb that everyone warns beginners about because of its spreading tendencies. But compared to chives most mints are tame. Peppermint especially is too poky for anyone to worry about. Even the rampant spearmint, one of the most aggressive of the group, can be controlled without planting it inside sunken flue tiles. I edge my clump every spring with a sharp spade and comb the surrounding soil for runners that have ventured out of bounds. And should it get out into the lawn, I suspect people prefer the smell of new-mown mint to the smell of new-mown chives.

Sage, which is also a mint, is not at all invasive. (The mint family, characterized by a stem that is square in cross section, contains a great many familiar herbs. An equally important family for herbs is the carrot family, with its characteristic, flat-topped flowerhead.) Individual plants will stay in one place, becoming woodier and woodier with age. I keep my plants young by cutting them back hard every spring, down to the lowest green shoots. The treatment looks drastic, but the plants soon send out new growth. If you don't cut your plants back annually you'll end up with long, sprawling branches.

I don't know whether the tarragon I am growing is French or Russian. I suspect it is French because I bought it as a plant and I like its smell. Russian tarragon is said to be what you get when you plant tarragon seed and is a vastly inferior plant. Here is an instance where you can't go wrong if you smell a plant before buying it. If the plant smells of anise and camphor, it is French tarragon; if it smells of summer savory, someone has mixed up the labels. Such mix-ups, though not common, are another good reason to keep your nose open. One tarragon plant is enough. You will be able to gift the entire neighborhood with tarragon vinegar. Just cut off a branch and put it into a bottle of vinegar. You don't even have to boil the vinegar first.

The last hardy herb on my list is thyme (or rather, are thymes, there being so many). These herbs thrive on neglect, spreading out over dry rocks and pavings. I grow three kinds: *Thymus vulgaris* is the standard culinary herb, *T.* x *citriodorus* is a lemon-flavored plant, and *T. herba-barona* is a plant possessing the startlingly pure smell of

caraway. Thyme plants take up little space, and one can justify planting a half dozen of them along the edge of a patio or atop a stone
wall. They will grow anywhere that they get the sun they need, sun
seeming to be their only requirement for success.

My two annual herbs are ones that this family would have a hard
time getting through the summer without. The first is dill. Dill is
actually two herbs, the leaves and the seed. The seed you can buy
dry, but the leaves are the reason to grow it yourself. Sow dill as you
would carrots, about the same time as you plant your cucumbers,
and you will have the thready foliage to mix into cucumber-and-
onion-and-sour-cream salad. Some years I don't get around to sowing
dill, and then I simply keep an eye out for volunteer seedlings sprouting up from the year before. However, seedlings don't transplant
well, so you have to leave them where you find them.

I have never had basil self-sow, perhaps because I assiduously prevent the plants from blooming by pinching out the flower buds as
soon as they appear. With basil you want the leaves, and the pinching
forces the basil plant to branch and produce more foliage. A single
basil plant can get to be two feet tall and nearly as broad. If you only
want a few basil plants, buy them already started. They transplant
well. If you intend to make pesto for the winter, sow a whole row
from seed. Direct-seeded plants grow nearly as fast as transplants.
Stay away from purple basil: it is showy but not as tasty as the green.
Basil is much more tender than dill and blackens with the first touch
of frost, so harvest the leaves and dry them or make pesto before it
is too late.

My final herb is rosemary, a plant that in Zone 6 and colder must
be moved indoors every winter. This year, having no pot big enough
to accommodate the generous root ball of a five-year-old specimen
and reluctant to drag the half whiskey-barrel in which it was growing
from the back deck into the living room, I trundled it down the
street on a hand truck for storage in a neighbor's cool greenhouse.
There its evergreen foliage dusted with blue flowers in early spring
was as much a treat as its fragrance. Although I have seen rosemary
growing as great bushes in the dry hills of northern Italy, I find the
plant particularly sensitive to drought indoors. If you are someone
who abuses your houseplants, as I do, be warned that it is possible
to kill a rosemary by underwatering. It is of course also possible to
kill one by overwatering.

The above is admittedly an abbreviated selection. Some of my omissions have been quite intentional. Parsley is missing. But really, does anyone eat it? I have also left out horseradish, an herb that grows as easily as crabgrass and that I eat a lot of. The problem is that I know of no way of eradicating the plant. Its underground roots, tenacious as a steel-belted radial, produce new plants from every broken fragment.

The herbs I have included are all worth growing. They will give you both pleasure and instruction. Spend a year with these herbs, and next year you will find yourself adding others. They will all flourish and so will your confidence. In no time you too will be writing an herb book.

Strawberries

FRUIT GROWING is the gardener's highest achievement. Vegetables can be mastered in a few seasons, flowers in a few years. But fruit can easily take a lifetime. Not only must you acquire the wisdom and cunning needed to better the birds, beasts, and blight; also there is the matter of waiting for the plants to begin bearing. "Plant pears for your children," goes an old saying. This is not an argument for putting the subject off. Quite the opposite. A French general upon retirement once ordered his gardener to begin planting an avenue of lindens the next day. When the gardener protested that the lindens would take a century to reach maturity, the general changed his mind and ordered that the planting begin that same afternoon. So it is with fruit. The best time to plant is at once, even if you are at the very beginning of your education as a gardener.

But while you are waiting for your fruit trees to begin flowering, you can reward yourself with strawberries, the tulips of the fruit world. Short-lived, fail-safe, and universally satisfying, strawberries are a short-term reward for those who have set out on the long road to fruit cultivation. Strawberries will begin flowering as soon as they are planted, even before they have had a chance to establish themselves, and the time between flowers and fruit is only four weeks.

However, even strawberry culture asks something of the grower. First is the matter of deciding what kind of strawberries to plant. It is a curious fact that the fruit is always sold generically. Everyone has learned to distinguish a 'Delicious' from a 'McIntosh' apple, a 'Bartlett' from a 'Comice' pear. But who can tell the difference between a 'Guardian' and a 'Scott' strawberry? What retailer has given us the chance to learn? There are hundreds of cultivars commercially available: a single catalog from which I buy plants offers thirty-one. And yet the harvest is all lumped under one word: strawberries. There are differences, of course, in fruit, in size, in color, in time of ripening, and, most important, in taste. There are also differences in the plants' hardiness, in soil preference, in the number of runners they set, and in disease resistance.

Over the years I have devised a system for sorting out the cultivars. It is a conservative system, one that no doubt misses a high note here and there, but it won't let a beginner fall flat. I start with the list of cultivars recommended for this area by my Cooperative Extension Service. This helps me weed out those cultivars that actually do best in Maryland or Arkansas, information that catalog writers sometimes seem reluctant to impart. Then I eliminate any cultivar with a noted susceptibility to disease. Red stele and verticillium wilt are two major strawberry diseases to watch for. Some cultivars have built-in resistance, and some don't. Beginning fruit growers have enough to worry about without raising plants that are genetically prone to getting sick.

I am still left with more choices than I can possibly plant, so I restrict the options still further. Next to go are the earliest-fruiting cultivars. I like early strawberries as much as anyone, but early fruiting means early flowering, and the earlier a flower appears the more likely it is to be nipped by late frost. A sign that a flower has been frosted is a black center in an otherwise normal blossom. When this happens, no fruit develops.

Finally, I am willing to forgo large-size, uniformly shaped fruit or bright red color in favor of taste. If you are planning to grow the best-tasting strawberries, there isn't much reason to select for freezing quality; I find there usually aren't enough berries left to freeze.

Most strawberries are so-called June bearers, but catalogs often devote extravagant prose to something called "everbearers." Everbearers actually bear two crops: one in early summer, followed by a second set of flowers that yield fruit in late summer and fall. The flowering and fruiting aren't perfectly synchronized, however, so a bed of everbearers almost always has a few fruits ripening in it, though the total harvest for the year is no greater than for June bearers. The difference between June bearers and everbearers is their response to day length. June bearers form their flower buds in fall in response to decreasing day length. Everbearers not only respond to decreasing day length but are also triggered to form flowers by days longer than 12 hours, so that the plants yield a second flush of bloom in midsummer.

Recently a third type of strawberry has been introduced: the day-neutral strawberry, so called because the flowers are formed almost continuously throughout the season without regard to day length. If you think of June bearers and everbearers as one- and two-crop strawberries, respectively, then think of day-neutral plants as three-crop ones since the plants produce flowers on a six-week cycle. These day-neutral strawberries appear to yield heavily, and the plants are attracting the attention of serious strawberry growers in ways that everbearers never have. 'Tribute' and 'Tristar', two new introductions from the USDA breeding program in Beltsville, Maryland, are both day-neutral plants, though catalogs tend to lump them in with everbearers.

Strawberry plants are sold in bundles of 25, 50, 75, 100, 200, and so on. The price per plant drops so rapidly as the bundle increases that it is always tempting to order more than you really need. Most June-bearing strawberries are originally planted 18 inches apart to allow room for the daughter plants to develop, so it takes relatively few plants to establish a good-sized bed. Twenty-five plants is plenty for three 10-foot rows, and since these rows should be a minimum of 4 feet apart that's a 120-square-foot patch. By the second year the original plants will have produced so many offspring that you will already be getting rid of some.

The soil for a strawberry bed should be prepared at least one year ahead to be sure that it doesn't contain perennial weeds, especially quack grass (which will be impossible to wipe out once the strawberries are planted). The soil should be well drained, and the more humus it contains the better the yield of strawberries. Just before planting apply 25 pounds of 10–10–10 fertilizer per 1000 square feet of future strawberry patch.

Strawberries should be planted as early in the spring as the soil can be worked. Your nursery usually makes the decision for you by shipping the plants you ordered at a time they consider appropriate for planting in your ZIP-code area. The plants will arrive tied up in bundles, straggly leaves at the top and a mass of tough, bare roots at the bottom. If you can't plant immediately, store the unopened packages in the refrigerator for two or three days. If you must delay any longer than that, you'd better unwrap the plants and heel them in, burying their roots in a shallow trench so that all are in contact with soil.

The most critical aspect of planting strawberries is assuring that the crown, that point from which the leaves arise, is level with the soil surface — neither too high nor too low. Half an inch either way will seriously restrict the plant's future growth. Also, the roots should extend continuously downward. It is better to shorten the

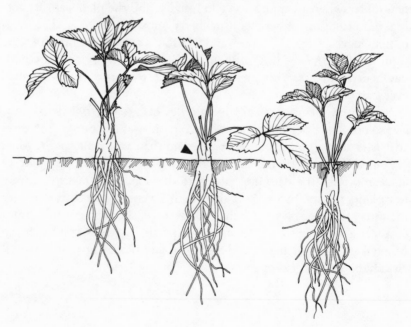

roots somewhat before planting than to bend them in the hole. I find that a trowel will open a slit deep enough to accommodate the entire root system vertically. If I find that the crown is a little low when I have backfilled around the roots, I simply tug the plant up a bit.

The plants, when they arrive, will still have a few leaves from the previous year. But once planted they will soon begin producing new ones. They will also begin producing flowers from the buds formed the preceding fall. As soon as these appear they should be pinched off. It may seem a shame to do this, but failure to remove them will inhibit the strawberry plants' production of runners. These are above-ground stems that travel a foot or more from their point of origin and terminate in a young strawberry plant, which puts down its own roots and becomes an independent offspring. It is these daughter plants that produce the bulk of next year's crop. The sooner they are formed, the sooner they will get established, and the greater their resources will be when it comes time for them to form buds in the fall. Everbearers can be allowed to fruit the first year, but flower buds should be picked off until early July to let the plants get established.

All strawberries are stimulated to produce runners by long days. The runners that form earliest in summer often go on to produce a second and even a third plant. Such strings of offspring have led to the spurious notion that there are such things as "climbing straw-berries." While one could conceivably train runners to a trellis, there is no reason to do so, and advertisers claiming to sell strawberries that climb have been prosecuted for fraud by the post office in recent years.

Runners that have not yet produced rooted plants at their tips can be repositioned and directed wherever the gardener wants. In what I consider the best training system for June-bearing strawberries — the spaced matted row system — runners are allowed to grow until the row is 18 inches wide, and plants are spaced 6 inches apart within the row. Additional runners that appear either within the row or between them should then be removed. Failure to do so will mean a smaller harvest with smaller fruit (because of competition). Further-more, the moisture trapped in the dense foliage of the row can cause premature rotting of any fruit that does develop.

Weeds are even more of a threat to a new planting than excess runners are. Commercial strawberry growers control weeds with soil fumigants and an arsenal of chemical herbicides. I rely on eternal

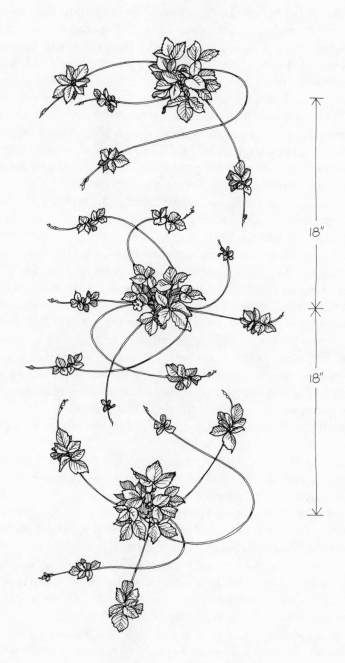

vigilance. Every Saturday morning I go through my strawberry patch, plucking out the weed seedlings while they are still tiny — before they have gained a foothold. As long as the strawberries are growing, the weeds are growing.

Strawberries retain a rosette of evergreen foliage all winter, but in the North they need some protection from seasonal extremes. Where snow cover always comes early and stays late there is no need for other protection. But where I live snow cover is a chancy thing, so I cover my plants with three inches of pine needles. Straw, from which the plants get their name, is an equally effective mulch, as is any other loose organic material. Don't use hay; it contains too many weed seeds. Leave the plants unmulched until temperatures begin to dip below 20 degrees Fahrenheit. Holding off allows the plants to take advantage of any last warm weather to set additional flower buds. Hereabouts, that usually means waiting nearly until Thanksgiving.

Remove the mulch in early April and pile it around the plants. This not only helps keep down weeds but it also adds organic matter to the soil as it decomposes, it prevents dirt from splashing onto the fruit, and it cuts down on soil compaction when people walk near the plants.

Presuming that a late frost doesn't blacken the hearts of the flowers; that flowering isn't followed by so much rain that the fruit all develops premature rot; that there isn't an invasion of slugs, chipmunks, or birds (netting helps), the gardener will be rewarded with fruit that year and every year after, so long as good fortune and the planting shall last.

A strawberry patch will bear fruit for many years (in theory, indefinitely), provided that the plants are kept free of competition from either weeds or their own kind, provided they have sufficient nutrients, and provided they haven't been infected by disease. Many growers find it is easier to start fresh with certified-healthy new stock every year. While this guarantees a uniformly large harvest, those of us not driven by economics can keep our strawberry patches bearing for three to five years with some annual attention.

The most drastic approach is the annual renovation given to June-bearing strawberry beds. This should be done as soon as the last berry is picked. The farther north you live, the more important it is that the renovation begin immediately, not two or three weeks later. With a rotary mower set to cut 1½ inches above the ground (or a scythe, or a pair of grass shears, depending on your patch), cut all the foliage from your strawberry plants. This sounds terrible, but do it. Trust me. Then broadcast 20 pounds of 10–10–10 per 1000 square feet of bare stubble. (Fertilizer should never be added to plants in the spring of their bearing year because it will produce excessive vegetative growth and reduce the amount of fruit.) With a spade, hoe, or tiller reduce the width of the rows to 10 inches, digging out, turning under, or otherwise destroying half the strawberry plants. This is also a good time to clean out any weeds you find — they are more visible with the strawberry foliage out of the way — and to add any decomposed organic matter you have handy. When you have done this, go along the row and thin out the plants that remain. Leave only the most vigorous plants. Frequently this will mean removing some of the ones you planted originally. (If your strawberries aren't growing in rows you will have to judge whether you have removed the requisite three-quarters of the plants.) Don't be afraid to be ruthless. Just remember how sparse the patch looked when you planted it and how quickly it filled in. The plants you leave, you are leaving as much for the runners they will produce as for any fruit.

When you have finished shearing, fertilizing, weeding, and thinning, make sure that the soil is moist to a depth of 6 inches. If it doesn't rain, water. The shorn strawberry plants will soon start putting out new leaves, followed by runners. From then on, treat the bed the same way you would a new planting, encouraging the runners away from one another and removing the excess plants once the row is 18 inches wide and filled with plants 6 inches or so apart.

Everbearing strawberries don't require such drastic renovation; indeed, it would destroy the fall crop. Everbearers tend to produce fewer runners than June bearers and are best spaced according to the hill system of planting. In this system the original plants are set 12 inches apart in double or triple rows with only 2 feet between rows. Any runners that form are removed. Periodic renovation is still necessary because the parent plants tend to form multiple crowns that compete with one another, reducing the harvest. An annual midsummer fertilizer application, combined with scrupulous weed control and periodic replacement of parent plants by runners, will keep a bed of everbearing strawberries going for several years. Day-neutral cultivars are sufficiently new that no one knows quite how to manage them, but the same principles as for everbearers should apply.

Whatever strawberries you are raising, plan on inspecting the patch every three days when the plants are fruiting. The hotter the weather, the faster berries will ripen. Frequent picking allows you to wait until the berries are fully red without risking their becoming overripe. Unless you intend to eat or otherwise process the strawberries immediately, pick them with the green calyx attached. Grasp the stem between your thumb and forefinger and pull with a slight twist. Don't grab the berry itself; it is too fragile and easily bruised. Containers for holding the fruit should never be deeper than 5 inches. The shallower the basket, the less likely are the berries to crush one another.

The great virtue of picking your own berries is that you don't have to put small or partially rotten fruit at the bottom of every box. When you pick, pick clean; but eat the skimpy ones and bite off the good half of those berries that show signs of decay. Don't leave any fruit to rot in the row; the mold will spread to other berries. When I am picking a lot of berries, I carry along an empty container to put the trash in.

Fresh-picked, fully ripe berries will keep uncovered in the refrigerator for three days, but it has been my experience that they rarely last half that long. A homegrown strawberry is equal to the finest plum, peach, or pear. To raise even a handful is to become a fruit grower, with all the rights and privileges of that highest category of gardening. The relative ease of strawberry culture makes the harvest no less an achievement, the fruit no less sought-after. In a world already filled with too much summer squash and too many marigolds, it is inconceivable that there could ever be too many strawberries.

Looking Ahead

GARDENING NEVER ENDS, but gardening books do. I began as a teenager reading books about vegetables when no one else I knew shared my enthusiasm for raising beets. I spent a great many hours in libraries and in the dusty stacks of secondhand bookstores, and grew as loquacious about the prospects for melons as others were about baseball. I owe much of my early success in the garden to books, but I reached a point where I realized that I was in danger of spending more time with words than with the plants themselves.

Gardening should not stop with armchair recreation. I still go to my bookshelf daily — to the single volume *Wyman's Gardening Encyclopedia* (Macmillan, 1986) or the ten-volume *Encyclopedia of Gardening* by Thomas Everett (Garland, 1981) — for there is only so much information that I can store in my head. But to the dismay of publishers everywhere, I believe that once you understand the basics, you are better off growing plants than reading about them.

Finding the plants to grow is easy. The number of mail-order seed companies and nurseries increases every year. The bigger ones pass around their mailing lists so that if you order from one you get the others' catalogs. I recommend the smaller specialty companies that advertise in the classified sections of gardening magazines. Their catalogs aren't full-color, but their prices are reasonable and their material excellent. Get in the habit of visiting local nurseries. Stop when you drive past a hand-lettered sign on a tree that says "Plants for sale." The cardboard-box-full of daylilies or rhubarb that you come away with will likely be accompanied by a full set of advice tailored precisely to the conditions in your own garden. Above all, ask yourself every spring what it is that you have dreamed of planting someday, and commit yourself.

Yes, when the crates and bundles start arriving it will be an inconvenient time. Nothing is ever delivered on a sunny Saturday morning, but always on a rainy Monday when you are headed out of town. You change your clothes and start sticking things in the ground as fast as you can only to discover that you have run out of space and will have to do an emergency enlargement of the garden. But any irritation that comes with having to dig holes when you are supposed to be somewhere else will be short-lived. Almost immediately it will be replaced with the pleasure that comes from knowing that whatever it is that you have planted — from grapes to peonies — is now a reality rather than a dream. Gardening is one-hundred-percent enjoyable in anticipation. If it sometimes is only fifty-percent enjoyable in execution, it invariably becomes two-hundred-percent enjoyable in retrospect. You are missing out on more than half of your due if you content yourself with dreaming of imaginary bouquets and future harvests. The best advice that I have to give is get out there and dig.

Index